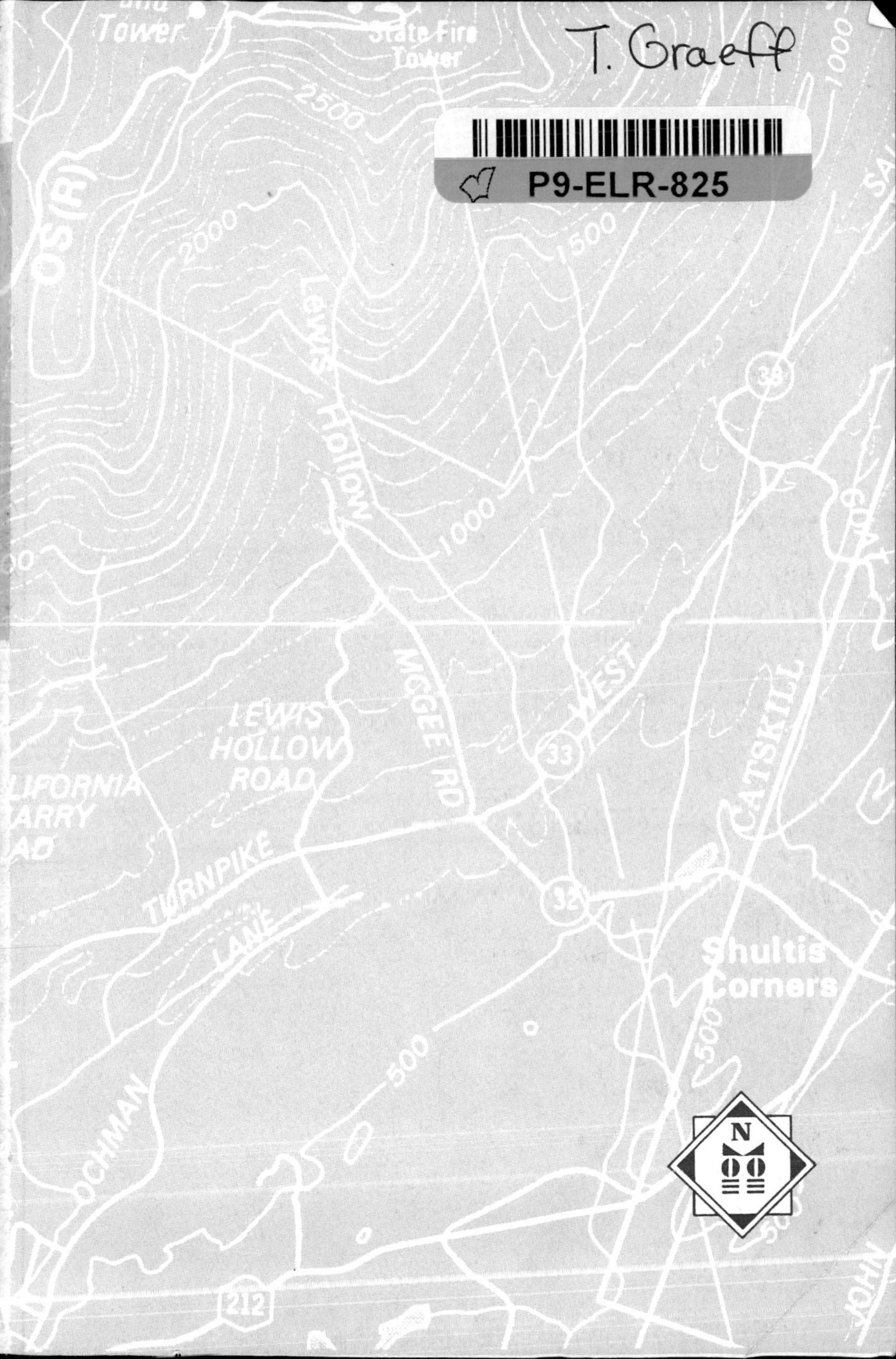

Tower
State Fire Tower
2500
2000
1500
1000
Lewis Hollow
LEWIS HOLLOW ROAD
MCGEE RD
WEST
33
38
32
CATSKILL
TURNPIKE
LANE
Shultis Corners
500
212

T. Graeff

published by **THE NEW YORK · NEW JERSEY TRAIL CONFERENCE**

HIKING
THE
CATSKILLS

*A Guide for Exploring
the Natural Beauty
of America's Romantic
& Magical Mountains
on the Trail and
"Off The Beaten Path."*

author **LEE MCALLISTER** • *associate author* **MYRON STEVEN OCHMAN**

Prepared and produced by The Whole Concept Design Studio, New York.
Designed & illustrated by Myron Steven Ochman.
Design associate Lee McAllister.
Photos by the authors.
Poems by Myron Steven Ochman.
Edited by Daniel D. Chazin.
Typesetting by Jason E. Genser, Starfleet Composition, New Jersey.
Composed in: Garth Graphic, Tiffany, Times Roman and Triumvirate.

Library of Congress Cataloging-in-Publication Data

McAllister, Lee, 1956-
   Hiking the Catskills.

   Bibliography: p.
   Includes index.
   1. Hiking--New York (State)--Catskill Mountains
--Guide-books.   2. Catskill Mountains (N.Y.)--
Description and travel--Guide-books. I. Ochman,
Myron Steven, 1957-   . II Title.
GV199.42.N652M376   1989   917.47'38   89-3129
ISBN 0-9603966-6-7 (soft)

Third Printing 1995

10   9   8   7   6   5   4   3

DEDICATION

Rainbows in all their infinite beauty
shine as they reach forever-more
and never-more than my heart reaches for you...

...Nathan Samuel, my dad,
for always pointing out the first buds of spring
...every spring!

...Cecile, my mom, for her everlasting zest for life!

...The Catskill Mountains,

Myron Steven Ochman

To my loving wife, Rosemary, for her support,
encouragement, assistance and patience; and in
memory of my mother, Helen, who instilled
in me the adventure that allowed me to
find the mountains.

Lee McAllister

THE AUTHORS

Lee McAllister is a native of Long Island and graduate of S.U.N.Y. College at Cortland; #434 of the Catskill 3500 Club; is also a member of the N.Y.-N.J. Trail Conference as well as the Catskill Center for Conservation and Development. Spends his free time hiking and exploring with family and friends. Runs, hunts, cross-country skis...just about anything outdoors. Enjoys doing slide show presentations and writing articles about the Catskill Mountains. Plans to do entire Long Path after its completion. Would like to retrace many of John Burroughs' original Catskill hikes.

Myron Steven Ochman is from North Woodmere, Long Island. Has a Bachelor of Fine Arts degree with a minor in Science from S.U.N.Y. Binghamton and has studied at Parsons School of Design. Founder of the Whole Concept Design Studio. Has updated and enhanced the N.Y.-N.J. Trail Conference's image by re-designing their entire line of trail map sets. #490 of the Catskill 3500 Club, as well as a member of of the N.Y.-N.J. Trail Conference and the Catskill Center for Conservation and Development. *Ever energized!*

ACKNOWLEDGMENTS

Special thanks:
Daniel D. Chazin
Howard Dash
H. Neil Zimmerman

Norman Carr
Madeline Dennis
Louis Ferrara, Sr.
Louis Ferrara, Jr.
Kingdon Gould
Gerald Hamm
Michael Kudish
Ken Kittle
Dennis Martin
Rosemary McAllister
Cecile W. Ochman
Evelyn L. Ochman
Marshall L. Ochman
Nelson Sears
Jack Sencabaugh
Bob Schrader
James Smith
Helen Tono
Hamilton Topping
Dick Van Laer
Matthew L. Visco
Dick Weir
Ray Wood
The Catskill Center
All the Fire Tower Observers!

PREFACE

We grew up in the suburbs of a large metropolitan area with a natural curiosity for outdoors and nature. We watched housing developments and shopping centers replace the meadows and woods. Each year there was less and less to explore. As we grew older, the automobile allowed us the mobility to discover Harriman State Park and the excellent hiking it affords.

Along with friends, we decided to try hiking in the Catskills. The mystique of these mountains looming in the distance, when viewed from the Hudson Valley, had always appealed to our sense of adventure. They were known to us as a place where the older crowd went to relax and fishermen coaxed trout with a fly rod. After seeing the view from a precipice near North Lake, we were hooked. Soon we were spending many a weekend exploring these mountains. We climbed all the required mountains for membership in the Catskill 3500 Club, but we did not stop there. We've hiked in all seasons and wandered around in many remote and out-of-the-way places. Somewhere along the way the thought occurred to write this book. Although we've hiked throughout the Northeast, the Catskills are like home to us!

Our love for the area combined with our enthusiasm for hiking is why we have written and designed this book. We want to share our knowledge and experience with the many hikers who may not be aware of the excellent hiking opportunities which the Catskills afford.

Our purpose is not just to recommend a particular trail or view, but to allow each hiker to choose where and when he or she would prefer to go, depending upon each individual's interests, ability and experience. This book will appeal both to the beginning hiker, who will be able to choose some fine introductory hikes, and to those more experienced, who will find suggested areas *"off the beaten path"* to explore.

You too can feel the tranquility and spirituality of the Catskills as well as enjoy the solitude of the little things that make life delightful, be it a small waterfall in the midst of a forest, a beautiful fern-filled col not shown on any map, or a fine light summit breeze during a spell of oppressively hot weather.

We offer more than mere descriptions of trails. We include notes on the history of the region, which will serve to add interest to hikes of particular areas. We also provide information on the types of vegetation and wildlife one is likely to encounter along the way, and on hiking equipment suitable to the various conditions. Finally, we interject short narratives of our own experiences throughout the Catskills.

The trail descriptions include mileage for the added convenience of the reader. We've also included the trail mileages list found on the backs of the New York-New Jersey Trail Conference's Catskill Trails map set.

This guidebook was designed for easy reading and easy access to needed trail information. We have, for example, italicized the trail-marker blaze colors, special views, water sources and other points of interest, as well as highlighted the trail names, mountains and relevant landmarks in a bold typeface. To avoid confusion on the trail we include in the trail descriptions directions with which you should turn at specific trail junctions, Left or Right; as well as North, East, South or West.

The descriptions of the trails and mountains are divided geographically into four chapters. Many of the suggested hikes entitled, *"Off The Beaten Path",* are in trailless areas or cross private property. As we repeatedly emphasize, it is important that anyone wishing to hike on private property secure permission and respect the landowner's rights. Moreover, those who decide to venture off the marked trails must be experienced and well prepared.

It is our sincere hope that all readers of this book, born of love of the Catskill region, will also enjoy the natural beauty of America's romantic and magical mountains as our families and friends will for years to come.

REGIONAL MAP

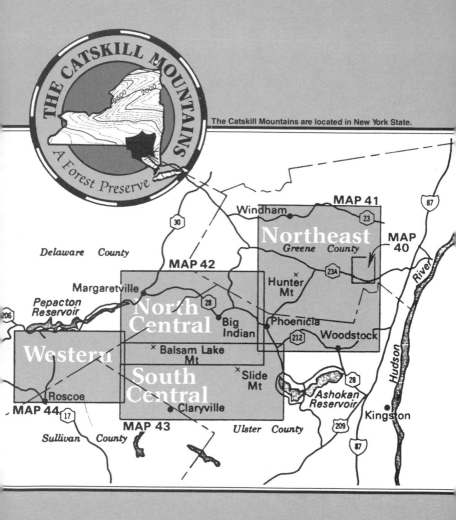

THE CATSKILL MOUNTAINS

A Forest Preserve

The Catskill Mountains are located in New York State.

MAP 41

Windham

Northeast

Greene County

MAP 40

MAP 42

Hunter Mt

Delaware County

Margaretville

North Central

Pepacton Reservoir

Big Indian

Phoenicia

Woodstock

Balsam Lake Mt

Western

Slide Mt

South Central

Roscoe

Ashokan Reservoir

Claryville

MAP 44

Kingston

MAP 43

Ulster County

Sullivan County

Hudson River

MAP LEGEND

Marked Trail & Terminus .... ⟶
Trail Name & Color ....**DB(B)**
Trail Color ....**R**-Red, **B**-Blue, **Y**-Yellow
Long Path Marker.. 🐾
Unmarked Trail .... ⎯ ⎯ ⎯ ⎯
Trail Parking...•**P**
Viewpoint...★
Leanto...•**L**
Water (spring) ....•**W**
Keep Out (private land) ....**KO**
Marked Elevation..△ 2663
Unmarked Elevation..× 2462
Primary Road..................................... ⎯ ━━━━━━
Secondary Road .... ━━━━━━
Route Markers (state, county) .... ⑳⑥ ㉴
Bus Stop ....•**B**

SCALE: 1:63,360 (1 inch = 1 mile)
Contour Interval 100 feet

Due to the magnetic
north all your com-
pass readings in the
Catskill Mountains
will read 13 degrees
west of the actual
north pole.

© 1989 OCHMAN

PHILOSOPHY

*"I go to nature
to be soothed
and healed and to
have my senses
put in tune
once more."*

John Burroughs

Why hike? Why camp out on the hard, cold ground among dirt and rock? Answers to these questions have always been obvious to outdoor enthusiasts.

In this "our electronic age," where television, home entertainment and fast foods often separate mind from body, there has been a renewal of interest, starting in the 1960's and accelerating in the '70s, in getting outdoors and back to nature. Today, there are more people taking to the outdoors than ever before.

There are several reasons for this. To begin with, a greater number of people than ever before have free time to pursue personal interests. Then again, many feel compelled by the pressures of the job and those created by our cities to escape to a quiet natural setting, seeking peace of mind. The fitness craze that has become popular in recent years also sends people outdoors, for exercise and to feel the exhilaration of clean air filling their lungs. Also, many people that view nature as a hobby or a science want to know and or feel somehow that life still goes on, in some places, as it did before man started tampering with the environment.

The challenge of hiking and camping is an excellent way to learn your own limitations, to teach yourself about yourself and to test yourself against the elements. We develop by learning new skills or learning more about ourselves each time we hike. Furthermore, there is a harmony and unison of all living things, including man, and this oneness with nature is a feeling we have often experienced in these mountains.

We have spiritually grown through our adventures, and time and again we return to the peace and tranquility that nature holds. We hope you too will experience these feelings. It is our responsibility to preserve this peace, not only for ourselves but for our children and our children's children. One thing is certain. Nature is here for us all, not just as keepers or preservers, but as a living part of it all.

©1989 Ochman

THE CATSKILL PAST

An Overview

"Geologically speaking, the Catskills are not true mountains but a plateau eroded down by millions of years of weathering."

*t*he Catskill Mountains rise west of the central Hudson Valley in New York State. To most, the Catskills conjure up huge resorts and popular nighttime entertainment. This misconception has caused many people interested in hiking to neglect the area entirely. The large resort hotels that some equate with the Catskills lie in Sullivan County, close to Route 17. The true mountains lie to the north, in northern Sullivan County, and in Ulster, Greene and Delaware Counties: a land of untamed mountains with aromatic, evergreen summits and awe-inspiring views, rich in folklore. It survives despite the seemingly endless years of uncontrolled tree cutting and burning without concern for the future, during a period in which the wilderness was believed to be inexhaustible. Trails traverse many of the higher mountains, but there are still several trailless mountains with summits in the same condition they were in thousands of years ago, open to the adventurous.

Geologically speaking, the Catskills are not true mountains but a plateau eroded down by millions of years of weathering. This area was beneath a shallow ocean during the Devonian Epoch (405-365 million years ago). As the North American and European continents moved slowly closer to one another, the buckling of the earth's tectonic plates caused the formation of the Appalachian Range. This went on for millions of years as water continued to run westward, forming an inland sea. The Catskill region was on the eastern fringe of this runoff and therefore retained coarse, resistant sediment buildup. The Catskills did not buckle with the rest of the Appalachians in the latter mountain-building episodes, yet they stand nearly 2,000 feet higher than the surrounding Appalachian plateau. It is believed the entire Catskill region uplifted during this time.

The proof can be found everywhere. Millions of years of sediment and life forms that collected at the bottom of this inland sea created a pressure so great that much of the sea's bottom was converted into sedimentary stone. As we now know, you can find these rock formations on any mountain in this region. They can be distinguished by their coarse parallel striated surface.

Sedimentary shale outcroppings like this are common throughout the Catskills.

Looking west down Black Dome Valley (Big Hollow) from Acra Point.

During the Pleistocene Epoch (commonly known as the Ice Ages), two million to fourteen thousand years ago, the northern half of North America was covered with great sheets of ice. These changed the lay of the land and weathered the mountains down to their present shape. Steep waterways formed to let melted ice escape as the great glaciers receded.

Evidence of these powerful forces of nature can be found throughout the region. For example, the so-named Goblin Gulch was cut on the eastern slope of Ashokan High Point by water tumbling southward to Olive Bridge Dam. *Drumlins* are elongated or oval hills formed by the movement of a glacier, such that its elongated shape parallels the direction of movement of the glacier. Van Loan Hill and Round Hill in the northern Catskills are examples. *Potholes* are smooth ovoid depressions in rock formed by the swirling action of water and gravel. Many were formed during the Ice Age from the billions and billions of gallons of glacial runoff.

The Catskills have a wealth of small streams and brooks which give way to several larger waterways.

These drain into major rivers such as the Delaware, the Mohawk, and, of course, the Hudson, the first major route into upstate New York. Henry Hudson, sailing for the Dutch crown, was the first European to sail up the river. In 1605, he made mention of seeing the prominent mountains that rose to the west.

The Dutch soon set up one of their first trading posts, called Fort Orange, at what is now Albany, and by 1655, Kingston (then called Sopus), located in the central Hudson River valley, was founded. They became important trading centers for trappers. However, settlement in the Catskills during this period was limited. Colonization and exploitation of the mountains was initially prevented by a series of skirmishes between the Dutch settlers and the local Indians that became known as the Esopus Wars (1655-1663). Then came the clashes between the Dutch and the English, who had taken control of New York.

But these were relatively minor obstacles to settlement of the Catskills, compared to what happened next. Through political and diplomatic maneuvering, in 1708 Queen Anne was persuaded to grant a patent for an allegedly small tract of land to seven individuals, including the influential Major Johannis Hardenburgh. The "small" grant turned out to be about two million acres, comprising most of present-day Sullivan, Ulster, Greene and Delaware Counties and including virtually all the mountainous terrain of the Catskills.

Difficulties began with the attempt to survey the land to divide it. The local Indians were not cooperative; they removed the stone markers set up by the surveyors. This became a cat-and-mouse game that went on for some time and culminated in the stealing of the surveyors' compass, thus making it impossible for them to complete their job. But the inevitable could not be put off forever and, when the surveying was finally completed, lawsuits over boundary disputes began.

When Hardenburgh died in 1748, the patent was still in dispute, and there were now numerous relatives of the original patentees claiming rights to tracts within the "Great Patent." Questions went on for years about this amazing land deal, and local people and historians still puzzle over it today. The arguments over title to the patent had a long-lasting effect on the region; they kept most settlers out and protected the land from exploitation until well into the 19th century.

Thus, the Catskills stayed an unchanged wilderness longer than one would have expected. Larger mountain areas, such as the White Mountains in New Hampshire or the Green Mountains in Vermont, were settled and accurately mapped before the Catskills were.

During the War of Independence there were many bloody battles at frontier outposts. Although the Catskills were not a critical area of dispute, guerilla warfare on the part of the Tories and their Iroquois allies from central New York kept the colonists of the Hudson Valley on their guard. After the war was over, settlers slowly moved into the area with leases from landlords who were descendants of the Hardenburgh patent owners.

With the coming of the Industrial Revolution, the virgin land was destined to be abused. In 1817, Colonel William Edwards bought some land on the Schoharie Creek and decided it was a suitable site for a tannery. Tanning (the process of turning hides into leather) was already prevalent in New England. The bark of the hemlock tree was needed for this process.

Large tracts of mature trees, growing in the shady valleys and cloves of the Catskills, were available to supply this bark for Colonel Edwards' tannery. The town that sprang up around the tannery was called Edwardsville. It is the present-day town of Hunter. Soon tanneries opened all over the Catskills, wherever suitable water supplies and hemlock trees could be found. The assault on the forest had begun.

There are many stories of the tanneries and the immigrants who worked in them. One interesting character was Zadock Pratt, who founded a tannery in a place which still bears his name, Prattsville. Pratt saw the huge quantities of wasted tree carcasses and the stripping of hillsides and valleys, and realized that this could lead to serious erosion, and large fires from the masses of dead trees left to rot.

Pratt replanted trees around the village of Prattsville, a method of conservation unheard of in his day. He also saw to it that his town was thoughtfully laid out, and he even tried to establish farming, with a local staple of butter as the premium product. In this way he hoped to have the town flourish long after the tannery was gone.

High on a hillside overlooking the site of the old tannery are engravings in rocks in which Pratt gave praise to the tanning life and all it had given him. Known as Pratt's Rocks, they can be reached from Route 23, just south of the village of Prattsville. A visit to them makes for an interesting excursion and provides insight into this unusual man and his life.

Tanning thrived in the area until shortly after the Civil War, when all reachable tracts of hemlocks were gone. Catskill-tanned leather played a very large role in the equipping of Union troops in that war. Today a virgin hemlock grove is a rarity for hikers to find; only a few have survived.

Another industry that flourished in the 1800's was quarrying, which supplied much-needed bluestone for major cities all over the United States. But this industry died late in the 19th century, after the discovery of the much less expensive portland cement. Only small-scale quarrying still goes on today. Meanwhile, the lucky hiker may come across abandoned quarries in the middle of the woods; they are interesting places to examine. Logging, another mountain industry, still goes on today. Other small industries which once flourished in the Catskills are acid wood plants, distilleries, and factories for making furniture and barrels. Many industries come and go; however, one industry that started in the 1800's lasted. This was the tourist industry.

"The assault on the forest had begun."

In the 1820's, America entered into her Romantic period. Much value was placed on the arts and the awareness of nature. A good view was held in high esteem. Despite the ravaging of the land that started at the time, the Catskills still held much natural beauty, and the aristocracy and intelligentsia of America found this area the prime place to meet. The rich and famous came to the few large hotels that flourished here.

As America moved westward, these great hotels closed, one by one. However, the many immigrant ethnic groups that poured into the country in the late 1800's started coming to boarding houses and small hotels. Irish, Italians, Germans and Eastern European Jews enjoyed the area. The railroads and steamships that had done so much for other local industries were now bringing the masses to the mountains. It was not unusual to see thousands of husbands commuting up to the Catskills from New York City on Friday nights to spend the weekend with their families. This was their getaway from the Industrial Revolution.

In 1885 the creation of the Forest Preserve changed the outlook of the land by saving it from the logger and lending it to the tourist. How this happened is an interesting story in itself. In the early 1880's a crusade was initiated by New York businessmen and sportsmen to save the Adirondacks from the merciless logging that was stripping the land. It was feared that uncontrolled logging would cause large-scale erosion which could possibly fill the Erie Canal and the Hudson River with silt, thereby crippling New York State's economic bloodlines. Little attention was given to the Catskills at that time.

Pepacton Reservoir in early morning.

However, it seems that once again political hankypanky was at work, much as it had been when the Hardenburgh patent was granted. Ulster County had incurred a large debt of unpaid taxes to the state for lands surrounding Slide Mountain. The details of the deal are sketchy, but the result was that these lands were turned over to the state to satisfy the debt and were included in the Forest Preserve.

The language of this historic bill is now found in Article XIV of the State Constitution. It reads: "The lands of the state, now owned or hereafter acquired, constituting the forest preserve as now fixed by law, shall be *forever kept as wild forest lands.* They shall not be leased, sold or exchanged or be taken by any corporation, public or private, nor shall the timber thereon be sold, removed or destroyed." So, although the Catskills were added to this bill as an afterthought, the state has been acquiring lands and enlarging the Forest Preserve to the present. Today, the Catskill Park, delineated by an imaginary "blue line" on the map, covers 705,000 acres, of which 272,039 acres (39%) are state-owned Forest Preserve.

"The lands of the state, now owned or hereafter acquired, constituting the forest preserve as now fixed by law, shall be forever kept as wild forest lands. They shall not be leased, sold or exchanged or be taken by any corporation, public or private, nor shall the timber thereon be sold, removed or destroyed."

Signs like these denote Forest Preserve boundaries.

The last big change to take place was the creation of the New York City reservoir system. The city realized that it could not accommodate its growing population with its existing water supply. It turned its eyes to the many streams and creeks that made up the Catskill watersheds, and bought large areas of land. To make way for the first reservoir, the Ashokan, which was completed in 1915, seven small hamlets and a number of farms were forced to move from their Esopus Valley home.

Furious at first, the people of the Catskills soon realized that there was money in this new project. The protests became murmurs and eventually died down. Five other reservoirs, Schoharie, Roundout, Neversink, Pepacton and Cannonsville, eventually joined the Ashokan. (The last of these reservoirs was completed in 1960). These are engineering marvels that actually add to the beauty of the area. The water is carried down toward the city in underground "aqueducts" which tunnel under large mountains in their course southward.

During the early 1900's, many more people became enthralled with the Catskills, largely as a result of the prolific writings of naturalist John Burroughs, a native of Roxbury. Burroughs' sensitive and amusing observations of the flora and fauna of the region, along with his own experiences, made him the most widely read naturalist of his time.

Small hotels and summer boarding houses continued to spring up throughout the Catskills and contribute to the region's reputation as a place to get away. The state continued to purchase large tracts of land that helped form the Forest Preserve as we know it today, and much of the land began to revert from farmland back to forest.

In 1975, a temporary state commission to study the Catskills was set up. This commission did a thorough study of the region to determine what plan should be adopted to manage the region and help the residents.

Today the Catskills are becoming recognized as a major source of year-round recreational activities. The area now offers many more fine hiking opportunities than ever before. The centennial of the Forest Preserve in 1985 helped showcase the region. With proper management from the Department of Environmental Conservation, the Catskills will continue to flourish as a hikers' paradise.

"Burroughs' sensitive and amusing observations of the flora and fauna of the region, along with his own experiences, made him the most widely read naturalist of his time."

New York State marker commemorating the centennial of the Forest Preserve.

©1989 OCHMAN

THE CATSKILLS TODAY

Flora & Fauna

"Today most summits above 3,500 feet in elevation are covered with virgin spruce and fir, remnants of the post-glacial forests."

When the last Ice Age receded, it left behind a layer of rock, clay and sand known as **drift** or glacial till on the mountains. A combination of this soil and climate allowed alpine plants to take hold. Later on, the area became dominated by boreal coniferous species, such as balsam fir and red spruce. The moderating climate eventually led to an invasion of other trees, including tall hemlocks and hardwoods, such as maple and beech, which grew in the valleys and on the mountain slopes. Today most summits above 3,500 feet in elevation are covered with virgin spruce and fir, remnants of the post-glacial forests. Indeed, according to Michael Kudish, Professor of Forestry at Paul Smith's College, who has made an in-depth study of Catskill vegetation, there are still a few scattered areas in the Catskills where alpine plants (such as alpine cinquefoil) may be found.

Today, three distinct vegetational groups may be found in the Catskills: **oak-hickory forest** (also known as southern hardwoods), **beech-birch-maple forest** (also known as northern hardwoods), and **spruce-fir forest** (also known as northern coniferous forest).

The oak-hickory forest consists of trees such as oak, hickory, black gum, tulip and flowering dogwood which are widespread in the southern part of the United States, but also are found further north at the lowest elevations in the major river valleys.

The beech-birch-maple forest is commonly found in the northeast along with black cherry and white ash.

In the Catskills, the spruce-fir forest, found mainly in areas above 3,500 feet in elevation, consists primarily of balsam fir and red spruce, along with a scattering of hardwoods such as paper birch, mountain ash and red cherry.

What makes the Catskills unique is that a hiker can pass through all three groups, normally found hundreds of miles apart, in a few hours!

The presence of evergreen trees on the summits is a welcome and refreshing sight to the hiker. These trees give the mountain tops of the Catskills a special character and provide a much appreciated change of pace.

Another feature of the Catskills which has given us much pleasure is the abundance of wildflowers. Any nature lover will be enthralled with the amazing diversity of wildflowers found in the Catskills. The famous naturalist John Burroughs used to go on many an outing just to find a rare or special wildflower known to bloom in a particular habitat.

Bee balm, also known as oswego tea, grows along streams and flowing ponds in late summer.

New York asters are often found in wet areas.

Bunchberry, also known as dwarf cornell, grows in cool woods near summits.

Painted trillium graces the forest floor in May.

Some wildflowers, such as the wood sorrel and spring beauty, are abundant in the Catskills; others are rarely found. Certain species, such as the jewel-weed (touch-me-not), are very conspicuous, while others, such as wild sarsaparilla and wild oats, are not quite as showy. Many wildflowers are known for their delicate beauty, such as the painted trillium and the goldthread.

From the first appearance of Dutchman's breeches and Canada violets, small, delicate spring wildflowers, to the large, colorful asters of autumn, keen-eyed hikers will be able to spot many and varied types of wildflowers. For those who wish more information on wildflowers in the Catskills, we've listed in the back of the book a few of the field guides available.

The Catskills also feature a wide variety of wildlife. The change in the landscape from the many farms and clearings of the last century to the thick second-growth forests and abandoned old pastures seen today has had a definite effect on the wildlife in the area. Alert hikers will perceive signs of mountain wildlife in the most inconspicuous and unlikely places. No matter how much noise you can make on the trail, you are bound to see some animal life.

Some of the creatures are common to most of us; others are secretive and mysterious. Keeping in mind that wildlife is everything from beetle to black bear gives you a whole new world to explore. Sometimes an encounter will take place so fast that you'll barely have time to take a quick breath, while other times you'll be able to relax and observe as the action unfolds before you...but don't count on it! The thrill that wildlife adds to a campout or hike is immeasurable. One thing is sure: nature will never fail to amaze those who take the time to observe it.

At one time, the Catskills were inhabited by wolves, mountain lions, lynx and possibly even elk. These have disappeared with the settling of the area, but a great diversity of wildlife still exists. Possibly the most popular animal associated with the woods is the **whitetail deer**. During the nineteenth century, a combination of year-round hunting pressure and the removal of much of the deer's natural cover helped bring them to the verge of extinction in the Catskills.

In the late 1800's, deer sightings made the local newspapers! An effort was made to restore some deer to the region by bringing a few in from the Adirondacks in 1889 and penning them on two hundred acres near Winnisook Lake at the base of Slide Mountain. Many folks would come to see the deer as a Sunday afternoon outing. Within a few years the protected deer multiplied and, by 1895, they were released. At the same time, white-tailed deer migrated to the area from Pennsylvania. When farming declined in the Catskills, leaving old orchards and abandoned clearings, the understory along the perimeter of the fields begin to grow back, enabling the deer to thrive again.

Today, due to this favorable habitat, there are far more deer than when settlers first entered the area. The absence of some of the deer's natural predators has also led to this population explosion. The state has a hunting season each fall to try to keep the deer herds from overpopulating their range. The firearms season is generally from mid-November to mid-December. Hunters fill the woods the first few days of the season, and hiking during this time of the year should be discouraged. Check the newspapers for the exact dates. If you want to hike during the hunting season, wear bright colors and make plenty of noise!

Whitetail deer see movement extremely well, have supersensitive hearing for anything out of the ordinary and are familiar with every inch of their terrain. They know how to traverse their area quickly and quietly. If you're lucky, you can spot deer any time of the year by walking quietly and watching for movement ahead of you. You are more likely to see

"...nature will never fail to amaze those who take the time to observe it."

signs of deer, especially prints in the snow or well traveled "deer paths" running along a steep hillside, usually on south or west slopes, where there is maximum sun exposure.

The largest animal found in these mountains is the **black bear**, which is quite shy and avoids contact with man wherever possible. It is amazingly quick and quiet, considering its size (large males can exceed 500 pounds!). This explains how it can live in close proximity to man without being discovered. The chances of seeing one are slim, although it is estimated that there are some 900 bears in the Catskill region. A sure sign that a bear is in the area is its droppings, which are large and dark. These animals hibernate in winter but can be stirred during warm wet spells.

Hiking the ridge line of West Kill Mountain, we once saw a tree with distinct claw marks higher than our heads. This is the bear's way of marking his territory. Unlike the situation elsewhere, you'll rarely hear of a Catskill bear coming to a garbage area in broad daylight. They usually head in the other direction when they smell or hear you coming. In sum, they pose little threat to the hiker and enhance the outdoors by just being there.

The **coyote** has an interesting story. It is unknown whether or not the coyote inhabited these lands prior to the 1940's. However, in the 1950's and 1960's it migrated eastward through Canada and spread its range into New England and New York. Today it is fairly common although rarely seen. One of us saw one while off the trail and resting on some steep ledges of Mary Smith Hill in the Western Catskills. It was fairly large and pursuing a whitetail doe. These keen hunters usually travel in small packs. The eastern species of coyotes rarely howl, so you probably won't hear one. You'd have to be in the right place at the right time to see one. Like most wild animals, they avoid people at all costs.

Another predator to inhabit the Catskills is the **bobcat**. It is the true wild cat of these mountains. Despite their rarity, we have seen many signs of them in most areas of the Catskills. Females leave their droppings on the tops of bare rocks to mark their territory. You'll see their tracks, particularly in the snow. We once found fresh tracks on a winter hike up Fir Mountain. Trying to follow them proved difficult and useless because these cats get in and around places people can't.

The bobcat is primarily nocturnal and can cover many miles in a night before holding up for a day. A forest fire observer in the Balsam Lake Mountain fire tower told us that a bobcat once ran out in front of his jeep on his way up one morning. He was impressed by the speed with which it took off. Bobcats prey on many small animals and on occasion a weak deer, yet their favorite meal is the snowshoe hare, which inhabits the higher elevations. Once heard, the piercing scream of this cat will never be forgotten.

There are several members of the weasel family that inhabit various areas of the mountains. **Mink** and **otter** are found along waterways, especially away from areas frequented by man. Both are long dark-colored animals, the mink being smaller. Mink are very active and can be found hopping along backwoods creeks and streams in search of fish, frogs, mice and anything else they can take for a meal. Otters are very playful and are often found in groups. They can be great fun to watch if you are lucky enough to find some, but they are fearful of people and should be watched from a distance. If you are bushwhacking along a stream, or camped in a backwoods area near running water, you should be aware of the possibility of spotting these critters.

Two types of **weasel** are found in the Catskills: long-tailed and short-tailed (also known as "ermine"). They both can inhabit woodlands or brushy farm areas. The long-tailed weasel is the larger of the two.

"Once heard, the piercing scream of this cat will never be forgotten."

Both animals are small, with the long thin bodies and short legs characteristic of much of the weasel family. They are ferocious hunters that can kill animals larger than themselves. One winter day, we found tracks in the fresh snow that indicated a den entrance on top of Plateau Mountain. The weasels utilized a few main trails from the den. We saw a similar situation on North Dome.

The **ermine** is a small predator that rarely gets over 13 inches in length. Its fur turns white in winter and is valued for this reason. The tip of the tail and eyes are the only parts of the animal that are black. As is the case with most woodland creatures, in order to see one you have to be quiet and lucky!

The **fisher** is another member of the weasel family that is little known and rarely seen. It has a very dark-colored body sometimes exceeding three feet in length, including a long tail. The fisher is not common in the Catskills, but DEC officials have assured us it is there. It favors mature forest wilderness areas and has a home range of 50-150 square miles, which is one reason there are not great numbers of these animals in the Catskills. It climbs trees well and is the only animal that has any success at flipping a porcupine over and killing it. For this reason, the state released a few of them in an effort to decrease the porcupine population. The program was not too successful, although at least one fisher set up territory near Hunter Mountain. Some have moved into the Catskills from the north. Although the fisher may be found in the Northern Catskills, it is still unlikely you'll get to observe one.

There is a **porcupine** problem in the Catskills. The few predators of the porcupine have failed to find a way to consistently subdue and kill them. They seem particularly prevalent along the Escarpment Trail in the Northern Catskills. They are one of the strangest looking animals in the forest, with white-tipped quills covering their bodies. We have had them waddle out in front of us on the trail, and even when hurrying to get away they don't move all that quickly. For this reason, you are likely to get some pictures of this animal if you have a camera handy. Porcupines move around day and night in search of food, eating the bark off trees. If you see a tree that is bare of bark in certain spots, examine it closely. If the damage was done by a porcupine, you'll see small teeth marks where the bark was cleanly stripped off. This is most noticeable on small beech trees.

"Porcupines love anything... We know of one friend who had a heavy pair of hiking boots chewed up."

Porcupines love anything with salt on it; in fact, it seems they'll try anything once. We know of one friend who had a heavy pair of hiking boots chewed up. The point is that porkies will chew up anything that has been sweated on. You may notice many of the old metal trail markers chewed and scuffed up. Porcupines seem especially fond of them, too!

These animals also make a good deal of grunting noises, as we can attest to. Even John Burroughs told of them keeping him awake his first night on Slide Mountain. One night on the Escarpment Trail, we awoke in the middle of the night to loud grunting and choking noises. Peeking out of the tent we saw nine or ten porcupines in a semicircle in front of the tent carrying on. Chasing them proved useless. When we got up early to watch the sunrise, we found one waiting to watch the sunrise with us. He clambered down and crawled into a nearby rock overhang as we took pictures.

Porcupines are harmless if left alone, but don't get too close for a picture. If you have a dog on the trail with you, we suggest you keep him leashed. The dog will likely come out on the short end of any confrontation. If the victim is struck, the quills will swell up. If by chance something of this nature should happen, it is said the barbs can be removed by cutting them about halfway and exposing the hollow core to relieve the pressure within. After you've seen one of these fellows clumsily lumbering about, you'll agree that they can make any hike more enjoyable and exciting.

You're also likely to see the **raccoon**. These little masked bandits inhabit the valleys and lower slopes, usually near streams. They are the true thieves of the forest and will go through anything left lying around. They have nimble fingers that can open zippers; therefore, no food should be left unwrapped or these fellows will find it. If you stay at a lean-to, you should expect one or more to drop by for a snack some time during the night. Although they appear playful, they can be vicious and should not be cornered or chased. Raccoons can carry rabies. There has been a serious rabies outbreak down south, and it appears to be slowly spreading northward. As of yet, it has not reached New York but it is quite possible that it may. Like all wild animals, raccoons should not be approached closely, especially if they appear tame. If you secure your packs, you need not worry about these animals. Their curiosity is their most troublesome trait.

While in the woods in the lower valleys, you might also come in contact with a **striped skunk**. Try to keep grinning as you slowly back off. If sprayed by a skunk, you may never get the smell out of your clothes and will probably lose your ride home! Skunks are best left alone. They are the number one carrier of rabies in the United States.

Other animals you're likely to see in the lower areas are the **woodchuck** and **opossum**. The woodchuck can be found in clearings and pastures. This plump animal, which farmers despise, never strays far from its den hole. The mound around the hole has caused many a horse to break a leg and much farm equipment to be damaged. Woodchucks favor clearings where they can see enemies approach. They are common throughout the valleys and farmlands of the Catskills. The opossum is a strange looking creature. The brightly colored hair on its snoot makes its face appear bare, and its tail is long and rat like. It climbs trees well and eats almost anything. It is mainly nocturnal and usually is only seen dead on the roads, since it feeds on road kills and does not avoid cars.

One of the more successful stories is that of the **beaver**. Its valuable pelts were a major source of income during early settlement. The fur was in great demand during the eighteenth and nineteenth centuries. Unregulated trapping resulted in this animal becoming extinct in all parts of the state except the Adirondacks. After a moratorium on trapping of any kind, a few were released in other parts of the state. Today, the animal has made a full comeback, even to the point of allowing for a trapping season again. We've come upon the beaver at scattered locations in the Catskills, such as the valley of the East Branch of the Neversink, the East Kill Creek south of Stony Clove, Long Pond and Alder Lake. There are noticeable beaver lodges evident in Kenozia Lake just north of Route 28 and a few miles west of the village of Ashokan.

Except for man, no other animal causes such an impact on the immediate environment. Beavers are constantly taking trees down and reinforcing their dams. They can turn a forest into a wet open meadow in a few months. They are fascinating to observe, and you'll want to spend some time checking out their areas. If you find a new dam, the cleanly cut branches can make excellent walking sticks or showpieces.

Another animal you may see in marshy, wet areas is the **muskrat**, which also builds dens by the waterside. It may look like a beaver at first, but the lack of the flappy tail will give it away. Muskrats are also trapped for their valuable pelts.

The **eastern cottontail rabbit**, a common sight to suburban dwellers, is also found in the brushy areas and thickets in valleys in the Catskills. The **snowshoe hare** is likely to be found in and around

"Except for man, no other animal causes such an impact on the immediate environment."

many summits just off the trail. Much larger than the cottontail, this hare inhabits higher elevations where snow will pile up and cause other animals to bog down. Their large well-furred feet keep them on top of the snow. They change from brown to all white in winter. This provides excellent camouflage in the snow, but during early melts in spring it can give them away. One of our hiking partners had one jump in front of him on top of Mill Brook Ridge. It was mottled white and brown but stood out no matter where it was. You'll see signs in tracks and droppings all over the higher peaks in winter time. We had one take off in four feet of snow right in front of us near the top of Panther Mountain. We'd swear he was wearing Sherpa snowshoes because of the ease and quickness with which he moved.

Among the smaller animals you'll see are the squirrels. There are three different species found in the Catskills. The **grey squirrel** is known to most of us. In the Catskills, they can usually be seen scouring the forest floor for acorns and other nuts. The smaller **red squirrel** lives in mixed stands of evergreens and deciduous trees. They are found at the summits of the highest mountains, especially in tall spruce and fir trees and in stands of hemlock. Though they are difficult to spot, they chatter loudly, and their movement in running from branch to branch usually gives them away. We once watched one on top of West Kill Mountain run from one end of our sight to the other without touching ground. They are the active go-getters of the evergreen forests. They'll also come into your camp and take any food left lying unprotected. The third type of squirrel is the **northern flying squirrel**. They are strictly nocturnal and glide from tree to tree without making a sound. For this reason they are difficult to observe. If you are lying on your back in the open woods around dusk, you may see one in flight between tall, mature trees. This is yet another example of an animal that is there, but rarely, if ever, seen.

A relative of the squirrels is the perky and hyperactive **eastern chipmunk**. They'll announce their presence to the unsuspecting hiker by chirping loudly, then suddenly scooting off through the leaves or ferns. They are curious and may come to investigate your campsite. They make a constant loud chipping sound (very much like the clucking of the wild turkey) which can be heard for some distance in the woods.

Other small woodland mammals are various species of field **mice**, **shrews** and **voles**. The mice are usually found in clearings near an old stone fence or structure. They have large eyes and thin bodies. Voles are rounder with very small eyes. Those found in the Catskills are usually reddish brown, while mice tend to be grey. Voles will travel under and around leaves along the ground. The tiny shrew is a voracious hunter for its size. They are small, narrow animals with a narrow snoot and small, almost non-existent eyes. They are grey and inhabit the woodlands. They scamper around the forest floor in search of something to eat. There are several species in the area. Any of these small animals can be seen only by sitting quietly on a rock and waiting for them to start moving around again. This can take up to an hour at times.

Wild turkeys are large native birds that have made a strong comeback after being restocked. They are shy and travel in flocks during the winter. They prefer to run along the ground and will fly only if threatened. Their large tracks are evident in the snow. They are very common in the hills of the Western Catskills. On Mary Smith Hill, one of us sat and watched a flock walk right past three deer. The deer didn't even blink their eyes. Turkeys can be found in the middle of the forest or in clearings.

Ruffed grouse are a favorite of hunters. They are extremely fast and explode into flight when flushed.

Normally thought of as a bird of woods edges and clearings, we've flushed them several times in deep woods where they had room to fly and manuever between trees. Keep a watchful eye, for it is possible to walk right by one without knowing it. This was almost the case one day as one of us walked right by a grouse on the trail. The second person stopped for a moment and the bird took off and thundered away in front of him. The most unusual place we flushed one of these birds was on the steep eastern slopes of Black Dome, at an elevation of about 3,800 feet.

There are several predatory birds in the mountains. Different species of **hawks** and **turkey vultures** can be seen drifting on the updrafts from open ledges. We once saw a rare peregrine falcon aflight over the Escarpment Trail. **Owls** are more often heard than seen. Their hoots can fill the ravines and valleys at night. One time on the Beaver Kill Ridge, we found a spot in the fresh snow where a grouse had recently been killed, most likely by a great horned owl. Feathers and ruffled snow were all that was left to see.

The alert hiker can have hours of enjoyment and memories by watching the antics of birds. One of us watched **cedar waxwings** pass berries down a line on top of North Point until all had eaten. On an early spring hike up Big Indian Mountain, we were suddenly surrounded by a flock of colorful **pine grosbeaks**. We remember the **chickadees** we hand fed in seven-degree weather on the summit of Slide; the flock of colorful **evening grosbeaks** we observed in winter at the base of Halcott Mountain; the **ruby-throated hummingbird** shimmering in the sun as it pollinated a crabapple tree in Woodstock. We could go on and on. The point is you can add a lot to the enjoyment of hiking by learning what's around you and appreciating it. To observe birds, a small pair of binoculars will help greatly.

The diversity of wildlife in the Catskills is endless. There are **bats** filling summer nights with mystery, **newts** floating at a pond's edge, **dragonflies** landing on wildflowers, and **brook trout** swimming in small isolated brooks. Few animals pose hazards. One that does is the **rattlesnake**. It would like to avoid people but people don't always avoid it. It is concentrated in a few areas (Vernoy Falls, Balsam Swamp, Tremper and Overlook Mountains) and chances of seeing one are slim. We discuss this further in the Tremper Mountain section of this book.

Last but not least, let's not forget about **black flies** and **mosquitoes**! They can really pain a person on an outing, especially in sticky, hot weather late in the spring or early in the summer. Another hazard to be aware of is the possibility of stepping on a **hornets'** nest built in the ground, usually alongside a stream. Some people are allergic to bee stings. These people should get their doctor's advice and carry medication or antihistamines with them. Being cautious as to where you step is also helpful. No one said hiking is without its pitfalls. You learn to take the good with the bad and hope the good memories and experiences linger on, and they usually do.

There are a good number of field guides available that will help in identifying animals and birds. We've listed some useful ones in the back of the book.

MANAGEMENT

The state land in the Catskills is maintained and protected by the New York State Department of Environmental Conservation (DEC). It patrols the lands, supervises the state campgrounds, maintains trails and enforces the regulations regarding the use of the area. The main office of the DEC is located in Albany. For administrative purposes, the DEC has divided the state into nine different regions. Unfortunately, the Catskills are under the jurisdiction of two regions. Delaware, Greene and Schoharie Counties are part of Region 4, with local offices in Stamford and Catskill; Ulster and Sullivan Counties are in Region 3, with an office in New Paltz.

As a result, coordination of management of the Catskills is more complex than it would be under one regional office. Like it or not, this is the present alignment, and we've been told it's unlikely to be changed.

A Catskill Park State Land Plan has been drawn up by the DEC to provide guidelines for proper management of the area. The plan lists four land classifications that indicate how the land should be managed: *Wilderness, Wild Forest, Intensive Use and Administrative.* The difference lies in the degree of human disturbance and the amount of outdoor recreational use allowed in each. Wilderness areas have minimal intrusion by people, and plans are to keep them as primeval and undisturbed as possible. **There are four designated wilderness areas**: The Slide-Panther Mountain Area, Big Indian-Beaverkill Range, North Dome-West Kill Mountain and Plateau-Indian Head Mountain Range.

Lands classified as Wild Forest, which represent a majority of the state land in the Catskills, are generally more accessible and allow a wider variety of outdoor recreational activity. It should be noted that there are several areas of Wild Forest that would have been classified as wilderness areas except for the fact that they are smaller than the required 10,000-acre minimum size established by the state. Intensive use areas are state campgrounds and other areas allowing concentrated outdoor activity. They represent a relatively small proportion of the Forest Preserve. Administrative lands are used for purposes other than those ordinarily permitted in the Forest Preserve. The State Fish Hatchery in DeBruce is an example.

The hiker may also come across signs for multiple use or reforestation areas. These are state lands outside the Forest Preserve itself that are managed for harvesting of trees or other purposes. These areas are not subject to strict regulations regarding vehicle use, while within the Forest Preserve all motorized vehicles are prohibited on state lands except where otherwise designated.

DEC trail cutting policies are very tight in wilderness areas, as they should be. A permit must be granted before any greenery can be cut to clear new trails. It is difficult to obtain permission to cut new vistas, and such permission must be obtained through the DEC's planning process, which allows for public input. Another task that has kept the DEC busy is the clean-up of the huge amounts of garbage found at trailheads and campsites in many areas in the Catskills.

The DEC has full-time forest rangers patrolling the Catskills as well as seasonal assistant forest rangers who work spring through fall. They are always checking for problems on the trails and making sure people don't camp above 3,500 feet elevation. Camping above that level was prohibited in the early 1980's in an effort to keep the fragile summit environments from becoming overused and scarred. At higher elevations, the plants are subject to very harsh conditions and regenerate more slowly. Before the establishment of this rule, many popular summits were subject to serious abuse, with some campers cutting down live trees to get wood for fires. We ask that you adhere to the 3,500-foot rule so that the mountain tops will stay as wild and natural as they were the day before you were there.

In 1969, the Catskill Center for Conservation and Development, a non-profit organization, was formed. Made up of independent citizens, the center is actively involved in Catskill affairs. It has helped to unify the area through legal and political efforts to protect

"...adhere to the 3,500-foot rule so that the mountain tops will stay as wild and natural as they were the day before you were there."

The Erpf House.

the social, economic and environmental well-being of
the Catskills. Proper planning for future goals, including conservation and enhancement of the region's
resources, has been a priority of the Catskill Center.
Through its efforts, many historic buildings have
been saved and restored. The Hanford Mills Museum
in East Meredith and the former home and studio of
Thomas Cole in Catskill are but two examples.

The Center has acquired large parcels of wilderness tracts for later state acquisition and has also
provided time and assistance to help revitalize several communities. Books and pamphlets pertaining to
the Catskills are available at the Center. Perhaps the
most important thing the Catskill Center has done is
arouse local and public awareness to the perils that
could befall the region. The best example of this is an
article printed by the Center detailing the purchase
and careless subdivision of land by out-of-state interests. It has stimulated many Catskill towns to
enact stricter legislation to protect their areas.

Our hats are off to the Center for its excellent
work. The Center is located in the Erpf House on Route

28 in Arkville. Located in the same building is the Erpf Cultural Center, which displays local crafts and art. Stop in when you're in the area.

Several hiking clubs also have ties to the area. The Catskill 3500 Club was formed in 1962 to encourage the climbing of Catskill peaks over 3,500 feet in elevation, including trailless summits. This gives people a chance to explore many different and interesting areas not seen by most hikers. The club has attached small orange summit boxes (known as "canisters") to trees at the top of these trailless mountains in order to enable those who bushwhack to the summits of these peaks to record their achievements. Many beautiful views can be found that you'd probably never have known existed if you hadn't bushwhacked these trailless mountains. We had fun every step of the way becoming members.

A major group is our own New York-New Jersey Trail Conference. It is a non-profit federation of over 70 hiking clubs and 6,000 individuals that helps build and maintain trails and promote conservation. Formed in 1920, the members of this association have always taken pride in their work. The founders of the Conference built the first section of the Appalachian Trail in 1923. Today they maintain some 800 miles of trail. In the Catskills, they oversee the maintenance of various sections of the Long Path.

Another hiking group interested in the Catskills is the Appalachian Mountain Club. They assist in trail cleanup, maintenance and construction throughout the Catskills. This club has a large membership with several chapters throughout the East.

There are many other benefits of membership, including maps and literature (such as NY-NJ Trail Conference's excellent Catskill maps) available at discount prices. Most importantly, your reasonable annual dues will go towards helping the club perform its valuable activities, including trail cleanup, maintenance and a bi-monthly news bulletin. ◣◉◉

"Many beautiful views can be found that you'd probably never have known existed if you hadn't bushwhacked these trailless mountains."

© 1989 ochman

HIKING

Possibilities

moments...
...unprepared moments
of peace

& futures beginnings
beauty of days
to come

pass silently
yet unprepared moments
pass

We would like to give a general overview on getting serious about hiking for the inexperienced. We've also got a lot of tips we've picked up that might help the more experienced. We're still learning each time we go out. No two trips are the same, as you'll find out. There is always something that will happen that will force you to make a decision or make do with what you have. You might be stuck in an emergency and forced to set up camp with no nearby water supply or to fashion a makeshift binding for a broken snowshoe. There is always an answer! Many minor problems can be solved by planning in advance. Some of our fondest and most humorous memories come from finding ourselves in and getting out of these situations.

We believe that knowledge is the key. This applies to everything related to your hike. Know how to read weather signs, know your trails and bailouts, know your own limitations and those of your party. Your enjoyment will be so much greater if you know something about the animals likely (or unlikely) to be seen or the name of the mountain range visible in the distance. As your interest increases, so will your readings on the outdoors. We've included in the back of the book a short list of related books that you might want to check out.

> *"...knowledge is the key."*

PREPARATIONS & PLANNING

In order to hike, you must be in shape both mentally and physically. This is not to say you have to be super athletic. It means that you must take reasonably good care of yourself so you'll be able to enjoy. To get physically prepared, probably the best exercise is some form of running or jogging on a regular basis. This helps develop your lungs and legs, the two things you're liable to need most. Aerobic activities such as bicycling, racquetball and swimming are all good. Don't underestimate the power of walking. Unlike the 1980's, most people of the United States during the 1700's and 1800's didn't have excess leisure time but they did have to walk virtually everywhere they went. It was not uncommon for preachers in the mountains to walk 20 or more miles a day in order to give their sermons in different towns.

A regular amount of vigorous walking can help ease the pain of sore legs the day after a hike. What we're saying is that your daily life routine will have an effect on how far or how fast you can push yourself when the time comes. It will also reduce the chances of injuring yourself. Recent studies have shown rowing machines to be very beneficial to hikers, especially those who backpack. Push-ups, sit-ups and stretching exercises are helpful as well. The keys to any exercise are discipline and consistency.

"It's important to be mentally prepared for your hike."

It's important to be mentally prepared for your hike. You don't have to psych yourself up, but if you're psychologically prepared for a ten-mile hike over three mountains, you'll find it a lot easier than if you're not. We've found this particularly true when you're hiking in an unfamiliar area. Check out the maps, re-check your food, clothing and equipment list and leave your problems at home. It also helps to know your limitations and those of your party. It might mean cutting the hike short of a desired goal. We once did a strenuous bushwhack up Balsam Cap and then over to Rocky Mountain. One of us wanted to push for Lone Mountain to close in on the 3500 Club membership. We looked at the situation rationally and realized we'd be scrounging back down to the car in the dark. We made the right decision by heading back.

We've found that having three people in a hiking party is ideal, especially if they are all experienced and familiar with each other. Never push an inexperienced or out-of-shape hiker beyond his limits or you could be carrying him out! One rule many follow is to let the slowest person lead. This doesn't always work and some of us find it impossible to hike slowly. In any case, go at a pace that is reasonable, and take plenty of rests. Be sure to communicate with your companions.

Preparing also includes studying your alternative auto routes. Auto access has been greatly improved in recent years. You'll find that most state highways and main roads to towns are kept in good condition, and are passable even during snowy winter weather. Some secondary mountain roads, however, are closed in the winter. If you're planning a winter trip, check the roads you plan to use to make sure they are open year round. In the spring, a flash flood can wash out a road, especially in the secluded valleys. Have a back up route should you need it. Observe the area you are driving through to get to your hike, not only to get ideas for future hikes but also to spot a place where you could have a good dinner on your return. We've found many a good restaurant this way. Learn to read a map. Knowing how to use a compass and altimeter is also helpful. Anyone venturing into the woods, on or off the trail, should have a compass and be familiar with its use. Learn to observe weather signs. (All of this is not as tough as it sounds). Start to hike with more experienced friends or relatives and read up on the subject. You'll learn a bit here and a bit there, and before you know it, you'll be teaching someone else.

"Never push an inexperienced or out-of-shape hiker beyond his limits or you could be carrying him out!"

There's more to planning than meets the eye. Always let someone know where you are going and when you expect to return. Know of any potential bailouts should you need them. Check the weather forecast before you leave. Have an alternative hike in the back of your head. We were once ready to set out for Indian Head Mountain when a large group pulled up and unloaded. They were destined for the same area as we were. After a quick discussion, we got back in the car and drove ten minutes to the base of Kaaterskill High Peak. We had the quiet weekend that we hoped for, with the view of the Hudson Valley we sought. Although some may think it snobby, this alternate route provided a solution to our problem. Flexibility is important to your enjoyment. Think out your options, take a look around when choosing a campsite, and take into account wind direction, sun location and water availability.

We'd like to stress the importance of everyone entering the woods to practice low-impact camping. *The idea is to cause as little damage as possible to the environment and leave no trace of your stay.* Be sure to camp within the rules set by the DEC; that is, set up your camp at least 150' off the trail and at least 150' away from streams, lakes and roads. Camp in a level area, doing as little damage as possible. Do not cut down ferns to make the bottom of your tents softer and never cut or damage any trees. It is not only unethical, but illegal! Try to use an area that has not been used often, so as to give the land a chance to heal. Remember to camp below 3,500 feet from March 21 through December 21.

If you must build a fire, clear all leaves from the area and make a small circle of stones. Make sure the fire is completely out before leaving, and disperse the rocks. The forest will be much better off if more people would use the portable gas stoves available. They are clean, efficient and easy to use. Every time a fire is made the earth is blackened for years. If you are staying at a lean-to, make sure you leave it cleaner than when you got there. The same rule applies for all campsites.

Be careful when near water supplies. Never wash your dishes in a stream or lake—take water from the water supply and do your washing some distance away. Pour the waste water far from the water source so that the earth can filter and purify it. It's best to avoid soaps of any kind; rather, scrub dishes with gravel or moss. The same goes for human waste disposal. Never go to the bathroom near or above a water supply (go a minimum of 150 feet away). Be sure to bury wastes 6-12 inches below the surface and cover them well. Nature will do the rest. Carry out your garbage in sturdy plastic bags and leave nothing behind! Always be careful in handling and packing food. Never leave food in your tent or sleeping area. You can cover your pack with a large plastic garbage bag and wedge it into a tree. Some might want to hang the packs from a sturdy branch. Remember, most animals have a remarkable sense

"The idea is to cause as little damage as possible to the environment and leave no trace of your stay."

of smell.

It is a good idea to learn how to use basic first aid, should it be necessary. This can be helpful any time and not just while camping. Know what conditions can exist the time of year you are out there and have proper clothing and equipment.

Clothing

To start hiking you really only need a few essential pieces of equipment and some basic clothing, de-

pending, of course, on the season. You don't need anything extravagant, although you will get more mileage and better performance from quality gear. We'd like to review some basics that will make your hiking more enjoyable and safer. If you know any experienced old timers that hike, you may find them to be the most valuable source of information you can find.

First and foremost to the hiker are his boots. There are many styles to choose from today. Boots with full leather uppers are traditional and have many advantages. Although they are fairly stiff at first and require a good deal of breaking in, they'll become your best friends on the trail, once broken in. Leather tends to

"You don't need anything extravagant, although you will get more mileage and better performance from quality gear."

conform nicely to your foot, can be treated to make it waterproof and is very tough and wear resistant.

Medium-weight boots give the support necessary for carrying heavy loads while backpacking. There are lightweight leather boots available that also do a good job at giving support while cutting down on weight. Vibram lug soles are most popular because of their durability and traction on open rock, but other types of hard rubber soles are also available. It is advantageous to buy a boot that can be re-soled when it wears down. This is economical and saves your well broken-in boots that have adjusted to your feet.

There are several lighter hiking boots made of a combination of leather and nylon, sometimes lined with a waterproof breathable substance like GoreTex. Boots of this nature vary from those that provide excellent support to no more than hightopped sneakers. For this reason, be careful in choosing lightweight boots. Your best bet is to inquire of a salesperson in a reliable outdoor camping store. The popular backpacking and outdoor magazines frequently review boots and will also be helpful.

You may want to bring a pair of old sneakers for

Unlike wool or silk, cotton socks absorb and retain much of your perspiration. Wet cotton can easily cause cold feet and/or blisters even on hot days.

campsite use. This gives your feet a breather from the boots. Most serious hikers will eventually own more than one pair of boots at a time. For example, you may want a medium-weight hiking boot for back-packing and for hikes in rocky terrain and a lighter boot for day hikes and faster paced outings. In the extreme cold or snowy conditions, you'll need a boot that is warmer. There are stiff-shelled expedition-type boots available, but we've found them unnecessary. A quality lug-soled, rubber-bottom leather-upper boot with removable wool felt liners will do the job nicely. (It will allow some breathability and flexibility). In short, you should take the time to buy the right boots for you and your needs.

In choosing clothing, remember that there are two essential factors involved in making hiking safer and more comfortable. They are staying warm and dry, both of which go hand in hand. To keep warm, you should dress in layers, instead of one heavy garment. This creates trapped pockets of air that heat up to keep the body warm. It also gives you the option to peel off one or more layers when you're going uphill and starting to heat up. You just put on a layer or two when you need to stop for a break. On most winter or cold weather hikes, you'll probably do this several times in the course of the day. Clothing with button-down fronts allows for ventilation and saves having to remove layers in some cases.

Just as important, if not more so, is the type of clothing you wear. In the winter, it is important to avoid cotton clothing. Cotton gets wet easily and takes a very long time to dry. It has a high capacity to absorb perspiration and, once wet, it actually draws heat away from the body. When you engage in vigorous activity such as hiking, you'll perspire profusely, even in the coldest weather. If you're wearing cotton underwear next to your body, the underwear will get soaking wet. Then, when you stop to rest, you'll soon get chilled from the clammy clothing as the moisture

---

"To keep warm, you should dress in layers..."

absorbs the heat away from your body.

Instead, wear underwear made of silk, wool or polypropylene. Wool is the traditional choice. It will keep you warm even when wet. However, many people find that some types of wool itch when placed next to the skin. A synthetic fabric known as polypropylene is another choice of winter hikers. Polypropylene does not have the same insulating qualities as wool, but it will keep you warm even when it's wet because it allows the moisture to pass between the fibers and be absorbed by your next layer of clothing. It also dries out amazingly fast.

Of course, you might want to combine polypropylene and wool. For example, you could wear polypropylene underwear and a wool shirt on top. To provide insulation and protection from the wind, you should carry an outer layer windbreaker (which could possibly double as raingear). A layer that protects you from the wind will prevent body heat from being carried away and help make your stay at an open windy viewpoint more enjoyable. By all means avoid down jackets. Like cotton, when they get wet they lose their ability to insulate. They also take forever to dry. Jeans are the worst thing you could possibly wear. They may look good on the Marlboro Man, but they could help cause hypothermia if it is wet and chilly.

In warmer weather, cotton may prove a satisfactory material. Even then, a cotton/polyester blend may be better, since it dries out more quickly. We've found old hockey jerseys made of this blend to be extremely durable and comfortable on warmer weather hikes.

Since the head is the area of primary heat loss, it makes sense to wear some type of headgear most of the year. There are countless options on cold weather hats. One is the traditional pullover wool watch cap type of hat. Another is the nylon shelled hats with ear muffs. These hats hug the head closely and keep the ears and back of neck warm. Hoods and pullovers act the same way. They are good for use around the camp-site or while resting. The alternative is wool or felt crusher style hats that do not fit on the head so snugly. They allow ventilation necessary when hiking. The felt wool crusher is an excellent wind and rain repellent with a wide brim for sun protection. Just about any hat will do: a hiking partner of ours wears an English Bangor type cap with matching scarf and high socks. It keeps him in style while on the trail. Despite the ribbings he has taken, the hat does the job. There are also lighter caps with wide peaks such as painters' hats that will keep the hot sun off your head and out of your eyes in summer.

In extreme winter conditions you'll need a scarf to protect the neck and face. A balaclava is also used for this purpose. It covers the entire head except the eyes and is very versatile in the winter. Hand protection in the form of gloves or mittens is essential in the winter. Mittens are warmest as the fingers can warm each other; however, gloves allow more freedom of movement. The skin as well as the eyes need protection from the wind in colder weather and from the sun all year round. Useful in this regard are sunglasses, lip balm and face guards (creams). After one blustery winter hike up Peekamoose and Table Mountains without face protection, we were red-faced for days. We had to fend off questions from friends as to what tropical island we had flown down to on the weekend. The point is to protect your face in the winter.

Two pairs of socks should be worn in cold weather. A liner of wool, silk or polypropylene works well to keep feet dry and warm. The second pair should be heavy wool socks. Avoid cotton socks because they cause a large buildup of perspiration around the feet. Wet skin causes blisters and tears much more easily than dry skin.

Lastly, don't forget to bring a few bandannas along. They come in handy for a countless number of things. Dipped in a stream and tied around the neck in summer, they help keep you cooled off. In colder weather they can keep your neck or ears warm. They can be used to secure a water bottle to your pack or as a pot holder. Their uses are endless.

Clothing a basic list:

☐ socks (2 pairs)
☐ boots (waterproofed)
☐ sneakers (for campsite)
☐ undies
☐ shorts
☐ pants (*no jeans!*)
☐ belt
☐ bathing suit
☐ t-shirt or jersey (cotton/poly blend)
☐ flannel (chamois)/sweatshirt
☐ wool shirts
☐ raingear
☐ towel
☐ windbreaker
☐ bandannas
☐ visored cap

Cold Weather

☐ thermal undies (wool, silk or polypropylene)
☐ unionsuit (great for sleeping in)
☐ wool jacket (medium weight)
☐ wool pants
☐ sweater (wool)
☐ lightweight parka (wind resistant)
☐ insulated jacket or vest (for campsite)
☐ gloves/mittens (2 pairs)
☐ hat

☐ scarf
☐ wool headband (for ears)
☐ balaclava
☐ gaiters

EQUIPMENT

Obviously, the kind of equipment you need will vary with the type of hike you have in mind. In gathering information for this book we became masters of the day hike, and we found that this can be an enjoyable and rewarding way to explore the mountains. People who have trouble getting an entire weekend free can fit in a day hike almost any time of the year. A few tips from our own experiences: Give yourself enough time. This could mean leaving during the wee hours of the morning. Properly planning the hike for your party can result in a great day in the Catskills. If you have two cars at your disposal, a fine end-to-end circuit can be made wherever you choose.

Once you have the right boots and clothing for your outing, you'll have to decide on some type of pack in which to carry your gear. On these excursions we used good sized **day packs** (also known as rucksacks). These are generally frameless packs made of nylon. Some are leather or canvas, but these are harder to find. Day packs come in many different sizes and shapes. Personal preference comes into play, but there are certain things to look for in a quality pack. First, choose a size that fits the type of load and weight you will be carrying. The biggest is not necessarily the best. You don't want items like a camera, binoculars or water container banging around in the pack and hitting your spine. If you have extra room, it is best to fill in the space with an extra shirt or sweater to keep the contents tight.

Ideally, the pack should have some sort of padding lining the interior of the side that lies against your back. In any case, always pack clothing against your back and try to keep any hard edges padded so they don't dig in. Our experiences have taught us that day packs with a top loading flap have the advantage of allowing you to shove those extra layers of clothing under the flap but not in the pack. This allows for quick access without having to open the pack. Unfortunately, this type of pack is hard to find, and the trend seems to be toward teardrop-shaped packs with zipper enclosures.

A good day pack should be tightly stitched and have well-padded shoulder and waist straps. Look for quick-release buckles on straps. Some of the larger day packs have exterior pockets, ice axe loops and lash patches which enable a small sleeping bag to be attached for overnight use. Another type of pack is the **fanny pack**, which goes around the waist. It has a limited carrying capacity but can be used for basic items or for a camera and film. It can be worn in addition to a day pack.

Overnight camping in the mountains? This means backpacking to your destination carrying a heavy load of food, clothing and gear. You have a choice between internal and external frame packs.

Internal frame packs have a frame system inside the body of the pack. They should be adjustable to the individual and have well-padded hip, spine and shoulder pieces. These packs are designed to hold the weight close to the body and to conform nicely to body movement. Internal frame packs are used extensively by climbers and cross-country skiers but in recent years they have also become very popular with backpackers. In these packs, the heavier weight is kept lower than in external frame packs, and this gives better balance on trails with poor footing. The pack is designed to keep most of the weight on the hips. Because internal frame packs lie close to your body they can cause the back to perspire even in cool weather. When choosing a pack you should try it on with the amount of weight you plan to carry and adjust it properly to get a feel on where it pulls most.

External frame packs made of light yet sturdy aluminum are designed to carry heavier loads more comfortably by keeping the weight in line with your spinal cord and alleviating any waste of energy from leaning forward. Properly fit, the frame will contour to your body curvature. The heavier weighted items should be close to the back but high up in the pack. These packs carry the great bulk of the weight on the hips where it is least likely to tire the hiker. Proper adjustment is obviously important. Look for well-padded hip belts and shoulder straps and good outside pockets for separation of items. Whichever pack system you choose, if it is a quality pack that fits properly, you will get good performance. We suggest renting both kinds and trying them on separate trips. This should give you an idea of what is right for you.

The next large item you may want to own is a **tent**. For backpacking, you'll need a lightweight tent that folds up small enough to strap onto your pack. Heavy duty elastic bunji cords work best for this. Ideally, the tent should weigh less than seven pounds yet be able to withstand the winds that can whip up any night of the year. There are many styles to choose from. Both the traditional A-frame tents and the newer dome tents are very popular. We've found that three average or thin people can fit into most two-man tents (except for the small ultra-light ones). Most tents need to be seam sealed to prevent leaks. You should also have some type of repair kit in case of an unexpected rip to the fabric or tear in one of the corners.

Many people prefer to sleep in lean-tos and this is fine if you don't mind company or visits from raccoon raiders in the still of the night. Have a tent along as a back-up. On really beautiful nights, nothing less than sleeping under the stars will do, but it is a good idea to have some type of covering in case of unexpected bad weather. Just be prepared for any situation that could arise and always be near some sort of shelter or have it available.

A **sleeping bag** is an important item in your equipment. Once again there is a choice, this time between down or synthetic fill. Each has its advantages and disadvantages. Down is, pound for pound, the warmest material for sleeping bags. That is, three pounds of down will keep you warmer than three pounds of synthetic fibers. Surprisingly, though, many of the synthetic-fiber bags are getting lighter, and you should be able to get a satisfactory one which weighs only four or five pounds. Down is very compact and makes a good bag for long outings with full packs. It will also last a long time if properly treated and cleaned. If it gets wet, though, down loses its insulating qualities and becomes virtually useless. In addition, it compresses so easily under the weight of your body that any bumps or uneven areas on the ground will be felt almost as if the bag weren't there. Finally, a down bag is generally much more expensive than a synthetic-fiber one.

Synthetic-fiber bags are made of Hollofil, Polarguard or some other type of polyester fill. They are being made lighter and warmer with each passing year. This makes them more compact and better for long trips than they used to be. Synthetic-fiber bags are very popular because they are reasonably priced. They are even used on expeditions to the Himalayas and other high mountain ranges. The lifespan of synthetic-fiber bags is limited because the loft of the bag usually starts to break down after about three years of use. Exposure to heat and general wear and tear contribute to this. But a lifespan of seven or eight years is possible with proper care.

In choosing a sleeping bag, you should look for one which gives you the warmth you require when a damp chilly night sets in, yet which is not too bulky or overly warm. Thus, you may wind up owning more than one sleeping bag. Winter bags require more bulk and warmth than the so-called three-season bags, but it is just plain uncomfortable to sleep with a winter bag on a warm summer night. You will perspire heavily and have to open the bag to ventilate it. If you are a serious winter camper, buy a good bag for winter camping. If you go out only occasionally in the winter, rent or borrow a winter bag. Don't get caught with a bag that will not keep you warm enough or you'll be in for an uncomfortable night. A bag with a temperature rating of five degrees or less is usually sufficient for winter camping, although you may be forced to don long johns and other clothing if it is extremely cold. Three-season bags range in temperature rating from 15 degrees to 35 degrees; summer bags have a rating of somewhere around 40 degrees, and are lightweight and compact.

Mummy bags may seem restrictive at first but they conserve body heat and are lighter than rectangular bags. A good mummy-style bag will give you, your feet and the warm air generated by your body enough room to move freely.

There are several types of **pads** to choose from that are lightweight and compact, but will cushion your bag and make for a more comfortable night. More importantly, they minimize loss of body heat to the damp, cold ground. Closed cell foam pads are recommended because they do not absorb water and are compact. Another popular choice is the self-inflating Therm-a-Rest pad, which is slightly heavier and more costly than foam, yet is very durable and unmatched for comfort. Pads come in different thicknesses; obviously, the thicker the pad, the more insulation.

The portable **backpacking stoves** available today make backwoods cooking easier and prevent the damage that might be done by making a wood fire. Most stoves are safe and efficient, are easy to use and will cook or boil water quickly. They also allow you more time to explore the area around your camp-site, instead of having to prepare a makeshift fire-place for the evening. And we've found them very handy for making hot chocolate to drink with lunch on cold-weather day hikes. All serious hikers should have a portable backpacking stove.

If you do insist on making a fire, however, be doubly sure to extinguish it. Do not make one on or near the trail, and try to remove all traces of the fire once you're through. Remember to have some type of fire starter material available for emergen-cies or in case of wet weather. There are many types of pastes or fire sticks that will assist in starting a fire even if the wood is wet. (Pastes are useful for priming stoves in cold weather.) Windproof matches, portable lighters and waterproof match cases are other useful items.

Mess kits are inexpensive yet essential for cook-ing, eating and drinking. You don't need anything fancy, just a durable, lightweight aluminum mess kit set, including a drinking cup and a small pot for boil-

Portable stoves are useful for making quick hot beverages on cold weather hikes.

ing water. When you choose **eating utensils**, look for the plastic type that is both melt resistant and unbreakable; a popular brand name is Lexan. (Always try to save on weight, even on the little things!) You should also have a **plastic water container**; avoid heavy metal ones. Bota bags (wine sacks) and canteens work well and can be strapped to the outside of your pack to save room. At least a quart of water should be carried by each person at the start of a hike—more, if there is no reliable water source within the day's walk.

Everyone develops his or her own system of pack storage and brings along unique items; this is part of the fun and individualism to which hiking and camping lend themselves. Nonessentials, such as a harmonica, a pipe and tobacco, binoculars, a special surprise dessert, a portable fishing pole or a drawing pad are likely to be brought along by the various members of a camping group.

But to return to the necessary items that every one should carry, the first of these is a good **folding knife** that will come in handy for a variety of things. The popular Swiss Army knife is especially useful. Other essential items are a **compass**, **maps**, **extra water**, a **flashlight** with **extra bulb and batteries**, a **foil emergency blanket** and some **high-energy food**. It also helps to have a small **sewing kit**, a **mirror** and a **whistle**. (Three loud blows on the whistle is the universal sign for HELP.)

We will continue to stress the importance of being prepared in case of an emergency or an injury to a member of your party. A full **first-aid emergency kit** need not be large but it should contain several necessary items. *Antiseptic cream, aspirin, bandaids/butterflies, gauze* and *tape* will obviously be useful for most of the cuts and bruises anyone in the party might encounter. *Decongestants* or *antihistamines* will not only help clear sinuses but will also reduce swelling from bee stings and insect bites. Other items you should carry are an *ace bandage, water purification tablets, a snakebit kit, nail clippers, portable scissors, safety pins, ammonia inhalants* and *aluminum foil.* Also, always keep some *moleskin* handy for those blisters that can make for a rough day. You will rarely, if ever, use the majority of these items, but knowing you have them and are prepared to deal with most problems is comforting.

Equipment a basic list:

- ☐ daypack/fannypack
- ☐ backpack
- ☐ tent
- ☐ sleeping bag
- ☐ backpacking stove & fuel
- ☐ firestarter
- ☐ extra matches (waterproof)
- ☐ candles
- ☐ mess kit/pot gripper
- ☐ eating utensils/can opener
- ☐ plastic water container/canteen
- ☐ barometer/altimeter
- ☐ compass
- ☐ maps
- ☐ binoculars
- ☐ camera
- ☐ flashlight/extra bulb & batteries
- ☐ foil-emergency blanket
- ☐ rope/nylon cord
- ☐ sewing kit
- ☐ mirror
- ☐ whistle
- ☐ first-aid emergency kit
- ☐ ace bandage
- ☐ snakebite kit

- ☐ water purification tablets
- ☐ water filter purifier
- ☐ insect repellent
- ☐ folding knife
- ☐ sunglasses
- ☐ toilet paper
- ☐ toothbrush/paste

POSSIBLE PERILS

This is a brief list of possible unforeseen emergencies that could arise. Most can be avoided by good judgement and knowledge of what to do while outdoors.

Hypothermia

This occurs when you are losing body heat faster than the body can replace it. A person can show signs of hypothermia with only a few degrees' drop in body temperature. Early warning signs are slow or incoherent and uncontrolled speech, shivering, continued stumbling and lack of finger coordination. Wet clothing (especially cotton) can speed this process along; dry clothing and hot liquid intake will help reverse it. It might also be a good idea to stop exerting energy by setting up camp and slipping into your sleeping bag to help minimize your heat loss.

While hypothermia is often thought of as a subfreezing-weather ailment, hypothermia cases can occur in 30-degree to 50-degree weather. Carry extra clothing, especially wool, and have raingear handy. The key is to stay dry and warm. If you are overheating while hiking, peel a layer off, but put it back on after you stop and before you start to feel a chill.

It is very important to avoid alcohol intake in cold weather. Alcohol lowers body temperature and causes the peripheral blood vessels to constrict, a very dangerous situation in frigid, windy conditions.

Frostbite

When exposed skin freezes and loses circulation because of exposure to cold, the condition is called frostbite. The obvious sign is loss of color to the affected area; it becomes pale and cold to the touch. To avoid frostbite, which is most likely to occur in cold, windy weather, you should protect the face, especially the nose and ears. Hands and feet can also become frostbitten. Slow warmup of the affected area is suggested; do not vigorously rub it, or permanent tissue damage can occur.

Snakebite

Although rattlesnakes inhabit a few spots in the Catskills, snakebites are rare. Snakes are timid animals and try to avoid contact with humans. If bitten, the victim should remain calm and not attempt to rush out of the woods; doing so will only result in the venom spreading more quickly through the system. If you are near a road, help the victim to get there with minimal exertion. A snakebite kit should be used if one is available. If not, make a small incision over the bite and suck the blood out. As already mentioned, snakebites are unlikely but you should be prepared for such an emergency if it happens.

Dehydration

There is no excuse for becoming dehydrated on a hike; ample water and other liquids should always be carried. Don't rely solely on water sources which are said to be available along the route. When you do reach them, replenish your supply, taking care to filter, purify or boil the water. Realize that dehydration is as likely to occur on cold dry days as on hot dry ones. Always drink when you are thirsty and don't try to ration your supply. The body uses water most effectively if it is replenished before a shortage occurs in your system. Again, at least a quart of water should be carried by each person at the start of a hike; more, if there is no reliable water source within a day's walk.

Giardiasis

This is an illness contracted from drinking water infected with a parasite called Giardia Lamblia. It is an increasing problem in the Adirondacks but it can sometimes occur in the Catskills as well. Giardiasis symptoms may take up to four weeks to appear, but when they do, you'll know it. Diarrhea, bloating and gassiness are the most common symptoms; vomiting, cramps, weight loss and loss of appetite are others. Many other ailments have similar symptoms, but if you consult a doctor about such problems, it helps to mention how long ago your last camping trip was. This will make him aware that your ailment may well be giardiasis which, once detected, is readily treatable with medication.

Giardiasis is sometimes known as "beaver fever" because that animal can spread the parasite, but it can also be spread by other animals. The major cause of this disease's recent increase is poor backwoods sanitation by campers, usually in heavily camped areas. But proper sanitation techniques can prevent giardiasis from becoming a serious problem in the Catskills, so do your part to safeguard the environment.

Never dispose of anything in a stream, lake or other body of water. Be sure to discard dishwater and bury human wastes at least 150 feet away from any water source and downstream from that source. Holes for feces disposal should be 6-12 inches deep and covered well. But do not bury wastes too deep or the decomposers in the soil cannot do their job. To prevent giardiasis you can boil water for ten minutes, or use chlorine or iodine tablets or one of the better portable filters available today. Generally speaking, the higher the source the safer the water.

Insect Bites

Insects are one of the facts of life from May through September. The black fly, so well loved in the north country, occasionally makes its way into the Catskills. These flies bite hard and often, and can ruin a trip. Mosquitoes are another problem. The worst time for these critters is the hot, sticky weather of late spring and early summer. There seems to be a first hatch in late May or, more often, early June that comes with the first really hot, humid spell.

Our experiences have indicated that weather is as important a factor as is the month. For example, one of us was virtually eaten alive by mosquitoes on Cornell Mountain during a hot spell in early June, yet two weeks later the other of us enjoyed a beautiful evening under the stars and a bug-free hike in cooler, drier weather while visiting Giant Ledge.

Bug repellents work to some extent and should always be carried with you. Experiment with different ones until you find the kind that works best for you. We have discovered that some hard-to-find brands (such as fly dope) made in Canada work especially well. The ingredient Diethyl-Meta-Toluamide (commercially known as DEET) has been proven to be effective against insects. Avoid stepping on hornet nests, often found along stream banks.

If you don't wear sweet smelling perfumes or bright colors, especially yellows, the bees are more likely to leave you alone. Insects should not stop you from hiking or camping in the summer months. Antihistamines have been proven to be effective against the swelling resulting from insect bites.

Poison Ivy

This shiny three-leaved plant is found in the Catskills but grows only in the low elevations of the valleys and is not common. Learn to identify it, avoid it and carry on with your business. Wearing long pants is an effective way to prevent getting poison ivy.

Lightning

Another rare and avoidable occurrence is lightning. If a thunderstorm should strike, get off exposed ridges and seek shelter. Be careful of damp caves or crevices, as they may attract a charge. Squat down under low trees to avoid being struck. If you feel your hair get staticky and stand on end, squat immediately because lightning may be about to strike your vicinity. If someone in your party is struck, he should be given C.P.R. or mouth-to-mouth resuscitation if necessary.

> "A compass and map should always be carried and checked frequently when you are venturing into an unknown area."

Flash Floods

Don't pitch a tent near a low spot by a creek or stream, and avoid dry stream beds. Heavy storms can produce rapid flash floods that can carry you and your gear down the mountain a lot quicker than you planned.

On Being Lost

Anyone spending time in the woods can become lost or disoriented. Anyone who has done a sufficient amount of bushwhacking can attest to this. A compass and map should always be carried and checked frequently when you are venturing into an unknown area. Learn to read the direction of the sun and be able to locate the stars. Summertime can be a particularly difficult time of year because the thick forest canopy makes everything look the same and stops you from seeing distant landmarks. Should you realize you are lost, take a moment to sit down and relax. Then try to mentally retrace your route. If you can't remember, try to find a stream or old road and follow it downhill; it will inevitably lead to a main road and some semblance of civilization. Do not panic or rush off without thinking. If bad weather or darkness sets in, find shelter nearby and make a fire. Lastly, and most importantly, always let someone know where you are going and when you expect to return. That way, a search and rescue team can be sent out to look for you if you don't return when expected.

"Learn to deal with situations calmly, and your time in the woods will be safe and enjoyable."

Learn to deal with situations calmly, and your time in the woods will be safe and enjoyable. It's a philosophy we should all carry into our everyday living.

FOOD

On any overnight trip, plan how many meals you'll need. Then allow for extra energy foods for the actual hike. Carry a little extra just in case you decide to stay longer than planned or in case you get lost or injured.

There are many freeze-dried foods on the market, but most don't taste like what they are supposed to. While their light weight necessitates their use on long backpacking trips, we do not recommend them for two or three-nighters. There are some dried foods that taste better and are more nourishing. In addition, cheeses, beans, pepperoni and certain fresh vegetables will last several days if kept wrapped and stored in the middle of your pack. Pastina is filling and nutritious and, with a few spices and bullion cubes added, makes a hearty soup. Other alternatives are ramen noodles and cous cous. Ramen noodles are light, contain pleasant herbs and salt, and require much less water for cooking than pastina. Cous cous is an inexpensive wheat pasta from the Middle East which cooks like pastina and is very filling and nutritious. It can be found in some grocery stores. Eggs can be cracked and put into a nalgene container where they will stay fresh a few days if tucked away and wrapped. You'll have instant scrambled eggs whenever you want. The plastic nalgene containers are excellent for carrying all sorts of foods safely and with little weight. Certain meats can be carried and eaten the first night. We'd recommend knockwurst and hot dogs.

We've also found English muffins and pita bread to be ideal for backpacking since they stay fresh longer than other kinds of bread and don't easily get crushed.

"Be sure to carry out whatever you carry in."

We know weight is a big consideration on any backpacking trip, but we have found it manageable to take a small number of cans on shorter trips. Beef stews, thick soups and vegetables can all be carried this way. Be sure to carry out whatever you carry in.

Whatever you choose to eat on your hiking trips, be sure to have plenty of high-carbohydrate foods. Balance this off with proteins and you'll be doing fine. Fats are also useful in small amounts since they are broken down and used by the body more slowly than carbohydrates and protein. If you are using freeze-dried foods or packet soups, you'll need plenty of water. Make sure you fill up whenever possible or camp near a reliable water source. There are juices available in paper containers that go great with lunch or breakfast. Keep an eye in the supermarket for lightweight foods like these.

Food a basic list:

- [ ] pasta or macaroni
- [ ] meat (first night)
- [ ] veggies (fresh or can)
- [ ] fruit
- [ ] bread or muffins
- [ ] pastina
- [ ] bouillon
- [ ] pop-tarts
- [ ] dried fruits
- [ ] granola bars/fruit rolls
- [ ] cheese
- [ ] pepperoni or salami
- [ ] butter (cold weather)
- [ ] beans (dry or canned)
- [ ] rice
- [ ] soup (packet)
- [ ] jelly
- [ ] sweets (chocolate)
- [ ] juice (soft containers)
- [ ] hot chocolate (packets)
- [ ] raisins
- [ ] peanut butter
- [ ] tuna
- [ ] sardines/kippers
- [ ] oatmeal (packet)
- [ ] eggs
- [ ] nuts or trail mix
- [ ] coffee or tea bags
- [ ] spices
- [ ] freeze-dried food

© 1989 Ocypman

THE MOUNTAINS

Rainbows

*Rainbows in all
their infinite beauty
shine as they reach,
forever-more &
never-more than
my heart reaches
for you!*

With all the mystery and legends the Catskills have bred it's no wonder that through the years so many have become enamored with the area. This is what inspired us to write this book and drove us into every corner of these mountains. The hiking is surprisingly good to those who scoff at the Catskills or have bypassed them while heading up to the higher Adirondacks or White Mountains. Other than in a few heavily used areas, the Catskills have a true wilderness character. There are many areas in the Catskills that receive little or no use. It is our hope that those wishing to enjoy the mountains will utilize some lesser-used areas, respect the land and practice low-impact camping. The Forest Preserve is fragile and can take only so much pressure before permanent damage is done. *This book helps enable hikers to choose an area best suited to their needs.*

Getting familiar with the area will enhance your trips. The Catskills are not as expansive as other ranges such as the Adirondacks, but this lends to their appeal. You get a cozy feeling that enables you to feel that the mountains are just big enough to know them all, but at the same time you can disappear into the mountains for days without seeing another soul. All of the high peaks are located within 50 miles of each other.

The hiker may opt for views of the same ranges from many different angles. It is a fun challenge to

"...you can disappear into the mountains for days without seeing another soul."

Plattekill Mountain with Roundtop and Kaaterskill High Peak in the background as seen from Overlook Mountain fire tower.

The Blackhead Range, Roundtop and Kaaterskill High Peak northeast from Indian Head.

Kaaterskill High Peak and Roundtop from South Mountain overlooking Kaaterskill Clove.

try and identify the peaks from completely different viewpoints. Each mountain takes on its own personality this way. Slide Mountain, the beacon that can be seen from so many sections of the Catskills, looks decidedly different when viewed from different locations. However, the majestic Blackhead Range, distinctive Doubletop or Round Top-Kaaterskill High Peak are just a few examples of mountains whose identification can often be easily made due to their simple silhouetted shapes. Learning to identify the mountains this way will also help you pinpoint your location if you should become lost or confused.

Most hikers are attuned to nature, or at least become attuned after a night or two out there. For many, it takes this long to re-acclimate the senses to nature after having them dulled by pressures of our techno-industrial society. In any case, the hiker can heighten the experience of the mountains by learning the various things he will encounter. Learning to identify animals, birds and wildflowers and to name the brightest stars or constellations in the night sky are all a part of the magic of "The Land in the Sky."

"The weather can change quickly and dramatically in these mountains."

CLIMATE & WEATHER

Mark Twain once said that the only thing that can be said about the weather is that there will be plenty of it. The key is knowing what can happen and being prepared for it. The weather can change quickly and dramatically in these mountains. It can spoil an outing if you're not ready for it (and sometimes even if you are!). Keep in mind that most of the weather changes are associated with the passage of fronts (cold or warm) and that these generally travel west to east. A small altimeter-barometer is a useful tool in forecasting weather. Team this up with with some simple cloud identification and wind direction and you can come up with a pretty good idea of the immediate (24-36 hour) weather forecast. Of course, this is not foolproof but at least you'll have an idea of what to expect.

Here are a few tips. (For more information check one of the books we've listed in the back of this book.) The appearance of high wispy cirrus clouds may foretell a change to come. If this is followed by a thickening of clouds and falling barometer, you've got a strong chance of rain within 24-36 hours. Low pressure denotes foul weather, while high pressure gives the fair weather that makes hikes so enjoyable.

You should always check the local forecasts before setting out and carry some type of rain gear with you. Another unexpected quick change in the weather occurs when summertime thunderstorms build up and move in quickly late in the day. This is caused by heating of the earth's surface and a build-up of moisture in the air. They can be identified by large cumulonimbus clouds that build up to massive heights in the sky and form anvil-shaped "thunderheads" that result in dangerous lightning. We discuss ways to avoid lightning on page 78.

The climate of the Catskills differs greatly from that of the nearby Hudson River Valley and is dramatically different from that of the New York metropolitan area. Studies have shown that the higher peaks receive nearly twice the precipitation of the nearby Hudson River Valley. On the average, these peaks receive 60-70 inches of precipitation annually, whereas only about 40 inches fall in the Hudson River Valley immediately to the east. This translates to more rain and snow on the mountain tops.

Higher winds and lower temperatures are characteristic of the ridges and high elevations. Keep in mind that the temperature drops about 3 degrees for every 1,000 feet of ascent. A drizzly day in Kingston can be a snowy cold day on top of a mountain. Combine this

"A drizzly day in Kingston can be a snowy cold day on top of a mountain."

Storm sequence west to east as seen from the summit of Windham High Peak.

The front fingers the earth, northeast of Windham, as it travels toward the Hudson River Valley.

Low to the land, the front is suspended as the sun shoots brightly by!

Here, the front barely grazes by the spurs of Acra Point to the east.

with higher winds and the unprepared hiker could be in trouble. On the summits, average temperatures vary from the lower teens in winter to the low sixties in summer. Of course, these are averages and the actual temperature can vary dramatically at any time of the year.

The Catskills are close enough to the ocean to feel its effects in terms of humidity. Although the ocean does not modify the temperature the way it does along the coast, a good deal of humidity is felt, especially in summer. This is not to say that cool dry weather does not occur, but it is not the rule, as it is, for example, in the Rockies.

THE SEASONS MONTH BY MONTH

Hiking the various seasons and observing the great changes that occur is one of the true joys of the Catskills. Each month has something different to offer.

Spring comes late to the mountains and usually first shows itself sometime in **April**. This is a month you can't trust to the weatherman; you must be prepared for almost any kind of weather. Snows often linger on the summits right through April. Heavy snows can occur at this time of year although they are often mixed with freezing rain and sleet. You can count on the wind blowing a good deal of the time.

This fickle month can have days with temperatures in the seventies and nights well below freezing. There are few hikers on the trails, which makes it a good time of year to check out some of the more heavily hiked areas and see them in the quiet stillness of their natural setting. Bushwhacking is easy this month because of the fading snow cover (usually) and the leafless trees that allow clear views.

The weather systems also move particularly fast

The awakening —
signs of spring as
first green plants
peer up at us!

in springtime, and this should alert the hiker to use caution in dealing with weather forecasts. We once went to sleep on a clear, calm evening and woke up to a windy monsoon-like deluge that lasted three days— no weather signs to read but plenty of rough weather.

May is a fine month for hiking. Wildflowers carpet the forest floor. Look for spring beauty, purple trillium, trout lily, wood anemone, Canada violet and Dutchman's breeches to name a few. The woods are wet and the leaves are starting to open up. The valleys will turn green, and the green will work its way up the mountainsides. There is plenty of water running all over. The bugs will make their appearance during the first warm spell. There are many clear days to enjoy views. It can still get cold at night, but warmer weather becomes more common in the mountains as the month goes by. Snow can linger into May. The latest we've seen snow on a summit was May 16, although we're sure it can linger even longer if the weather stays cool.

"The latest we've seen snow on a summit was May 16th..."

May is a good month to observe birds migrating through the Catskills. More can be seen since foliage is thin and there is a lot of movement going on. Birds like the scarlet tanager or rose breasted grosbeak, which are tough to spot in summer, can be viewed quite easily this month.

Sometime towards the end of May, or beginning of **June**, a real hot sticky spell often hits. This leads to a large hatch of mosquitoes or flies and can make for a rough time. This is the kind of weather to avoid camping if you can. June also has cool spells, though. A day in June with dry, cool weather (days-70's, nights-50's) can be as close as you'll get to paradise. When songwriter Van Morrison wrote "Rave on, fill the senses on nature's bright green and shady path," he must have had a June day in mind. Wildlife abounds; birds are singing and breeding. Bunchberry, yellow clintonia, starflower, goldthread and foamflower light up the forest floor.

Keep an eye out for the elusive scarlet-colored wild columbine growing on a rocky ridge beneath the tree tops. The hobblebush on the ridges become showy for a while early in the month and along the ledges the colorful mountain azalea emits a distinctive bouquet. Bogs and swamps can be explored for rare orchids and other plants. Many will take to the trails in June, and it is probably a good time to look up a secluded favorite spot you have.

July puts summer in full swing in the Catskills. Ground cover becomes tall and thick, and ferns dominate much of the forest floor. Learning to identify ferns can be fun. The most common fern found in the Catskills is the spinulose wood fern. The hay scented fern and the New York fern can also be found easily.

In all, there are more than 20 different types of ferns found in the area, although some are very rare. Because of these ferns, an almost jungle-like look prevails in some sections of the forest.

Hot spells are prevalent in July, but a walk on a shaded ridge will expose the summer breezes that can make your trip tolerable. The weather is about as dependable as it will ever get in the Catskills. Other than evening thunderstorms, weather systems generally move pretty slowly and their signs are readable. The long days provide more time to explore and set up camp. Night temperatures rarely go below the upper 40's, so a light sleeping bag will usually do. Look for wood sorrels to line the trails near the summits. From June through mid-September, you can observe the birds of the summit conifers as they raise their young and sing loudly.

August can continue the hot muggy weather, yet cool dry spells do occur. Swamps and wet meadows will boast tall flowers. Queen Anne's lace and tansy brighten the fields and pastures. Sometime during late August, there is usually a cool spell to let us know that summer's end is not far off. In late August and early September, the woods are at their driest, so caution must be used with any type of flame.

September brings the return of real cool weather and the first changing of the leaves at upper elevations. Hot spells can occur, but they are rare. Wildlife seems to be everywhere and in full gear in preparation for the coming cold weather. A good hiking month, September sees the end of crowds at state campgrounds, but many seasoned hikers are taking to the trails with their cameras. By the end of September the fall foliage changes are underway at upper elevations. This varies depending on the weather.

October can have brilliant days of color and more color. Cool weather dominates and the forest is ablaze. If you had your camera out in September, you'd still be clicking away in October. Wet weather can

"If you had your camera out in September, you'd still be clicking away in October."

stay for several days, so be sure to check the forecast. The first light snows can appear on the summits, but they do not last long. This is a good month to hike, camp, or just be outdoors to see the changes going on. By the end of the month, the forest will be burned out of brilliant colors and **November's** somber grays will take over.

Cold fronts and clear weather can make a November outing an enjoyable and invigorating one. The leaves are now gone from the trees and many views open up to the hiker. It's a good time to do a fast-paced hike, but try to avoid the cold dismal spells that can occur at this time of year.

The big game hunting season usually starts the Monday after the 15th of November. It's advisable to stay out of the woods during its 3-4 week length. Check with the DEC to get the exact dates. If you must venture into the woods during this period, wear bright clothing and make plenty of noise. This is also a good idea in October, as small game hunting season is open.

December usually brings the first appreciable snows to the Catskills. Some years little or no snow has fallen in December. It's a good time of year to get some solitary hiking in, if you've got your holiday shopping done early.

If it hasn't snowed much in December, you can bet your paycheck it will in **January**. Cold, clear weather allows superb visibility and enables you to observe animal tracks in the snow. Try to get out soon after a snowstorm to enjoy the pristine beauty of snow and sky. Those properly prepared can try winter camping. Camping above 3,500 feet is permitted between December 21 and March 21 (although open fires are still prohibited).

Despite the obviously frigid weather, there are several warm spells during the course of the winter. **February** usually has several of these, and hiking with snowshoes is fun and challenging. We've had some great hikes during February thaws and we rarely encountered other hikers. The weather can also be vicious this time of year, so caution is to be advised.

March may see a gradual shrinkage of snow in the valleys, and the weather may be mild or very cold. March is a windy month but hiking can be rewarding. Days are lengthening and visibility is unusually good. Look for flocks of chickadees, juncos and kinglets noisily to pass by. Brown creepers and nuthatches will give themselves away as they move along from tree to tree. As April approaches, the first green plants begin to poke through the ground as the cycle of life continues.

Whatever time of year you choose, there is always something to observe. *Happy Hiking!*

©1989 OCHMAN

NORTH-EASTERN CATSKILLS

A Dark & Silent Forest

Cool to the touch
we touch,

Silent to the ear
we listen,

Darkness to the eyes
we look,

Yet warm to the heart
we feel,
we touch,
We feel.

*t*he northeastern section of the Catskills lies north of Route 28 and as far west as a line drawn between West West Kill Moun tain and North Dome, and is covered by Map #41 of the Trail Conference Catskill Trail Maps. (The area around North Lake is covered in greater detail on Map #40). This section of the Catskills contains two long trails, the Escarpment Trail and the Devil's Path. These connect to many side trails which provide a great variety of options to the hiker. The area showcases the Kaaterskill and Platte-kill Cloves, steep dramatic gorges slicing through the "Great Wall of Manitou" from the Hudson Valley. Most of the area lies within Greene County, with the balance in the northern part of Ulster County.

Rich in history, the Northeastern Catskills were settled early by transplanted Yankee New Englanders and contain some of the oldest trails in the country. This region inspired America during the Romantic Period of the nineteenth century, spawning the first of the great mountain hotels. Most of the trails are close to a road or town, yet offer great views of the Hudson Valley. There are good bushwhacks for those wanting to get off the trail and explore. All the higher peaks have excellent growth of red spruce and balsam fir on their summits.

Challenging hikes, wide views and rich local history combine to make this area extremely popular all year round.

NORTH LAKE AREA

High above the Hudson Valley, between North and South Mountains, lie **North** and **South Lakes**. It was here that the white man made some of his earliest explorations in the Catskills. Much of the Catskills' mystery and lore was born here. This area is rich in historic value and natural marvels. Indeed, nowhere else in these mountains can you find so much in so small an area. A book written on the Catskills would be remiss if it did not devote particular attention to this special area.

The native Indians used the Catskills for hunting and passage between the Hudson River Valley and more westerly sections of New York State. The dark hemlock-filled valleys and wooded slopes were plentiful in game but not suitable for tribal life. Instead, the fertile valleys of the Hudson, Mohawk, Susquehanna and smaller river valleys were cultivated. It was here that crops could be grown easier and earlier.

The Indians called these mountains "Onteora," translated as the "land in the sky." The Indians linked the North-South Lake area with the Great Spirit "Manitou." What we now know as the Escarpment was called "The Great Wall of Manitou." Indian lore has it that a great giant was felled and his body became the mountains. North and South Lake were said to be the eyes of this giant. Understandably, the area was considered hallowed and sacred.

During the 17th and 18th centuries, the first Dutch settlers in the Hudson Valley grew curious about the mountains that seemed to spring up from the river valley to touch the clouds. It was said that one could predict the weather by the color of the mountains and the surrounding cloud cover. "Blue Mountains" was sometimes used to describe the hazy shade of blue given off by the Escarpment to signify good weather. A change to purple meant bad weather was on the way. The farmers of the Hudson Valley may have had a better weather forecasting system than our modern forecasters! Their livelihood certainly depended on it.

Up to this time, except for the occasional hunter, few had strayed into the mountains. For one thing, the famed Hardenburgh Patent kept many out, and the mountains were forbidding, a poor environment to farm for a living.

In 1742 a young man named John Bartram, who was sent to America to collect samples of indigenous plants, hiked up the Escarpment to the North-South Lake area and discovered what a unique natural area it was. He gathered the cones of a tree with a pleasant smell and sticky resin, known in its day as the "Balm of Gilead," today known as the balsam fir. It is often associated with the Christmas holiday season because of its characteristic smell and shape. Bartram was collecting samples that would be brought back to England and planted in the fashionable gardens of his time period. Bartram made many notes on his excur-

"The Indians called these mountains 'Onteora,' translated as the 'land in the sky.'"

sions and was one of the first active naturalists in America.

As more settlers wandered into the mountains, the North-South Lake area became a magnet for the romantic and creative. It was here that painter Thomas Cole was inspired to sketch and paint many landscapes. Cole was the founder of the Hudson River School, America's first school of landscape painting. Other artists such as Asher B. Durand and Frederick E. Church also painted this area. Poet William Cullen Bryant immortalized the Kaaterskill Falls in a poem. Henry David Thoreau spent a summer in 1844 at a small house above the Falls and found the "quietness and cleanliness and coolness...to be all one." The view from the Escarpment is described by James Fenimore Cooper in his novel, THE PIONEERS (1823), by character Natty Bumpo, also known as Leatherstocking. From here, Natty "could see the carryings on of the world" and see "all creation."

The Catskills played an important role in the birth of American Romanticism and the philosophy of the times. They were becoming known to America and the world and became *the place to be!*

The view from the Escarpment also stimulated a man named Erastus Beach to realize what a good place it would be to set up a hotel for those wishing to share this view and pay for it! The *Catskill Mountain House* started in 1824 as a simple structure. It became an American landmark within 30 years and existed much longer. Located near North and South Lakes in an area known as Pine Orchard, the Mountain House continually grew in size and popularity. It became a place for the rich and famous. Its dining room would eventually be capable of seating 500 people at one time. For the wealthy, it had all the comforts of home. The elaborate trail system that was developed in the area allowed all guests to get a close first hand look at nature. Most pictures show its gleaming white facade with 13 large Corinthian col-

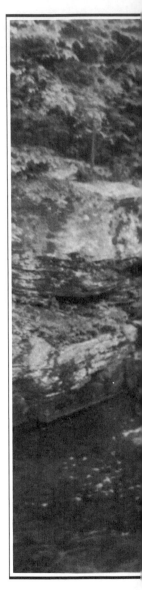

Small cascades typically found throughout these mountains.

umns. What a sight this marvel must have been for those traveling up the Hudson River!

One could gaze in awe at the Mountain House from the river 12 miles away and 2,200 feet below. From New York City, a boat would take people to the village of Catskill where a bumpy and steep stage coach ride would take them up the Escarpment to the Mountain House. To cut travel time and effort, in 1892 the Otis Elevating Railway laid its tracks directly up the Escarpment. Today, the scar left by this engineering feat can still be seen.

Despite visiting Presidents, poets and aristocrats, the Mountain House declined in stature as America moved west on wheels. It changed hands and fell into decay. The DEC torched it in January 1963 to prevent any further danger to the curious.

Today a large commemorative sign stands in an open meadow, and all that remains are the two stone gate markers at the entrance on the west side. It is amazing to think of the size of the hotel in this location...truly a wonder in its time. Think of all the important people that spent nights at this spot. One can almost see the Hudson River filled with sails on a sunny summer day. The Mountain House is gone, but the view is still there for all to enjoy!

The Catskill Mountain House was the first in a long list of great mountain hotels that sprung up all over the Catskills, developing into the classic resorts of the mid-late 1800's.

An interesting story that pertains to the North Lake area is the story of the *Hotel Kaaterskill*. The story, oddly enough, begins at the Catskill Mountain House in 1880. George Harding was a well-known aristocrat and regular guest at the Mountain House. His daughter was not in good health and was on a diet that stressed eating chicken. One night, he wanted her to have fried chicken instead of the menu staple, and was told he could not. He wound up talking to the owner, Charles Beach, and an argument ensued that would begin what has been called the "Fried Chicken War." Harding left the premises, never to return.

He built another hotel on land he purchased on top of South Mountain about one mile southwest of the Mountain House. It opened in 1881 and was even larger than its rival with more modern facilities. Harding saw to it that guests could find access to this giant structure as he purchased his own access roads and even a railroad station at Palenville. Its list of guests was even more impressive than that of the Mountain House, as Presidents and politicians, entertainers and inventors all mixed here. Guests enjoyed a view overlooking Kaaterskill Clove from the many porches and terraces. Many would stroll the easy paths to the views over Palenville or to the Mountain House. The hotel brought much business into the area and was built at the height of the Catskills' enlightened period.

Both Hotel Kaaterskill and the Mountain House continued to prosper until the early 1900's when both owners died in 1902. The Hotel Kaaterskill burned in 1924. It is said the blaze atop South Mountain could be seen from up and down the distant Hudson Valley, even as far north as Albany!

Let's take a look at the area as it is today. The easiest access is by car via Haines Falls and Mountain House Road (County Route 18). Approaching the area from the west, you'll reach a gatehouse where the DEC charges a fee (for the summer season) to enter and park your car near North Lake. The state runs a campsite for car campers on the north shore of the lake. We can't argue that it's not a good place for a campsite, but it is sad to think of what a beautiful tranquil place this could be if left to grow back to a natural state.

It seems that North and South Lakes have always been used for profit since their discovery by pioneers. Back in the 1790's, a settler named John

Cairo Roundtop and Hudson River Valley looking north from the Escarpment.

Ashley built a cabin on the shore of North Lake and started brewing spruce beer from the needles of the spruce trees. Later on, the hotels in the area used it for recreation and to supply water, but we suspect the area was better off back then.

One hot Sunday afternoon in September, we were ending a long backpack trip and passed an elderly woman vehemently arguing with a DEC officer over a small green tree that she had hacked down to use for firewood. She scolded the officer and said she had come all the way from the Bronx and he had no right to ruin her day.

Attitudes born from ignorance like this not only give the city dweller a poor reputation, but ruin the area permanently for the next hiker. We suggest hiking this immediate area in the off season or during the week when it is more quiet so you can get a feeling for the place as it once was. On weekends in the summer, it can resemble a day camp!

Nevertheless, the views and natural beauty of this area shouldn't be neglected. There are many easy-to hike trails that encircle the area, most of which begin at the North Lake parking area, but keep in mind that you can choose to start out from other parking areas (which will be mentioned in the trail description) and explore whatever strikes your fancy.

These sections of trail are off limits to camping but make excellent day hikes to get acquainted with a beautiful and historical area.

The site of the Catskill Mountain House can be reached by walking south from the North Lake parking area. In a few hundred yards you'll come to a large clearing on the left with two stone pillars, one on each side of an imaginary entrance. Just beyond was the site of the Catskill Mountain House. A large marker sign erected by the DEC designates this historic site and lists its elevation as 3,000 feet just as owner Charles Beach once did. The true elevation is 2,200 feet. As we noted earlier, this area is known as Pine

Orchard, a remarkably unique area for those interested in the distribution of plants and trees in New York State.

Pine Orchard is named for the pitch pine that once grew on this elevated plateau. They still do grow along the nearby Escarpment. However, the pitch pine is a tree of the southern forests and in this same area, oddly enough, northern hardwoods such as maple and beech can be found along with summit vegetation such as fir and spruce. This is the only place in the Catskills that we are aware of in which all three forest types are found in one spot.

After you enjoy the expansive view of the Hudson Valley from the Mountain House site, you have a choice of proceeding either south or north on the Escarpment Trail. We'll first describe the hike to the south, which leads to the magnificent Kaaterskill Falls. This will be followed with a description of the hike to the north, which goes to North Point. Either hike will reward you with spectacular views and many interesting natural features.

"...this area is known as Pine Orchard, a remarkably unique area for those interested in the distribution of plants and trees in New York State."

ESCARPMENT TRAIL

South to Kaaterskill Falls

North to North Point

North Point to Windham High Peak

"*The Kaaterskill Falls are considered by some to be the most beautiful natural spectacle in all of the Catskills.*"

*f*rom the Catskill Mountain House site, proceed south on the *blue-blazed* **Escarpment Trail**. Soon you'll pass into a wooded rocky area, and you'll see many unmarked old side trails that go off to the right (west) into an area that is fun to explore.

This section of South Moun-tain was owned by the Mountain House, whose guests used to walk these trails and gave names to some of the most interesting features. One area known as "*Puddingstone Hall*" has some features comprised of conglom-erate pudding stone. Names from the Romantic period such as "*Druid Rocks*," "*Elfin Pass*" and "*Fairy Spring*" can be found on many old maps. "*Druid Rocks*"

Overlooking Kaaterskill Clove towards Hunter Mountain from South Mountain.

is the name given to three large rocks which resemble stone-hedge monoliths built by the ancient Druids. "Fairy Spring" is a cold clear spring nearby and "Elfin Pass" is a very narrow pass between rocks also called the Lemon Squeezer.

We won't tell you exactly where they are, but if you explore this area southwest of the Mountain House site, you'll most assuredly have fun rediscovering this once very popular area.

Continue along the Escarpment Trail southward and soon you'll junction with a *red-blazed trail* that takes a shortcut only to merge with the trail you are on further along. If you continue along the blue-blazed Escarpment Trail, you'll come to two fine lookouts that are close together. These lookouts **"Split**

Rock" and "**Boulder Rock**" are often bypassed by hikers. We enjoyed lunch at this spot as the views of the many farms below danced before our eyes. To the south, you can see the ridge of the Shawangunk Mountains in the distance, not a common sight from the Northern Catskills.

The trail will now turn to the right (west) and in another 0.75 mile, after reaching the second junction with the red trail, a large clearing will appear on the right. This is the site of the Hotel Kaaterskill. Shortly thereafter you'll reach a junction with the *red-blazed* **Schutt Road Trail** which will take you 2.55 miles to Schutt Road and a parking area. The gatehouse you passed on the way in is another 0.1 mile further.

To continue on the Escarpment Trail, turn sharply to the left (southeast) and descend gently for about a quarter mile until you reach a sharp turn to the right. At this point, a horse trail maintained by the DEC descends to Kaaterskill Clove. This trail forms part of the Long Path. There is a great view here overlooking Kaaterskill Clove, which is almost as steep and dangerous as Plattekill Clove to the south.

View overlooking Kaaterskill Clove of the private mountain communities of Santa Cruz and Twilight Park from Inspiration Point.

The trail runs along the top of the clove for 0.3 mile until it reaches **Inspiration Point**, a favorite of President Grant. To the south and east, the peaceful plain

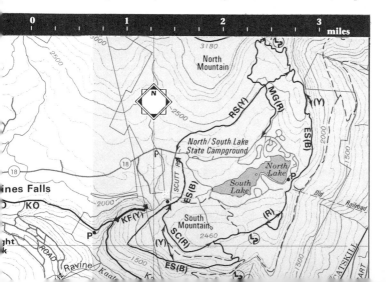

of the Hudson River Valley gives way to the ever rising mass of Kaaterskill High Peak. The peak gently rolls westward until it rises again, cresting at Roundtop Mountain. Although the shorter of the two, Roundtop appears taller from this vantage point. Hunter Mountain, recognizable by its ski slopes, is also visible to the west. To the right of Hunter is Onteora Mountain which stands above the back of Kaaterskill Clove.

Here, the drainage system funnels into the depths of the clove and out into the Hudson Valley. This perspective is what gives Inspiration Point its name. The area below and across the clove to the coast is called the "Amphitheater" because of its spacious cavernous shape. We hiked this area in mid-April when there were several small waterfalls visible across the clove on the slopes of High Peak as winter snow was in a run-off stage.

The trail continues along the ridge and, in another 0.7 mile, reaches a stone monument dedicated to Frank Layman, who died at this spot fighting a forest fire on August 10, 1900. From here, Hunter Mountain is clearly visible to the west and, on the slopes across the valley, you can see the private mountain communities of Santa Cruz and Twilight Park.

The trail now curves to the right (north) and passes through an attractive area of white birch trees. In another 0.45 mile, you'll come near the top of **Kaaterskill Falls**. You are now 4.0 miles from the North Lake parking area. The trail goes very close to the rocky area at the top of the falls, and you may wish to follow a herd path which leads to the very top. Caution is urged here, however, as many fatalities have occurred at this location. If you're not careful, you might end up following the water over the edge!

The Kaaterskill Falls are considered by some to be the most beautiful natural spectacle in all of the Catskills. The Falls consist of two separate waterfalls that together are higher than Niagara Falls. The first drops 175 feet into a pool, from which the water spills another 85 feet in a second fall.

The Falls have not changed much since the days when Henry David Thoreau stayed at a saw miller's house near the top of the Falls, absorbing the tranquility. During the height of the hotel era, a wooden staircase led to the bottom of the Falls.

The third hotel in the area, the **Laurel House**, stood at the top of the Falls. Modest by comparison to the Mountain House

A southeasterly view from the Escarpment.

and the Hotel Kaaterskill, it nevertheless was very popular, largely because of its unique location. The owner, Peter Schutt, had a dam built to control the flow of water to the Falls. He charged a fee to turn on the water and show spectators the Falls, and was apparently successful for some time. The Laurel House was burned by the DEC in 1966 after the state acquired the land.

Today, the same Kaaterskill Falls can be viewed in all their glory without your having to pay a fee to have them turned on.

With the decline of the hotels, the Falls became somewhat forgotten. Renewed interest in the history of the area, in part the result of the book THE CATSKILL MOUNTAIN HOUSE, written by Roland Van Zandt in 1966, has once again made the Falls a popular place.

Possibly the best view of the Falls is from *Prospect Rock* on the north wall of the gorge. This vantage point can be reached by following the abandoned railroad bed west from the south end of Laurel House Road, and then picking up a short side trail on the left that goes down a few hundred feet to the viewpoint. (The DEC plans to construct a marked trail to this spot in the near future).

Until recently, the Escarpment Trail followed a steep, eroded path down to the base of the Falls and ended at a hairpin turn on Route 23A. However, in accordance with the management plan for this area, the DEC recently closed the portion of the trail connecting the top of the Falls with their base.

The Escarpment Trail has been rerouted, and it now terminates at a parking area on Schutt Road just south of its junction with Mountain House Road (County Route 18), about 0.75 mile from the top of the falls. (Schutt Road is now closed to vehicular traffic south of this parking lot). This point is 4.75 miles from the North Lake parking area.

If you've followed the Escarpment Trail to this point from the North Lake parking lot, you may wish to take an alternate route to return to your car. Continue on Schutt Road north for a short distance to Mountain House Road. Turn right and continue past the gatehouse, then take the right fork and follow a paved road which runs parallel to and south of the lakes, and which leads you in a little more than a mile to your starting point at the North Lake parking lot.

If you wish to see the Falls from their base, you'll have to approach them via a *yellow-*

Winter morning near the top of Kaaterskill Falls with view of Roundtop.

blazed trail (formerly blue-blazed and part of the Escarpment Trail) which leads from Route 23A. The trail begins at a hairpin turn in the road, about 2 1/2 miles west of Palenville. You can't park at this point, but a parking area is located on the left side of the road a short distance further west. (If you park here, be careful walking back along the road to the trailhead. The road is narrow and the traffic is often very heavy.) The trail immediately passes the small but attractive **Bastion Falls** (which can be seen from the road) and, in another 0.4 mile and 400 feet of climbing, reaches the base of Kaaterskill Falls.

For the really adventurous, there is an *unmarked trail* which leads to the edge of the chasm and under the upper falls. If you manage to find this trail (and you'll have to bushwhack to get to it), be extremely careful, and make sure of your footing. There is little to hold on to, and the trail can be very slippery. Indeed, peo-

ple have fallen to their deaths from here! But if you go slow and keep your wits about you, it will be worth the effort to stand under the Falls and see the water plummeting past, blurring the sky as it goes.

Of course, winter hiking should not be attempted here except by experienced ice climbers with crampons. The mist from the tumbling water freezes on contact, resulting in a layer of ice on all exposed surfaces. ◣▲ ⚥⚥

North to North Point

Another popular day hike is along the Escarpment north to North Point. This hike captures the mystique and grandeur that has made the Catskills so special to so many. We suggest that you try to get out on this section of trail early in the morning, while the sun is still yawning on the expanse of the Hudson Valley.

From the parking lot at North Lake, follow the *blue-blazed* **Escarpment Trail** to the north, passing a register box in a few hundred yards. Keep your eyes open in early June for the

---

" ...try to get out on this section of trail early in the morning, while the sun is still yawning on the expanse of the Hudson Valley."

---

lovely orchid called Indian moccasin or pink ladies slipper. (If you started at the Mountain House site, just follow the blue blazes a short distance to the north until you see the parking lot to the left, then continue straight ahead on the blue-blazed trail). In about 0.3 mile from the parking lot, you'll reach **Artist Rock**, made popular by Thomas Cole, the founder of the Hudson River School of landscape painting. From here, you'll pass a series of rock ledges overlooking the Hudson Valley to the east.

Near these ledges you can find five different species of evergreen trees growing together. Hemlock, white pine, pitch pine, red spruce and balsam fir can all be identified on the same site. This is an unusual find indeed, and as previously mentioned it may be the only place in all the Catskills where summit conifers

Newman's Ledge.

exist with southerly species.

In another half mile, the trail climbs steeply through large rock formations, with a steep, rocky area to your right. At one time there was a ladder here, known as "Jacob's Ladder," which enabled Mountain House guests to climb up to **Sunset Rock**, which provides an impressive overview of North and South Lakes.

This scene, the Mountain House against the backdrop of High Peak and Roundtop Mountain to the south, has been immortalized in many 19th century paintings. The adventurous can still clamber up the rocky slope, but for those who want to keep their feet on solid ground, a short *yellow side trail* leads off to the right about 100 yards further up the Escarpment Trail and proceeds back (southward) to Sunset Rock.

From this point, the Escarpment Trail continues north, with many views of the Hudson Valley to the east. We think that the most impressive and prominent view is from **Newman's Ledge**, about 0.2 mile past the junction with the yellow side trail. This ledge is a rock which juts out from the Escarpment. The view from this point is magnificent, but there is a sheer dropoff, so please be very careful.

We were once there on a clear day, when the Taconics and Berkshires of Massachusetts and Connecticut, some forty miles to the east, were visible. The Hudson River in the valley below gleamed as red-tailed hawks caught free rides on the updrafts which are common in this area.

You'll notice a low wooded ridge below and to your left (north), with a rocky outcrop on it. The valley just south of this ridge is known as *Sleepy Hollow* (or Rip Van Winkle Hollow). Legend has it that *Rip Van Winkle* slept in this hollow for twenty years. There is some dispute as to whether Rip came from Palenville, at the mouth of Kaaterskill Clove, or the village of Catskill, due east on the Hudson River. In any case, the legends of the Catskills are forever bound to this area.

> **"Legend has it that Rip Van Winkle slept in this hollow for twenty years."**

If you look to the north, beyond Sleepy Hollow, you will see a small round hill alone in the valley. This is Cairo Round Top, and it appears tiny despite the fact that it rises about 800

> *"The Hudson River in the valley below gleamed as red-tailed hawks caught free rides on updrafts..."*

feet above its surroundings to an elevation of 1,400 feet. To the right (south), you can see the remains of the Mountain Turnpike, the old carriage road from Sleepy Hollow which once was the primary means of access to the Mountain House. The portion of the road you see from here was known as the "Long Level," since it ran along the side of the mountain at a contour elevation of about 1,900 feet. What an arduous trip this must have been for both man and horse!

From Newman's Ledge, the trail proceeds to the northwest and moves away from the edge of the Escarpment. Although you're never far from the edge, you won't see the Hudson Valley again until you reach North Point. The trail climbs 140 feet and comes out on a level, open area. Soon you'll pass a small clearing on your left. Close inspection will disclose a swamp, which is well worth exploring. Among the interesting plants you'll see blooming in the early summer are wild irises and

Looking north from Newman's Ledge just after sunrise.

mountain laurel.

Just beyond this clearing, you'll reach the *yellow-blazed* **Rock Shelter Trail**. This trail is named for a large rock overhang, known as **Badman Cave**, which was reputedly a hideout for outlaws in the 1700s. Several people can comfortably fit underneath, and it can provide temporary shelter in bad weather. The Rock Shelter Trail leads in 2.0 miles to the gatehouse at the entrance to the North Lake area, descending 500 feet in that distance. It intersects with the red-blazed Mary's Glen Trail in 0.45 mile, and the combination of these two trails provides a pleasant return route to North Lake if you've had enough hiking for the day.

Continue on the Escarpment Trail, which ascends over rocky terrain and passes through another open area too rocky to support any trees or large plants. The trail here is at an elevation of about 2,700 feet, but it passes through areas of spruce and fir that usually are found only at elevations of 3,500 feet and above.

In 0.6 mile from the junction with the Rock Shelter Trail, you'll reach a junction with the *red-blazed* **Mary's Glen Trail**. This is a very beautiful trail which leads in 1.6 miles to

Mountain House Road at the west end of the state campground. In 0.45 mile, it intersects the yellow-blazed Rock Shelter Trail, and soon passes a small

---

"This primeval setting is unusually cool in the hot months of the summer."

---

waterfall near moss-covered rocks in a dark and silent forest. This primeval setting is unusually cool in the hot months of the summer. The trail then goes through Mary's Glen, following a stream in a wooded area, until it reaches Mountain House Road. For much of the way, the trail is paved with large stones...a reminder of the day when it served the guests at the Mountain House who expected a gentle, easy-to-follow path. It provides an excellent return route to the North Lake area.

If you choose to continue on the Escarpment Trail, a very steep climb lies ahead. You'll ascend only 240 feet in 0.25 mile, but it will seem a lot longer. The trail up to North Point is very eroded, and you'll find yourself grabbing onto trees for support. This section of trail is especially difficult in wet weather. But if you persevere, you'll soon reach the open rocks and wonderful views from the top of **North Point** (2.45 miles from the North Lake parking lot and just under 3,000 feet in elevation).

To the south, you can see North and South Lakes (they now are really one large lake, but they used to be separated). You can also follow the path along the easterly edge of the Escarpment which brought you to where you are now. To the east, you are afforded a *magnificent view* over the Hudson Valley. On a clear day, you can see New York's state capital, Albany, to the north. With binoculars you'll be able to clearly identify the Empire State Plaza buildings and the four white towers of the SUNY at Albany campus to the left (west) You'll also notice the Blackhead Range looming to the northwest (left).

When you've had enough of the beautiful views, retrace your steps down to the junction with the Mary's Glen Trail, which makes an excellent return route (see above). ◣◢

North Point to Windham High Peak

In the previous section, we've described in detail two sections of the Escarpment Trail which make excellent day hikes. But the Escarpment Trail is actually a 23-mile trail which provides a real trek for those who desire to spend several days backpacking.

For almost its entire length, this trail follows along the top of the Escarpment of the Northeastern Catskills. Also known as the "Wall of Manitou," this escarpment (a steep slope or cliff formed by erosion) begins at Overlook Mountain, just north of Woodstock, and continues northward to Route 23 near Windham. It is penetrated by only two major notches or "cloves," Plattekill Clove and Kaaterskill Clove. The Escarpment's sudden rise is the result of an abrupt change in bedrock from the hard sandstones and conglomerates found in the mountains to the soft shales and limestones found in the valley.

Of course, the location of this trail at the edge of the Escarpment provides many beautiful views. Water is scarce, so you'll want to bring along plenty of

"The Escarpment's sudden rise is the result of an abrupt change in bedrock from the hard sandstones and conglomerates found in the mountains to the soft shales and limestones found in the valley."

fluids.

Camping is limited at the southern end. The ease of access and beauty of the North Lake area, resulting in heavy trail use, has forced the DEC to close the southern end of the Escarpment Trail to camping. The only place south of North Point where camping is permitted is at the North Lake State Campground. Because of this, you might want to do the section from Schutt Road to the Mountain House site as a day hike.

If you want to do the entire trail in one shot, start from the southern terminus at the parking area on Schutt Road, just outside of the North Lake gatehouse. You'll reach a trail junction in 0.55 mile. Take the right fork which leads in 0.2 mile to near the top of the falls, and proceeds to the edge of the Escarpment at Layman Monument. It continues along (or near) the edge of the cliff to the Mountain House site, which is 4.5 miles from the beginning on Schutt Road. (For a more detailed description of this section, see pages 106-113 above).

Many backpackers choose instead to begin their hike from North Lake, near the Mountain House site. From the parking lot at North Lake, the trail proceeds northeast and continues along the top of the Escarpment towards North Point. (Again, this section of the trail has been described in detail on pages 113-119 above, so we will not repeat this description here).

North Point, which is 2.45 miles from the North Lake parking lot, is the first area along the Escarpment Trail at which camping is permitted. It makes an excellent campsite, with the open, pollution-free skies providing clear views of the lights in the Hudson River Valley to the east. You might want to bring a small alarm clock to ensure that you're up in time to catch the sunrise over the valley. Because of the popularity of this site, which already bears scars of overuse, you should take special precautions to protect it from further abuse. Use a backpacking stove rather than build a wood fire. You'll probably find it quite difficult to find wood in this heavily used area, anyway.

Leaving North Point, which gives you the last view over North and South Lakes, the Escarpment Trail turns to the west and slowly climbs over North Mountain. The trail continues through brushy areas and up steep rocky slopes to **Stoppel Point** (elevation 3,420 feet), which is 1.7 miles from North Point (4.15 miles from the North Lake parking lot).

Stoppel Point, about 400 feet higher than North Point, is covered with a mixture of spruce, fir and hardwoods, and makes a very pleasant spot to eat lunch or to camp. Although the view from here over the Hudson River Valley is not as extensive as that from North Point, the small ledge facing east provides a certain coziness. Jutting out to the right (south) is North Mountain, which you just came from.

———

"In the evening, a full harvest moon rose over the Hudson River Valley, bathing us in a pale glow..."

———

We once spent an enjoyable night on Stoppel Point and were joined by a deer for dinner! Amazingly, she grazed a mere 10 to 15 yards away. In the evening, a full harvest moon rose over the Hudson River Valley, bathing us in a pale glow, as the lights of the village of Catskill sparkled in the distance and owls hooted from all around. It is these kind of experiences, which will linger in our minds forever, that have made the Catskills a special place to us. One note of caution, however: Porcupines are prevalent in this area. We've even heard of a heavy pair of Fabiano hiking boots and an axe cover being chewed up one evening by a porcupine! Take care not to leave such items, or any edibles, outside at night.

From Stoppel Point, the trail goes west for a short distance. Before you start to descend, you'll get a view (at least if there are no leaves on the trees) of the Blackhead Range to the north, with its striking skyline made up of Blackhead, Black Dome and Thomas Cole Mountains. The Escarpment Trail will eventually lead you to the top of Blackhead. The trail then turns northward, descends rather steeply for a vertical distance of about 300 feet, and then levels off. You'll continue for about half a mile along a level area, with a mixture of summit and slope trees. We found this a good area for observing many different kinds of birds, especially early in the day during their migration season. The trail then descends another 300 vertical feet and again levels off.

Soon you'll come upon an *excellent lookout* to the east, with rocks to sit on and permit you to enjoy the view. To your right (southeast), the piece of land jutting out in front of you is actually a spur leading up to Stoppel Point. On the other side of this spur is Winter Clove. Looking back, you can see that you've made a substantial descent from Stoppel Point to get to your present location. The steep valley immediately in front of you seems to lie at your feet.

During the warmer seasons, you can usually observe large turkey vultures gliding the air currents created by the abrupt rise of mountains from the valley.

A short distance past this lookout, the trail steeply descends another 200 feet into **Dutcher Notch**. This is the low point between two mountains. You are now at an elevation of about 2,500 feet and 6.4 miles from North Lake (11.15 miles from Schutt Road). To your right, the *yellow-blazed* **Dutcher Notch Trail** drops about 1,500 feet in 2.4 miles to its terminus on Floyd Hawver Road.

The importance of this trail to the average hiker lies in the fact that there is a *reliable spring* 0.35 mile down the trail (on your right). This spring, which has cold, clear water year round, is the first source of water since North Lake. You'll almost certainly want to make the rather steep trip down to the spring to replenish your water supply. To your left, the relatively new **Colgate Lake Trail**, also *yellow-blazed*, descends to the west. After about 2.0 miles, the trail passes an unnamed lake, with much beaver activity visible in the area, and then turns right to skirt privately-owned land around Lake Capra. It reaches a parking area near the state-owned Colgate Lake in 4.25 miles.

Dutcher Notch makes a nice sheltered place to camp. Although the area is not abused, the bare ground that we observed in the notch leads us to conclude that it has been camped in often.

Looking ahead, a false summit seems to jut up like Mt. Everest. The hike ahead may appear impossible, but it's not quite that bad. Although the climb is tedious, and you gain about 800 feet in only 0.75 mile, the trail is not excessively steep and there are few, if any, places where you'll have to pull yourself up and grab a hold for support. Along the way you'll pass large rocks with attractive campsite potential. When the trail finally begins to level off, you'll see a *short side trail* to your left which leads to a viewpoint, with *excellent views* back towards Stoppel Point. You can also see Lake Capra and Colgate Lake in the valley to the southwest (right). The elevation of the viewpoint is about 3,200 feet. One of us, to his surprise and amusement, once stumbled upon some nude sunbathers at this spot. After introducing themselves, they humbly carried on with their business.

The Escarpment Trail will now climb very gradually through areas of balsam fir and white birch. At one point, you'll start to descend slightly. The trail will pass through a few open areas surrounded by thick shrubby vegetation. We noticed several campfire rings in these areas.

Blackhead Mountain will become more apparent and loom taller in front of you as you enter each clearing. The climb of over 600 feet in about half a mile gets increasingly exciting as you stop to catch your breath and get a look at the Hudson Valley to the east. The best view awaits near the top of Blackhead itself.

Although you are looking out over tree tops, it feels like being in a small airplane. At 3,940 feet, Blackhead gives a close-up *view of the huge valley* at the highest point on the Escarpment.

On a clear day Albany can be spotted with the naked eye and easily with the aid of binoculars. As mentioned before, Cairo Round Top is the only round hill straight out between the Hudson River and yourself. You can also trace the course of the trail back

On the frozen summit of Blackhead Mountain.

to North Mountain to the southeast.

After a rest, you'll move along the summit of Blackhead amongst the gnarled balsam firs that are stunted from being wind blown and dehydrated. We were once up there in zero degrees Fahrenheit weather. The sky appeared to be within arms reach due to the heavy snow cover that lifted the trail at least three feet. This made the trees seem that much smaller. The top of Blackhead is amazingly unspoiled and the trees have grown very close

Southwest towards the Devil's Path from upper slopes of Blackhead Mountain.

is a required winter peak for the Catskill 3500 Club.

From the summit, the *yellow-blazed* **Blackhead Mountain Trail** drops off to the west and descends about 520 feet in 0.6 mile to Lockwood Gap between Blackhead and Black Dome. We'll continue on the Escarpment Trail, which turns right and drops steeply northward off the airy summit of Blackhead, revealing an occasional glimpse through the trees of the trail ahead that goes over Acra Point. The 1,100-foot descent on the north slope of the mountain sees little sun, and is therefore cooler than any other side of the mountain. Snow will last here long into the late spring.

Near the base of the descent, you'll pass *two fine lookouts* over the Hudson Valley. You'll then continue to descend for a few hundred feet through a forest of mixed fir and assorted hardwoods, and pass through a beautiful grove of white birch

together for protection from the wind. You really cannot wander off the trail and this is all for the good. If hikers were to leave the trail, great damage could be done to the fragile, thin topsoil and the plants that grow in it. Blackhead's trail is heavily hiked and

North towards Acra Point and Burnt Knob from just below summit of Blackhead Mountain.

"No matter what season, the valley blossoms in a patchwork of shapes rising from the mix of field and forest."

Gazing westward over Big Hollow from Acra Point.

trees. Soon you'll reach a junction with the **Batavia Kill Trail**. This *yellow-blazed trail* will drop off to your left (west) and pass the Batavia Kill Lean-to in 0.25 mile. This lean-to is situated next to the *Batavia Kill* which is a *reliable water source*, a commodi-

ty not common to the Escarpment Trail. The **Batavia Kill Lean-to** makes a nice campsite and provides an opportunity to get off the ridge line of the Escarpment and experience a change in terrain.

In 0.65 mile past the lean-to,

Rainy, foggy day on Acra Point Ledge. Burnt Knob is barely visible to the west behind our friends.

the Batavia Kill Trail merges with the *red-blazed* **Black Dome Trail** which leads in another half mile to Big Hollow Road and a parking area. This makes for good access on day hikes. The Escarpment-Batavia Kill Trail junction is a full 14.65 miles from Schutt Road and the beginning of the Escarpment Trail, and 9.9 miles from North Lake parking lot.

You'll now continue north on the Escarpment Trail and come to another *fine lookout* over the Hudson Valley. This one is well shaded due to the presence of tall evergreens. When we were there we noticed a large tree felled by a recent storm. This served to open up more of the northward view toward Albany. No matter what season, the valley blossoms in a patchwork of shapes rising from the mix of field and forest.

As the trail continues north there are no views to be found, even though the Hudson Valley is just about a stone's throw away. If there are no leaves in the trees, you'll be able to get a glimpse of the valley, which makes an excellent backdrop, especially on winter hikes with snow on the ground.

As the trail begins to turn west, take note of the elevated area on your left (west). This is a sign you are nearing **Acra Point**, elevation 3,100 feet. The open rock summit is reached with little climbing. The high growth of small trees and ground cover obscures a clear view. Acra Point is 16.45 miles from the start of the trail on Schutt Road, and 11.7 miles from North Lake parking area.

If you follow the trail a little further as it turns west, you'll find an *excellent view* down the Big Hollow (also known as Black Dome Valley). You'll notice Black Dome and Thomas Cole Mountains on the left (south) side of the valley. The small hills at the west end of the valley are Van Loan Hill and Round Hill. They are "drumlins" formed by glacial debris and action during the Ice Age. Now follow the trail down a few hundred yards and you'll see a short path to the left that leads to an *open rock with a view* similar to the one just mentioned.

If you look to the northwest (right) side of the valley, you will see Burnt Knob, with Windham High Peak beyond it. This is a great place to rest. We feel this is an *unheralded* but *excellent viewpoint*. Another treat a short distance down the trail is an excellent view off to the right (clearest when there are no leaves on the trees) towards the distant Adirondack Mountains in the north. The valley below is spattered with farms and silos as well as woodlots.

The trail will now drop off a few hundred feet to an unnamed saddle between Acra Point and Burnt Knob. At 17.15 miles from Schutt Road, you'll reach *a junction* with the *red-blazed* **Black Dome**

North towards Albany from Burnt Knob.

Trail which descends 1.0 mile to the parking area at Big Hollow Road, a descent of 600 feet or so.

Continuing along the Escarpment Trail, you'll start to climb to the right and then you'll switchback to the left and proceed steeply up. If the trees are bare, you'll notice the valley on your right as you get higher up. You'll eventually level off and the trail will pass just below the summit of **Burnt Knob** (elevation 3,180 feet). There is a *fine viewpoint* looking over Big Hollow to the Blackhead Range. This is about 18.4 miles from the beginning of the Escarpment Trail and 13.65 miles from the North Lake parking area.

The trail will descend about 200 feet and then climb up to a false summit with another outlook over the valley. After another drop and climb you'll finally be ready to start the final climb toward Windham High Peak, the last mountain on the Escarpment Trail (or first, if you choose!)

When you first approach the level summit of Windham High Peak, you'll be taken by *a great panorama* from an open rock on this, the northeast side. At this point, most of the climbing is over, if you're following our course. Notice the engraved initials in the rocks dating back to

the 1800's. As for the view, it is one of the most open found anywhere in the Catskills. Burnt Knob and Acra Point are to the east. We have seen various weather disturbances, from trapped fog to black clouds in a passing cold front, form in the valley just

Sign marker post between Acra Point and Burnt Knob.

Southeasterly view following the Escarpment Trail overlooking Burnt Knob and Acra Point towards Blackhead Mountain from summit of Windham High Peak. A hollow between Burnt Knob and Acra Point acts as a flue, channeling the warm air from the valley up to the cooler air of the Escarpment ridge, forming clouds.

> *"It was quite an experience, beneath the swift, dark opaque clouds, to be peppered by wind-driven hail."*

north of Burnt Knob and Acra Point. Some days the buildings of Albany can be seen to the north.

The summit of **Windham High Peak** is rather open, as one of us found out when caught in a thunderstorm. It was quite an experience, beneath the swift, dark opaque clouds, to be peppered by wind-driven hail. We don't suggest you seek this kind of fun!

You'll notice a few scraggly fir trees on Windham High Peak. These are remnants of the once dominant evergreen top that crowned the mountain. In time they will probably be replaced by the ever-invading summit hardwood species.

Following the summit for a few hundred yards, you'll pass a partial view south towards Black Dome and a more *open view* to the northwest a little further on. This latter view is near the true summit at elevation 3,524 feet, marked by a USGS marker embedded in the rock. You've now gone 19.85 miles on the Escarpment Trail and 15.1 miles from the North Lake parking lot. We'd strongly recommend that you do Windham on a nice clear day, so that you can appreciate the views.

The trail will now drop off the summit and descend moderately until it reaches two thick groves of mature, tall Norway spruce trees with a small peace-

Blackhead Range from Windham High Peak.

The roots of the spruce trees.

ful meadow between them. We suspect that these trees were planted by the Civilian Conservation Corps in the 1930's. Their root systems are exposed and one must walk on top of them.

On a warm spring day we passed through this cavernous canopy atop pools, roots and melting snow with the smell of the evergreen everywhere in the dark, chilled air as a three-foot-high fog formed an unearthly eeriness before us.

In a little over two miles, you'll pass the **Elm Ridge Lean-to** (elevation 2,300 feet) to your left. This lean-to makes for a nice place to camp with a quiet setting. Just beyond the lean-to is a junction with the *yellow-blazed*

Elm Ridge Trail. This trail is a remnant of an old turnpike that traversed this area and has a *pipe spring* a few hundred yards down the trail (on the right side). The 0.85 mile trail leads to a parking area on Peck Road in Big Hollow.

We'll continue on the blue-blazed Escarpment Trail down to a register box and through a meadow to its terminus on Route 23 (elevation 1,760 feet). The parking area is across the road. You're now 23.15 miles from the beginning of the Escarpment Trail, or 18.4 miles from the North Lake parking area. The village of Windham is 3 miles west (left) on Route 23.

Of course, you might choose instead to start from Route 23 or from one of the access trails in Black Dome Valley. There are also several interesting day hike possibilities available in this area. Whichever route you choose, the views from the Escarpment Trail are worth the climb.

BLACK DOME RANGE TRAIL

"The majority of this hike is spent in high elevations above 3,000 feet."

*i*n the Northeastern Catskills, running east to west, three mountains comprise what is commonly called the Blackhead Range. They form a distinctive profile visible from many vantage points in these parts. As one travels south on the Northway near Albany, this distinctive range may be seen from many miles away.

The Blackhead Range as seen from West Kill Mountain.

Black Dome, **Blackhead** and **Thomas Cole** are the third, fourth and fifth highest mountains in the Catskills. Each is over 3,900 feet in elevation. They make for excellent two or three-day backpacking trips, or they can be broken down into exciting day hikes. The majority of this hike is spent in high elevations above 3,000 feet. The Black Dome Range Trail was cut by the DEC in 1967, making it one of the more recently cleared trails that traverse major Catskill peaks.

A good place to start a day hike is from the end of Elmer Barnum Road. This point may be reached by traveling south from the village of Maplecrest on Maplecrest Road, and continuing straight (rather than turning right) at the sharp turn in the road. Parking is available at the end of the road where the *red-blazed markers* designating the **Black Dome Range Trail** (also called the Blackhead Range Trail) lead into the woods. This point is at elevation 2,300 feet. If you have two cars, it's a good idea to leave one at the parking area on Big Hollow Road, where our hike will terminate. If not, you'll have to backtrack, which is what we did, enjoying every step of the way. (Or you might choose to return on Big Hollow Road, which makes for a surprisingly pleasant roadwalk through a tranquil farm valley).

At the beginning of the trail, south of Elmer Barnum Road, there is a beautiful meadow. We found it filled with wildflowers and bustling with birds. It is a strong contrast to the lofty views ahead.

In the beginning, the trail will climb slowly. Keep an eye out for low-growing wildflowers in the spring and early summer. We found the unique scarlet wild columbine growing just off the trail in mid-May. Spring beauty, purple trillium and assorted wild violets are also easy to spot at this time of the year.

You'll soon pass the register box and, as the trail makes a turn to the left (northeast), you'll start a steep hike through a mature hardwoods forest. Before reaching the first false summit (elevation 3,300 feet), you'll come to a *beautiful viewpoint* over the valley below...an excellent spot to take a breather. Cave Mountain is prominent to the west. When you get to the false summit, you'll have climbed 1,200 feet in 1.3 miles.

Push on another 0.65 mile and you'll really feel on top of things. At 3,500 feet, this false summit is a spur of Thomas Cole Mountain named **Camel's Hump**, which is appropriate since it has a distinctive hump shape when seen from a distance. A short unmarked path to the left will take you to an area of scrubby primary growth, with *views in every direction* (although

> "We found the unique
> scarlet wild columbine
> growing just off
> the trail in mid-May."

For more detail see map on pages 120-21.

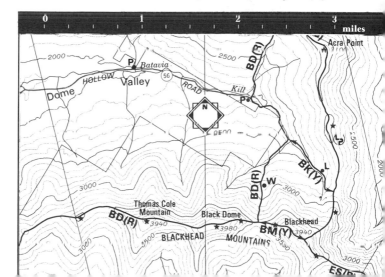

Windham High Peak from Camel's Hump.

the growth of vegetation has cut down the views considerably in recent years). Looking east, you can see the spur the trail follows up to Thomas Cole. Windham High Peak and the route of the Escarpment Trail can be seen across Big Hollow to the north. To the west, looking down the wide valley, there are numerous mountains to be seen. This makes an excellent place to have lunch or just relax and enjoy the view.

Back on the trail, you'll follow a level ridge line through an open area for about half a mile. Some of the trees are dead from weathering and poor drainage. You'll then start to climb the final 500 feet to the top of **Thomas Cole Mountain**, passing over bare rock and finally reaching the 3,940-foot summit, 2.9 miles from the start of the trail. At the summit, just to the right of the trail, a short side trail leads to a *good view southward*. The DEC has obviously cut the trees at this spot to widen the view and in doing so has sacri-

ficed some of this spot's beauty. Nonetheless, it is the only view we could find from Thomas Cole Mountain. The mountain is named for the famous painter who founded the Hudson River School of Painting.

From Thomas Cole you'll drop a few hundred feet, pass a viewpoint to the south, and start a quick, relatively easy climb, traveling 0.75 mile to the summit of **Black Dome** (3,980 feet), which is 3.65 miles from the start. After you level off at the top, you'll notice a short side trail to your right (south) that comes out on a large rock with a *southward view* similar to the one from

> *"...this view was apparently popular with 19th century hikers who inscribed their names for future view-seekers to read."*

Thomas Cole, but much more impressive because of its wider scope.

Another interesting fact about this rock is the engraved names that date back to the 1800's. Although there were no official trails up Black Dome un-

Devil's Path at the horizon from summit of Black Dome.

til recently, this view was apparently popular with 19th century hikers who inscribed their names for future view-seekers to read.

The Devil's Path, which dominates this view, can be seen in its entirety. You can easily see the steep drops into Mink Hollow (between Sugarloaf and Plateau Mountains) and Stony Clove (between Plateau and Hunter Mountains). You'll also notice Kaaterskill High Peak and Roundtop to the southeast. Looking straight down in front of you in the valley you'll see Lake Capra and Colgate Lake. You can also pick out the smaller Parker and Onteora Mountains just beyond the nearby valley.

The summit of Black Dome is beautiful and level enough to take a short stroll before it starts to drop again. On one of our hikes, the summit was shrouded in fog, which gave a mystical aura to the scene. While exploring off the trail, one of us had the fortune to flush a bobcat out from under a small fir tree.

From the summit, the trail drops 200 feet or so to some rock ledges that jut out of the east slope. In our opinion, these ledges provide one of the most *impressive views* anywhere in the Catskills. The hulk of Blackhead Mountain stands out before you, with the expansive Hudson River Valley as a backdrop. Acra Point and Burnt Knob can be seen

Blackhead Mountain from Black Dome across Lockwood Gap.

down to your left (north) as they wind around the Black Dome Valley. You'll also see a small clearing with a white house in it. There is a parking lot near it that the trail will take you down to. This view is definitely one of our favorites and should be seen on a clear day to really appreciate it.

On one late October hike, all the leaves in the higher elevations were down, leaving Blackhead draped in an impressive assortment of earth tones. These ledges make a great place for lunch (be careful not to slip or to drop anything as it is a very steep drop here!). The trail descends steeply from these ledges, and you will need to use your hands for assistance in your descent.

When you reach **Lockwood Gap** (4.25 miles), which is the col between Black Dome and Blackhead, the elevation will be 3,420 feet. A marker sign indicates that the *yellow-blazed* **Blackhead Mountain Trail**, a popular day-hike, will take you to the top of **Blackhead Mountain**. This steep climb of 520 feet in 0.6 mile is interesting and provides *excellent wide views* southwest toward Hunter Mountain and vicinity. You'll also get a first hand look back at Black Dome. Be careful if it's wet or below freezing, as you will cross open rock at several points with little or nothing to hold on to.

We'll follow the red-blazed Black Dome Range Trail as it turns northward and descends steeply from Lockwood Gap. Watch your step, as there is loose rock on this section of trail. A few hundred feet down, you'll pass a *small pipe spring* on the right, a fairly reliable water source. At 5.40 miles the *yellow-blazed* **Batavia Kill Trail** goes off to the right (see page 128). The Black Dome Range Trail continues down and levels off alongside the *Batavia Kill*, reaching a parking area at 6.0 miles.

If you're making a day hike, you'll probably want to end it here. The trail will climb northward to the other side of the valley, terminating in the col between Burnt Knob and Acra Point, 7.0 miles from its start. Here it junctions with the Escarpment Trail. This section can be used as a bailout for those on the Escarpment Trail or for access by day-hikers.

The Black Dome Trail, together with the Blackhead Mountain Trail and the Escarpment Trail, can provide an excellent two or three-day circular backpacking trip. Start at the parking lot at the end of Elmer Barnum Road, and proceed along the Black Dome Range Trail to its junction with the Blackhead Mountain Trail. Follow the Blackhead Mountain Trail to its junction with the Escarpment Trail at the summit of Blackhead. Then take the Escarpment Trail to its junction with the Batavia Kill Trail, and follow the trail down

Black Dome Mountain from Blackhead.

Devil's Path from County Route 16.

DEVIL'S PATH

"According to legend, the cloven feet of the Devil made it possible for him alone to traverse this steep and sometimes dangerous terrain."

to the lean-to, where you may choose to stay overnight.

The next day, retrace your steps back to the Escarpment Trail, and continue north and east over Acra Point, Burnt Knob and Windham High Peak to the Elm Ridge Lean-to. If you're taking a three-day trip, you'll spend the second night here. From the lean-to, follow the Elm Ridge Trail south to Peck Road. Take Peck Road to Big Hollow Road, which you'll follow to the village of Maplecrest. Proceed south on Maplecrest Road, then turn left onto Elmer Barnum Road and follow it to the parking lot at the trailhead. You'll find the road walk a welcome contrast to the ridgetop hiking.

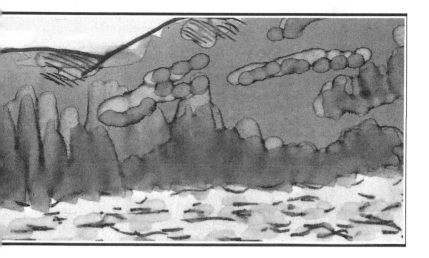

*t*he early Dutch and German settlers brought many religious superstitions and beliefs to the Hudson River Valley. Among these was the belief that the Devil himself inhabited the Catskills and indeed had favorite haunts where he roamed. According to legend, the cloven feet of the Devil made it possible for him alone to traverse this steep and sometimes dangerous terrain. It was here that he retreated to find rest from the invasion of men living in the gentle valleys below. Thus the Plattekill Clove and Stony Clove areas, and the mountains between, became known as the Devil's Path.

Today we know the **Devil's Path** as a 23.6-mile long trail that surmounts seven mountains, six of them over 3,500 feet, with substantial drops into some of the deepest notches to be found between mountains in the Catskills. The trail abounds in views and is crossed by many side trails, making day hikes in sections a very feasible alternative to the punishment of trying to backpack the entire Path. A good place to start is Prediger Road, near Plattekill Clove, at the eastern end of the trail.

"Clove" is a Dutch derivative meaning a cleave or "cleft" in a mountain wall or range. Plattekill Clove, which cuts deeply into the mountains, is often *consid-*

> **"The entire Hudson Valley was shrouded in an ocean of bright white haze…Oh, the wonders of weather!"**

---

ered to be one of the most rugged areas of the eastern United States. The Platte Clove Road is always susceptible to slides. Because of the danger of icing and the precipitous drop to the bottom of the clove from the road, it is closed in the winter.

Hiking in the clove is not safe. However, you're going to want to pry around to see the spectacular geological marvels that the Devil's Kitchen contains. This area is located just off Platte Clove Road, near the head of the clove. At one time people were charged a fee to see the formations within **Devil's Kitchen**. Please be careful should you choose to scramble in this area, since some serious accidents and even fatalities have occurred here.

The *red-blazed* **Devil's Path** sets out from the end of Prediger Road at approximately 2,000 feet elevation. Be sure to sign in at the register on the trail. In about 0.5 mile, a junction is reached with the *blue-blazed* **Jimmy Dolan Notch Trail**, which climbs for 1.5 miles southward to rejoin the Devil's Path in the

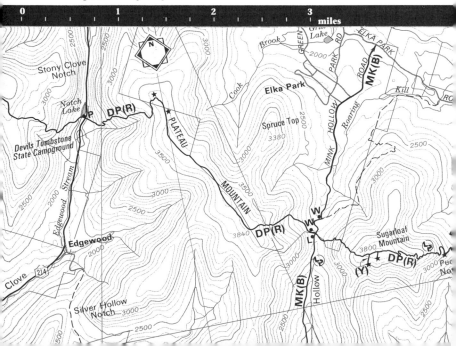

notch between Twin and Indian Head Mountains. We'll continue east along the Devil's Path, gradually winding and rolling up and down for almost two miles, and eventually turning right (south) on a wide old road.

In another 0.2 mile, you'll come to a sign indicating that the Devil's Path turns right (west) and starts its ascent of Indian Head Mountain. If you would like to set up camp nearby, the **Devil's Kitchen Lean-to** is 0.2 mile along the old road (now *blue blazed*) from the junction. This blue-blazed trail continues to Overlook Mountain, but we'll talk about that in detail later.

From the junction, the Devil's Path gradually climbs

Indian Head from Plattekill Clove.

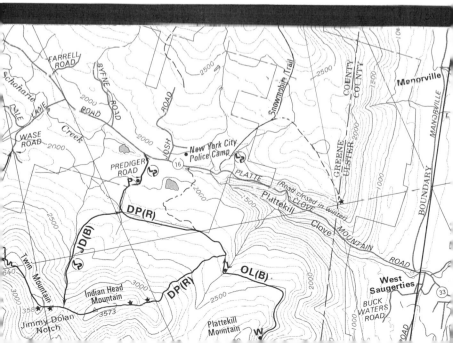

over brooks and through hemlock groves. After climbing more steeply through the woods, you will come upon a refreshing opening with a *view northward* of Kaaterskill High Peak and Roundtop. To your right lies Plattekill Clove, which opens into the expanse of the Hudson Valley. The large building at the base of High Peak is the old New York City Police Camp, now known as Indian Head Lodge, that some unsuccessfully attempted to convert into a prison in the early 1980's.

We were at this lookout on a warm sunny February day. The entire Hudson Valley was shrouded in an ocean of bright white haze. Even more amazing was the way the fog rolled in and filled the clove such a short distance away while we enjoyed a great sunny day of "thaw." Oh, the wonders of weather!

From here, the trail winds around the east end of Indian Head, with views of Plattekill Mountain to the east, the Hudson Valley beyond, and Overlook Mountain to the southeast. Notice the fire tower on top of Overlook Mountain.

Soon you'll climb through evergreens and pass a *fine viewpoint looking south.* This is not the summit of **Indian Head**, but it is a small prelude to the many wide vistas that you'll encounter on the Devil's Path.

The trail will drop a bit, and then climb very steeply through

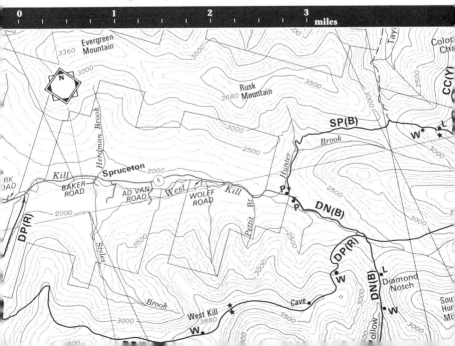

North from first open view on Indian Head Mountain, with High Peak and Roundtop.

an eroded crevice up to a ledge where you can stop and get your wind. If you look back at the first part of the mountain you just climbed, you can distinguish the chin of the "Indian head" which gives the mountain its name.

The trail continues to wind

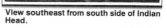

View southeast from south side of Indian Head.

Climbing Indian Head on the Devil's Path from the south face.

through the evergreens and up another ridge. It levels off and winds past a steep short dropoff of 15-20 feet on your left. This area has large climax red spruce trees that grow unusually large because of their sheltered location. You may go past the 3,573-foot summit without knowing it.

Soon, you'll start a moderate descent of a little over 400 feet into Jimmy Dolan Notch. At this point, you've gone about 6 miles and may want to bail out. You'll find signs for the *blue-blazed* **Jimmy Dolan Notch Trail** which will take you 2.0 miles back to the parking area on Prediger Road. It's not an especially tough trail, although it is a bit steep for the first 0.3 mile or so.

If you continue on the Devil's Path, you'll start a stiff climb of almost 500 feet in a little more than 0.5 mile to the first summit of Twin Mountain. You'll pass some interesting rock ledges on your left and, when you stop to get some much needed oxygen, be afforded a look back out towards the Plattekill Clove. This will give you a feel of why the Devil's Path is so named.

When the trail levels off, you can look down over the notch you've just come from and take a last look at Indian Head Mountain.

Soon you'll reach the summit of **Twin Mountain**, which is covered with a thick growth of very short spruce and fir trees, the characteristic summit evergreens. The small size of these trees may possibly be attributed to a massive blowdown which occurred during a hurricane in November 1950.

The trail comes out to a *wide viewpoint that is one of the finest on the Devil's Path*. To the south is the Ashokan Reservoir and the Burroughs Range, while Panther Mountain is in the distance to the west. Closer to you is Olderbark Mountain, attached to the south side of Plateau Mountain. Sugarloaf Mountain is between you and Plateau. Nearest to you is the north summit of Twin, which may appear further than you'd think from looking at a map. From here, the trail descends

Chilled fog-filled valleys from Twin.

slightly into a lovely hollow-like area and then ascends to the *true* (north) *summit* of Twin Mountain (elevation 3,640 feet). Just below the summit, you will reach *another viewpoint to the west*, with a close-up view of nearby Sugarloaf. The Hunter Mountain fire tower can be seen in the distance. Approximately 200 feet below the summit you will find a rock overhang which may be useful as a wind or rain shelter. The trail then steeply drops an impressive 800 feet to Pecoy Notch. You'll be glad if you choose to come down this way instead of up! Pecoy Notch, at elevation 2,800 feet, represents the low point between Twin and Sugarloaf and another bailout point. The *blue-blazed* **Pecoy Notch Trail** leads in less than 2 miles back to Platte Clove Road.

You'll now start a 1,000-foot winding assault on Sugarloaf Mountain. About halfway up, there are some small ledges which allow a look back up and across the notch at Twin, rising like a natural skyscraper. The summit of **Sugarloaf** (elevation 3,800 feet) offers a *view south* towards the southern Catskills. The trail then starts a descent of 1,100 feet into the gap between Sugarloaf and Plateau Mountain. After about a mile, you'll junction with the *blue-blazed* **Mink Hollow Trail** which goes off in both directions (north and south). (This trail is described in more detail on pages 160-162). The **Mink Hollow Lean-to** is a short walk south on the Mink Hollow Trail.

You might have noticed that we haven't mentioned anything about water sources yet. That's because, up to this point, there are no reliable ones in dry weather. As we said before, if you're hiking in spring or early summer, you usually won't have problems finding water. Howduring the other seasons it can get tricky.

There are *two reliable water sources* near the Mink Hollow-Devil's Path junction. One is about 0.25 mile north (right) down the Mink Hollow Trail and about 300 feet ahead of you off to the left of the trail. The other is a spring about 0.35 mile up the Devil's Path toward Plateau Mountain.

Proceeding on the Devil's Path up Plateau Mountain, you'll

Woodland sunflower.

have to scamper up a hefty 1,200 feet in the next 0.75 mile or so. Be sure to stop and get water at the spring on the way up, for the next water source is a long way off. Right before the trail crests,

"...cluttered with boulders, a darkened impasse engulfed by hemlocks; a fearful place inhabited by the Devil."

Notch Lake in Stony Clove.

there is a *good viewpoint* north-east towards the distant Hudson Valley and nearby Sugarloaf.

The summit of **Plateau Mountain** is a nice two-mile stroll that offers soothing shade, especially in summer. This level "plateau" is a great place to observe wildlife year round, and has very large climax red spruce trees, the most mature to be seen at this elevation in all the Catskills.

There are two other *fine viewpoints* near the western end of the long summit, with views north toward Kaaterskill High Peak and Roundtop, and an excellent shot of the Blackhead Range. At one time, there was a lean-to on the long summit of Plateau, but the DEC dismantled it because of the 3,500-foot rule and the amount of garbage that was accumulating from thoughtless campers.

Just before the trail starts its descent, it comes out on **Orchard Point**, a large open rock with *views of several mountain ranges* south and southwest, the Burroughs Range, Panther Mountain and the Balsam-Big Indian Range, all of which are visible on a clear day. See if you can pick out Graham and Doubletop in the background. The view west is blocked by the massif of Hunter Mountain. You can see that the ski area (north side) comes nowhere near the summit of this huge mountain.

The drop into **Stony Clove** from Plateau Mountain is a steep 1,700 feet in only one mile. During its descent, the trail crosses several open areas that have resulted from slides. Finally, you will reach Route 214, which bisects Stony Clove between Hunter and Plateau Mountains. You've now gone 14.15 miles from the start, and are at approximately 2,000 feet in elevation.

The clove is a wonder to those who pass through it because of its steep walls on each side. Try to imagine what it was like more than 150 years ago, cluttered with boulders, a darkened impasse engulfed by hemlocks, a fearful place inhabited by the Devil.

When the pioneers first moved into the area, they recognized Stony Clove to be the most inhospitable place in the Catskill frontier. Indeed, it was so narrow that it was actually blasted in the early 1800's to make it wide enough for horse-drawn wagons to take hides into the towns of Tannersville and Hunter. The clove has often appeared in postcards and photos of the area through the years. For many, it has captured the essence of the Catskills.

The state-run **Devil's Tombstone Campsite** is just to the left (south) of where the Devil's Path intersects Route 214. It gets its name from the large rectangular "tombstone" standing just off the road. Keep in mind that many car campers use this popular state campsite.

At this point, the Devil's Path starts another steep ascent up **Hunter Mountain**. The trail climbs through a section known as the **Devil's Portal**, winding up steep rocky areas that make you work for each step. At about the 3,000-foot level, however, the grade begins to moderate.

At about 2.1 miles from the road (16.3 miles from the start), you'll meet up with the *yellow-blazed* **Hunter Mountain Trail** which climbs the final 500-plus feet to the summit. We'll continue upwards on the Hunter Mountain Trail, passing through thick fir trees. About 1.3 miles up this trail, you'll pass the *blue-blazed* **Becker Hollow Trail** which leads to a *good spring* in about a quarter mile and continues 2.3 miles back down to Route 214 north of Stony Clove. It is the shortest and possibly the steepest route to the top of Hunter. Soon afterwards, you will pass a foundation in a small clearing where the old fire tower once stood to the right of the trail. There was

once a lean-to at this spot.

The Hunter Mountain Trail ends at this point, and we'll continue on the *blue-blazed* **Spruceton Trail**, which leads into a large cleared area at the 4,040-foot summit where the *fire tower* now stands. Notice how windy it gets as you climb the eight flights of stairs to the top. Hopefully, it will be a nice day when you go up into the tower.

There is often a forest fire observer on duty in the tower in the warmer months, and he'll be glad to point out any mountains or landmarks you're looking for. He might tell you of the bear claw markings on the telephone poles leading to the tower. The particular day we were up there, the observer told us a story of when he was caught in the tower during a fast developing thunderstorm, an experience he didn't care to go through again!

The view from the tower is superb, since there are no obstacles to obstruct your vision from this, the second highest mountain in the Catskills. Spruceton Valley can be observed to the west. The distant southern Catskills around Slide Mountain are to the south, and Plateau Mountain is immediately to the east. Just north of Plateau is Kaaterskill High Peak and its companion Roundtop. Further to the north (left),

"Once in the tower...the endless expanse and silence sends one's thoughts to reflect upon the ages."

Diamond Notch Falls on West Kill Creek.

you'll notice the North and South Lake areas. Just below and to the left, you'll see a small dark area and with binoculars (if the sun is high enough) you might be able to see the two glistening ribbons of water of the Kaaterskill Falls. It's a view you will never forget, especially if the water catches the sunlight just right. To complete the view, the Blackhead Range and Windham High Peak are also visible to the north. If you have binoculars, look to the distant west and find the fire tower on Mt. Utsayantha. This is as far west as a fire tower can be found on a major peak.

Back down on the summit, you'll notice a *blue-blazed jeep trail* which goes off northward. This is the continuation of the

Spruceton Trail, which is a wide jeep road all the way down to Spruceton Road, which it reaches in 3.35 miles. In another mile, it passes the *yellow-blazed* Colonel's Chair Trail, which goes for one mile to the top of the famous Hunter Mountain Ski Area on the spur known as the Colonel's Chair.

Soon after the junction with the Colonel's Chair Trail, you come to the John Robb Lean-to, which stands in a small open area at about 3,500 feet. There is a *spring* about 0.2 mile further down the trail (the spring is 300 feet to the left on a *spur trail*).

Let's retrace our steps and return to the Devil's Path. When you reach the fire tower foundation we previously mentioned, you'll see some light through the trees to the right (west). There is a rock you can go out to which provides a *close up view* of West Kill Mountain and Spruceton Valley. This would make a nice place to have lunch or just take a break.

We'll continue to the junction with the Devil's Path and head west. Soon you'll come to a lovely clearing where we found a pleasant surprise in mid-August —it was filled with yellow-green cone flowers and purple New York asters. We found it very photogenic and decided that the adjacent Devil's Acre Lean-to, with its limited view south, would be a nice place to spend a night.

If it's summer, look for interesting flowers in the nearby swampy clearings, like the strange looking turtleheads that bloom in August. The lean-to is at 3,500 feet elevation, so if you're looking for a place to pitch camp, keep it below this mark.

As you continue down the Devil's Path, you'll start to descend through summit hardwoods and you'll feel the trail wrapping around the mountain. The trail will level off for a while and then you'll come to an *open view* on the left looking west toward a mountain known as **Southwest Hunter** (elevation 3,740 feet), which has recently been added to the 3500 Club list. It makes an interesting bushwhack. This lookout is a particularly good spot to observe birds that nest in fir trees on the tops of the higher peaks.

The trail will soon bear left and downhill at a steady pace, passing through a beautiful area of white birch. Eventually, it reaches a junction with the Diamond Notch Trail. The Devil's Path has now gone 18.6 miles from its start.

At this point, the **Diamond Notch Trail** goes straight ahead

out to Spruceton Road on a dirt road wide enough for a vehicle. The lovely *West Kill Creek* runs alongside, and there are often people camping along this area despite signs banning camping.

The area is receiving special attention from the DEC due to public overuse and the accompanying environmental damage. (Recently, the DEC designated some sites north of the dirt road in which camping is permitted).

The abuse of this area is largely attributable to some people who feel they must camp within a short walking distance of their car. This breed of camper usually lives out of an ice cooler and shows little regard for the environment around him, as seen from the young hacked-up trees and the abundance of empty beer cans.

We do not mean to say that all car campers are like this; rather, those who respect the environment will find designated campsites where they can camp without breaking the rules established by the DEC.

The Diamond Notch Trail comes out onto Spruceton Road and ends at a parking lot which can be used to gain access to the Spruceton Trail mentioned earlier. This parking lot is an ideal place to start a day hike up Hunter Mountain or the sur-

West Kill Creek.

rounding mountains.

Spruceton Valley is a beautiful dead-end valley with mountain ranges on either side of it. Spruceton Road runs through the valley for several miles beginning at Route 42 in the tiny hamlet of West Kill. There are pleasant fields that run right to the foot of the mountains, making this an enjoyable ride any time of year.

Let's go back to the Devil's Path-Diamond Notch Trail junction. There is a sign-in box here. Turn left and cross the wooden bridge over the *West Kill*. There is a *beautiful waterfall* here just west of the bridge. The Diamond Notch Trail continues straight ahead, passing the **Diamond Notch Lean-to** in 0.5 mile. It crosses the height of land between Southwest Hunter and West Kill Mountains and then drops down into Diamond Notch Hollow, running along *Hollow Tree Brook* until it reaches Diamond Notch Road, which leads to Route 214.

Almost immediately, the Devil's Path turns right and leaves the Diamond Notch Trail. For a short distance it parallels the West Kill, which runs over large open rocks. The West Kill pools up in this area, making it a useful place to cool off. A narrow channel can be seen where the rock has fractured and worn away by the eroding power of water. Be careful filling up here with water, as the current is more powerful than it appears. This is the last dependable water supply for some time in the dry season.

The next mile of trail is a steady, steep ascent of 1,200 feet to the ridge. There is a *spring* after 0.75 mile (on left of trail), but it might be dry in late summer. Near the crest, you'll pass a *rock overhang*, large enough for two or three people. The worst is over, but you'll still have to walk another half-hour and ascend 400 feet to get to the summit of West Kill Mountain.

Just before you reach the top, you'll pass an excellent viewpoint called **Buck Ridge Lookout**. Facing south and east, it looks right over a glacial cirque much like the one seen from Panther Mountain. Across Diamond Notch, one can see Hunter Mountain (identified by the fire tower) and Southwest Hunter.

A short walk to the north side of the mountain provides *views* of the Blackhead Range, the Rusk-Evergreen Range and all that lies beyond. Nearby there's a large rock that makes for a good place to rest and take it all in. There is a classic spruce-fir conifer mix growing at this eleva-

> ***"The higher elevations of a few coniferous Catskill peaks represent the farthest south this bird breeds in North America."***

tion. If it's summer, it is a good place to listen or look for the blackpoll warbler. The higher elevations of a few coniferous Catskill peaks represent the farthest south this bird breeds in North America. Any of the several field guides will help in identifying it, and once its song is recognized, you'll never forget it. Little things like this have helped us enjoy these mountains so much more.

The true summit of **West Kill Mountain** (elevation 3,880 feet), 21.15 miles from the start of the Devil's Path, is a few hundred feet past the lookout. The trail then starts a slow descent. A

Late afternoon sun taken from a tree looking west from West Kill.

Wispy cirrus cloud over Blackhead Range from Lee's Ledge on West Kill Mountain.

few hundred yards below the summit there is a *small spring* off to the right of the trail. We wouldn't suggest relying on it in late summer or during a dry spell. After descending gradually for about two miles, the trail climbs abruptly up 200 feet to the 3,420-foot peak sometimes called **West West Kill** or **St. Anne's Peak**. We didn't find any views when we were there in the summer, but when the leaves are down, you'll easily be able to spot nearby North Dome, with its steep ledges.

The trail then drops off steeply, descending 800 feet before coming to a swampy area in the other (and lesser known) Mink Hollow. It turns right (north) and descends gradually for 1.5 miles to a parking area on Spruceton Road (County Road 6), where the Devil's Path ends, 25.85 miles from its start.

Western terminus of Devil's Path.

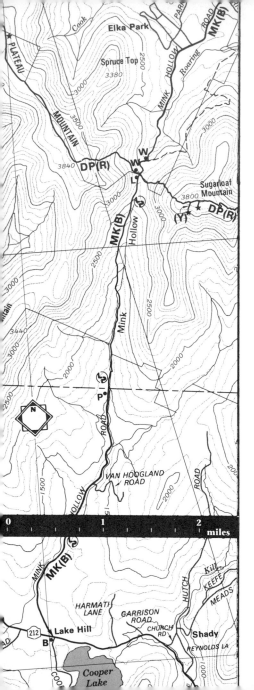

MINK HOLLOW TRAIL

> *"Indeed, many colonists took up witch doctoring as a regular practice to rid the area of the Devil's mischief."*

m*ink Hollow* runs in a north-south direction through the col between Plateau and Sugarloaf Mountains of the Devil's Path. Streams run through the hollow both north and south from the col, and it is likely that its name is derived from the mink that inhabit these waterways.

The **Mink Hollow Trail** follows the route of one of the most noteworthy Indian trails in the Catskills. Even before the Revolutionary War, this area was settled by pioneers. The hollow was the scene of many skirmishes between the Tories and

Mink Hollow slices between Sugarloaf and Plateau Mountains.

their Iroquois Indian allies, on the one hand, and the colonists, on the other. The hollow was also reputed to be inhabited by the Devil, and the early settlers developed many superstitions and myths regarding the Devil and the ghosts thought to dwell in the area.

Indeed, many colonists took up witch doctoring as a regular practice to rid the area of the Devil's mischief. Subsequently, the trail through Mink Hollow was used as a route to ship hides to tanneries in Hunter, Tannersville, Prattsville and the surrounding areas.

Today the Mink Hollow Trail extends 8.3 miles from Lake Hill on Route 212 to Elka Park Road. However, the southernmost 2.8 miles and the northernmost 1.5 miles follow paved roads, so that the trail proper is actually only about 4 miles long.

Even the road-walking portion of the trail is quite interesting, following a dead-end road as it winds through a quiet valley. The Mink Hollow Trail makes an interesting day hike, or it can be used to gain access to the Devil's Path (or as part of a circular hike).

We'll start from Route 212 in Lake Hill, which is a few miles west of the village of Woodstock and near scenic Cooper Lake, which supplies water to the city of Kingston. The trail begins at the intersection of Route 212 and Mink Hollow Road, just west of the lake. We'll proceed north on Mink Hollow Road, following the *blue markers* on telephone poles along the road.

In about three miles, you'll reach a parking area at the end of the driveable road (elevation 1,500 feet). This is the best place to begin the hike. The trail follows an old woods road along a brook, climbing gradually to the col between Sugarloaf and Plateau Mountains.

Although you'll gain a little over 1,000 feet in elevation by the time you reach the col, the climb is at no point overly steep. Just before the intersection with the Devil's Path at the col (about three miles from the parking area; elevation 2,600 feet), you'll pass the **Mink Hollow Lean-to** to the left of the trail.

The best source of *water* is a little further to the north (about 0.25 mile beyond the col and 300 feet to left of trail), just off the Mink Hollow Trail (although water is also available to the west a short distance up the Devil's Path). To the north of the col, the trail descends moderately, reaching the end of the road (passable to vehicles up to this point) in about a mile. No parking is available here; however, cars may be left along the side of the road about 0.3 mile further north. From here the trail follows Mink Hollow Road for about 1.5 miles to its end at the intersection with Elka Park Road (where the elevation is just under 2,000 feet).

The Mink Hollow Trail is enjoyable year-round, and makes for excellent cross-country skiing in the winter.

RUSK MOUNTAIN

*j*ust west of Hunter Mountain lies Spruceton Valley. **Rusk Mountain** (elevation 3,680 feet) is on the north side of this valley and northwest of Hunter Mountain. Rusk is a trailless peak, but it is easily reached by bushwhacking from the state-maintained parking lot just before the eastern end of County Route 6 (Spruceton Road) in Spruceton Valley. To reach this point, turn off Route 42 at the village of West Kill and continue east on Route 6 for about 6.5 miles. Pass a "dead end" sign, and continue as the road becomes all dirt. Turn left at the sign indicating the parking lot and the trailhead of the Spruceton Trail.

Follow the *blue-blazed* **Spruceton Trail** north for about half a mile to a sharp hairpin turn a short distance beyond a bridge over *Hunter Brook*, then turn left, cross the brook, and take a compass bearing to the top of Rusk. The climb to the fairly flat, fir-covered summit is not difficult, and in springtime you'll be rewarded with many beautiful wildflowers growing along the mountainside. We've found trout lilies, cut-leaved toothwort and the inconspicuous blue cohosh.

You'll also be able to see many birds during their spring migration, such as the rose-breasted grosbeak, the scarlet tanager and the black-throated green warbler.

When you reach the summit, you will be rewarded with *views in every direction*, especially before full foliage. Particularly noteworthy is the fine view to the southeast over Diamond Notch and Hunter Mountain. One word of caution: The summit canister of the 3500 Club is attached to the trunk of a tree with many low-hanging branches, and it can be a little difficult to find.

We spent an enjoyable May afternoon in a trance while lying on soft moss-covered rocks just northeast of the canister. The clouds drifted by, providing a clear view of the Huntersfield Mountain range to the north. It must have been a similar setting that put Rip Van Winkle off for 20 years!

To the west of Rusk Mountain is **Evergreen Mountain**, which forms a part of the same ridge. Despite the absence of trails in this area, Evergreen and other mountains to the west can easily be hiked, and they provide *excellent open views* of Spruceton Valley to the south.

OVERLOOK MOUNTAIN

"A climb up the fire tower opens a delightful new perspective..."

*a*t 3,140 feet, **Overlook Mountain** only ranks 71st in height of all the Catskill peaks, yet it offers a striking diversity of first-class views. This mountain has played an important role in the history of the region.

At the base of Overlook lies the village of Woodstock, which historically and romantically has been linked to the famous artist colony, Byrdcliffe, founded by Ralph Whitehead early in the 1900's. Thomas Cole, the founder of the Hudson River School of Painters in the 19th century, is said to have favored the ledges of Overlook Mountain as a place to take it all in. More recently, the area has inspired musicians such as Bob Dylan and The Band, who lived near the base of the mountain. These and other artists were

First glimpse of hotel from trail.

Ruins of the Overlook Mountain House as it stands today.

Steps into the past.

Scarred window frames...a picture portal into a bygone era.

a part of the 1960's counterculture of peace, love and brotherhood which was centered in Woodstock. Today, many of the shops still have an upbeat look, and you'll be able to find many unusual items.

In 1870, the *Overlook Mountain House* joined the growing numbers of great hotels in the Catskills and, at 2,978 feet, boasted being the highest of all. It could house up to 300 guests. The hotel flourished in the early 1900's but then fell into disrepair, as did all the great hotels in the area. It almost became a sanitorium for tuberculosis patients but was bought by new owners who began to construct a new building. Just as work was progressing, it was halted by "Black Friday," the stock market crash of 1929. Much looting and pillaging has occurred, leaving us with a large skeleton of a bygone era.

Today the ruins of the partially completed building are still there, but great care must be taken if you want to explore them as the floor is gone and metal and broken glass are scattered about. The state owns the land around it and is trying to buy the "house" itself so they can demolish it, as they feel it poses a threat.

There are two trails to the top of Overlook Mountain. The easiest is the **Overlook Spur Trail**, a *red-blazed wide jeep trail* that goes up from Meads. This is the trail that goes past the Overlook Mountain House ruins not far from the summit.

It is a good starter hike for an inexperienced hiker or someone just wanting to get acquainted with hiking the Catskills. It ascends a vertical distance of 1,400 feet in about 2.5 miles, passing a *spring* on the left after half a mile. Soon after passing the ruins of the Overlook House, the trail turns right as the *blue-blazed* **Overlook Trail** continues straight ahead. From this point, it's another 0.5 mile to the summit.

You'll soon see the fire tower start to rise through the trees on

Hudson Valley from tower steps.

Summit trail.

your left. Notice that the summit is covered mainly by hardwoods, especially northern red oak which is more prevalent in the lower elevations of the valleys.

A climb up the *fire tower* opens a delightful new perspective of the area. The Hudson Valley lies eastward as far as the eye can see. Mountains lie to the west. Most impressive is the close up of the long evergreen-topped Indian Head Mountain.

An experienced DEC ranger told us that the abrupt rise of the mountains from the valley reminded him of the Black Hills of South Dakota. If you look in a line towards the smaller Plattekill Mountain (to the east of Indian Head) and then down into the valley below, you can get a glimpse of a small body of water. This is Echo Lake, which makes a nice destination for lunch if you have the energy to continue.

If a ranger is present, be sure to ask him any and all questions. Rangers are experts on the terrain, and every ranger has many interesting stories and anecdotes

Picnic and/or peace at base of tower.

> ## *"Bats fly in the twilight..."*

he loves to share.

From the base of the tower, head a few hundred feet east to the open ledges that face the Hudson Valley. They make a good place to relax and maybe soak up a little sun. They also make a nice area to camp for the night. If it's late summer, pick some of the blueberries that grow along there.

A note of caution, though: this area is one of the few places

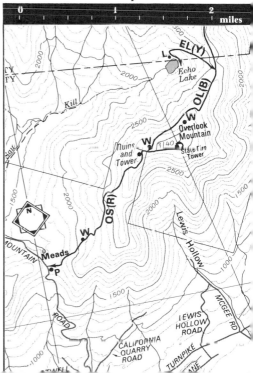

*"It almost became
a sanitorium
for tuberculosis
patients..."*

in the Catskills where rattlesnake dens are found. There's no need to be scared off...just look before placing your hands or feet in an area that you can't see, such as a sunny rock ledge. These creatures want even less to do with you than you want of them.

An interesting side trip would be to *bushwhack* down to a large rock ledge (at about elevation 2,500 ft.) called *Ministers Face*. This open rock ledge has close-up *views of the Hudson Valley*.

If you've decided to go to Echo Lake, head back down the way you came until you reach the trail junction we mentioned earlier. Go right (north) on the blue-blazed Overlook Trail. Note that it is 3.6 miles to the junction with the Devil's Path and another 1.5 miles to the nearest parking area. The Overlook Trail is an old carriage road which used to give access from the north to the Overlook Mountain House. It makes a nice trail in winter for cross-country skiing, as you can see through the trees to the west

---

"*The creatures of the water and surrounding area sing in chorus, echoing the night till dawn.*"

---

at various points and it isn't too steep.

In 1.4 miles, you'll reach a junction with the rocky, *yellow-blazed* **Echo Lake Trail**, which will take you down some 500 feet in 0.6 mile to a lovely, placid area. **Echo Lake** rests nestled in the mountains at an elevation of 2,100 feet. You'll notice that, due to overuse and abuse of the area, you can camp around the lake only at certain designated sites, including a lean-to on the north side of the lake. The DEC is hoping this program will preserve the natural beauty of the area. We urge people to follow the rules so that Echo Lake will always remain as peaceful as it was when we were there.

A late sunset over the lake in the warmer months is something you'll remember. When the lake is calm, it reflects the sky like a mirror. Bats fly in the twilight in their erratic butterfly-like search for insects. The creatures of the water and surrounding area sing in chorus, echoing the night till dawn.

Let's head back up to the blue-blazed Overlook Trail. You can either retrace the route you took back past Overlook Mountain to Meads (3.4 miles) or go north and junction with the Devil's Path, possibly camping at the **Devil's Kitchen Lean-to** near Platte Clove some 2.3 miles distant. If you do return to your car at Meads, by all means stop at Woodstock to browse in some of the unique shops or enjoy a good dinner at one of the local places. Woodstock has long been a cultural center of the Catskills and is always an enjoyable place to pass the time.

Kaaterskill High Peak and Roundtop from Overlook Mtn. fire tower.

KAATERSKILL HIGH PEAK & ROUNDTOP

"Known simply as 'High Peak,' this mountain was believed to be the highest in the Catskills until the 1870's, when Hunter Mountain was measured."

*k*aaterskill High Peak rises 3,655 feet over the Hudson Valley with expansive views in all directions for those who are willing to scrounge to the top through thick summit evergreen growth. Known simply as "High Peak," this mountain was believed to be the highest in the Catskills until the 1870's, when Hunter Mountain was measured.

It is one of the most prominent mountains to be seen from the New York State Thruway when approached from the south. This view, similar to that seen coming up the Hudson River by boat on a clear day, undoubtedly caused early travelers to believe High Peak to be the highest mountain in the entire area.

Later on, politics came into play as the owners of the great mountain hotels nearby boasted High Peak to be the tallest mountain in the area and refused to accept any news to the contrary. Having an establishment close to the highest peak was a big selling point to them and added to the glamour of their location. There was even an attempt in the late 1800's to have High Peak renamed after former President Lincoln, but the idea never caught on with the locals.

Although there is no official marked trail up Kaaterskill High Peak, a state-maintained *snowmobile trail*, also used by the **Long Path**, leads up to the 3,000-foot elevation, and an unofficial trail, with blue markings, goes from there to the top of the mountain.

The snowmobile trail begins on Platte Clove Road just east of the old New York City Police Camp, now known as Indian Head Lodge. (The State once planned to convert this structure into a prison, but abandoned the idea in the face of widespread opposition. The property has since reopened.) There is no designated parking area at this point, but there is room to park a few cars on the side of the road just south of the small stone bridge. The snowmobile trail ascends gradually on a wide old dirt road. Notice the signs on your left designating the Platte Clove Preserve of the Catskill Center for Conservation and Development.

After about a mile, as the trail turns to the left, you'll see a *trail marked by white-painted can covers with red dots* leading to the right. This little-used trail leads in about a mile to an *excellent viewpoint* overlooking Plattekill Clove, known as **Huckleberry Point**. True to its name, the viewpoint is covered with blueberry bushes whose fruit ripens in August. We spent a warm afternoon here as turkey vultures soared below us in the clove. From here you can see all of the mountains comprising the Devil's Path as far west as Hunter, the Minister's Face on Overlook Mountain, the clove 1,500 feet below, and the Hudson River Valley to the east.

Another interesting feature of this hike is the pitch pine forest the trail passes through just before reaching Huckleberry Point. This forest brings to mind what the "Pine Orchard" near

North Lake must have looked like before it was cleared for the Catskill Mountain House. This side hike to Huckleberry Point makes an enjoyable short day hike.

To continue to Kaaterskill High Peak, return to the snowmobile trail and follow it for about another two miles. At about elevation 3,000 feet, you'll reach a point where the trail divides into two branches, which lead in a circle around Kaaterskill High Peak and its neighbor, Roundtop Mountain. Take the left fork, and continue for about another mile and one half On the way, you may pass the wreck of a small airplane that crashed on the trail in June 1987. If you look carefully, you will find a *faint trail marked with blue blazes* crossing the snowmobile trail. (Be careful here, as this trail can be very difficult to find). Turn right on this trail and proceed upward. Soon you'll come to a short strenuous climb, but you won't have to use your hands to pull yourself up.

A little further on you'll come to a steep area where you'll need your hands to pull yourself up. At the top of this area, stop to get your wind and, if there are no leaves on the trees, look back to the southeast for a glimpse of the shimmering ribbon we know as

> **"...look back to the southeast for a glimpse of the shimmering ribbon we know as the Hudson River."**

the Hudson River.

The best is yet to come, though. Soon you'll begin to ascend a precipitous vertical rise of rock that will lift you up and out of the tall hardwood trees and place you in an open grassy area. Be careful climbing in this area, as sure footing and hand grips must be maintained to prevent

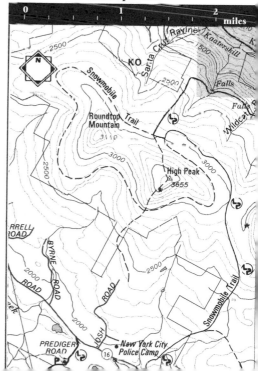

> **"A famous painting by Thomas Cole entitled 'Sunny Morning on the Hudson' was undoubtedly inspired by this view from Roundtop."**

losing your balance. The help of your hiking partners shouldn't be turned down if you require it.

Soon you'll reach a small grassy area just before coming to a large clearing. On one of our hikes, this small grassy knoll heated up from the sun to about 70 degrees despite the fact that it was still late March. We found it a great place to lay back and catch 40 winks!

From this open area one can gaze southeast down the Hudson Valley until the river disappears in the distance. This exposed area is known as *Hurricane Ridge* due to the winds that can whip around the mountain. However, on a calm clear day, there aren't many better places we can think of to relax, get sun and enjoy the mountain scenery.

You'll get an incredible eye-level close-up view of the mountains of the Devil's Path as they line up as far back as Hunter Mountain, some 7.5 miles distant. Especially prominent are Indian Head and Twin Mountains. Can you see the profile that gives Indian Head Mountain its name? From this viewpoint, the valley seems to slide right into Plattekill Clove.

The open area where you're standing is quite large and goes up for at least a hundred feet. This is about the 3,500-foot limit for camping. From here you have less than a 200-foot ascent to the top of this evergreen-clad mountain, which is marked by a small clearing. From the top, make your way eastward through a nearly impenetrable forest. The trees are not too tall but grow very closely together and make the going tough. You'll eventually come out to *wide open views* looking northeast and east across the Hudson Valley. The Berkshires of Massachusetts is the mountain range to the far east. Be sure to look for North and South Lakes and, with the aid of binoculars, try to find the open rock area known as North Point (page 123). If you work your way along these ledges, you'll find the wreck of a small airplane near an open view on the northeast side of the mountain. It has been gnawed by porcupines and partially covered with vegetation, and serves as a sad reminder that small airplanes occasionally strike the eastern wall of the Catskills in bad weather.

If you should choose to return to your car via a different route, continue on the blue trail as it descends the north side of the mountain to its end on the northern part of the snowmobile trail loop. When you reach this point, turn right on the snowmobile trail loop, proceed a short distance to the junction with the southern part of the loop, then turn left and follow the snowmobile trail back to your car.

Another possibility is to bushwhack over to nearby **Roundtop Mountain** to the west. A view of the mountain can be had through the trees from the west side of the High Peak summit. From this *vantage point*, you can also see Onteora Mountain and the East Jewett Range to the north down the valley. Roundtop is 3,440 feet in elevation and affords views of High Peak and the valley beyond. It is only about a mile from High Peak, and you shouldn't have too much difficulty in reaching it.

A note of interest is that during the Revolutionary War, a small fort stood on top of Roundtop and was manned by the British-backed Tories and their Indian allies. Supposedly, the good view of the Plattekill and Kaaterskill Cloves made this fort a strategic vantage point to watch colonist

activities and movement in the Hudson Valley. It also afforded quick escape to the British-run territory to the west. Prisoners taken from the Hudson Valley often spent their first night in captivity there.

Traces of earthworks and of foundations of the old fort can still be found. This alone would make for a very interesting excursion. A famous painting by Thomas Cole entitled "Sunny Morning on the Hudson" was undoubtedly inspired by this view from Roundtop.

THE LONG PATH

Platte Clove to Kaaterskill Clove

---

*t*his section of the *Long Path*, which is the NY-NJ Trail Conference's through trail from the George Washington Bridge to Windham, is the newest trail in the Catskills. Constructed in 1986 and completed in the spring of 1987, it connects Platte Clove and Kaaterskill Clove, two of the most dramatic places in the Catskills. From **Platte Clove** to just north of Kaaterskill High Peak, the Long Path uses the eastern leg of the High Peak-Roundtop snowmobile trail system. North of High Peak the trail descends to **Kaaterskill Clove** and follows an old quarry road down into Palenville. This section of trail features some of the most *picturesque waterfalls* in the Catskills. For most of the way, the trail is marked with the DEC *blue plastic markers*, but at the northern end (near Palenville) there are *turquoise paint blazes*.

We'll begin our hike from the Platte Clove end. There is a small parking lot with room for about six cars on Platte Clove Road just at the head of Devil's Kitchen (a short distance east of the entrance to the snowmobile trail). The best way to reach this point (except in the winter) is to take the Platte Clove Mountain Road from West Saugerties. The climb up on this road is without question the most spectacular in the Catskills (if not in the entire eastern United States).

As you approach Devil's Kitchen, the view will literally take your breath away as you peer either down 1,000 feet to the bottom of the Clove or up 2,000 feet to Indian Head Mountain. Be careful here as careless motorists have driven off the road to their deaths! If you hike here in the winter, you will have to approach Devil's Kitchen from the west, as this section of road is closed in the winter.

From Platte Clove Mountain Road, the Long Path proceeds north, following a snowmobile trail for about 3.5 miles. The first part of the snowmobile trail follows the old Steenburg Road, passing through lands owned by the Catskill Center for Conservation and Development before coming to the state land boundary. This section is wide and it goes through many sections of old forest. After about one mile, the snowmobile trail makes two right turns, leaves Steenburg Road and continues north on another old woods road.

Shortly after the second right, an old poorly marked trail to the right (east) leads to **Huckleberry Point** (see page 172). Continuing along the snowmobile trail, you will follow a short level stretch. Soon you will pass through an area with some very old hemlocks, cross *two small creeks on wooden bridges*, and then begin to ascend the southern slopes of Kaaterskill High Peak. At about the 3,000-foot mark, the trail levels off and passes through an area known as *Pine Plains* (after the long stretches of hemlocks found here). The trail continues almost level, descending very slightly for almost a mile and passing through a number of wet areas, in season.

At 3.5 miles from the start, you will reach the point where the snowmobile trail turns left (south) and ascends to intersect the *Kaaterskill-Round Top Snowmobile Loop Trail*. If you plan to climb High Peak, you will want to continue along the snowmobile

trail and follow the route up Kaaterskill High Peak (see page 171).

To continue on the Long Path, proceed straight ahead. After a short distance (about 0.2 mile), the trail will intersect an old trail that formerly ran from the private community of Twilight Park to High Peak.

This is another approach to High Peak and you can turn left (north) here if you wish to climb the mountain. To continue on the Long Path, turn right (south) and descend along the old trail for about 0.5 mile. The Long Path then turns right to avoid Twilight Park property and descends steeply to the north, switchback-

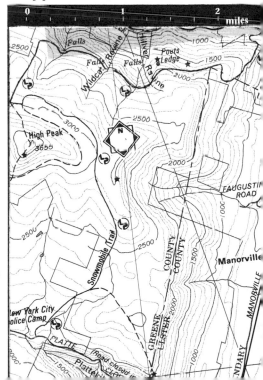

ing through a number of rock ledges. After descending to about 2,200 feet elevation, the trail intersects an old woods road, known as Red Gravel Hill Road, and turns right (east) along it. This road, which the Long Path follows for the remaining 4.4 miles into Palenville, was originally built in the 1800's to transport bluestone. This old road follows the escarpment of Kaaterskill Clove, and for most of its way is over 1,000 feet above the bottom of the clove.

It passes by the top of a series of beautiful waterfalls that descend into the clove. The area is very wild! One spring day we found fresh bear tracks, both large and small, along the trail, obvious evidence of a mother and her cub.

The first waterfall you will come to, after about 0.5 mile along the road, is **Buttermilk Falls**. It is possible to approach the top of the falls to get a *view of the clove below*, but this must be done with extreme caution as there is a drop of over 100 feet off the top of the falls. It's also possible to climb down to the bottom of the falls by descending along the ledges just to the east. Be very careful if you do so, as this area can be wet and slippery. However, your descent will be rewarded by a *view of a series of spectacular falls*, just as dramatic as the Kaaterskill Falls, on the other side of the clove. Do not attempt this descent when the area is very wet or in the winter! If you are backpacking, there is an excellent campsite just east of the falls.

After following the trail along the ledge for another 0.5 mile, you will come to the second waterfall, **Wildcat Falls**. In dry season it is possible to walk out to the top of these falls where you will be rewarded with a *grand view of Kaaterskill Clove* and the Hudson Valley to the east. Early one summer, we found mountain laurel in bloom on the east side of the stream leading to the falls.

Shortly after Wildcat Falls, the trail turns left (north) and descends a small ledge, passes a large boulder, and swings right (east) along the next ledge. In about 0.5 mile you will come to Hillyer Ravine where you cross two brooks, *the last sure water source* along the trail into Palenville. As you continue east through a hardwood forest, you will intermittently follow a brook which is dry most of the season. You'll then pass through a hemlock forest before turning left (east) away from the brook and descending through more hemlocks.

After descending a series

of small ledges, you will come to a partial view into Kaaterskill Clove through the trees to the left. Soon afterwards, you will pass a series of *old bluestone quarries* off the trail about 100 yards to your right. This area is fascinating, with slag heaps of bluestone piled everywhere. There is evidence of an old camp here with a level, cleared area just to the right of the road.

Bluestone from these quarries was transported on the old Red Gravel Hill Road you are following and was used to pave the streets of New York in the 1800's.

From the quarries, the trail follows the east side of the ridge and makes its final descent into Palenville. As you descend, you will intersect a number of other woods roads. At the 1,100-foot level, you will cross the state land boundary where the blue plastic DEC markers end and the Trail Conference's *turquoise paint blazes* begin.

The Trail Conference has received permission from the private landowners to mark this section, and you will be following these blazes the remaining 0.5 mile to Malden Avenue in Palenville. When the trail exits in Palenville, it passes between two houses. Be sure to respect the privacy of these landowners that have allowed the trail to be there! Turn left on Malden Avenue and continue 0.4 mile to Route 23A. While there is no designated parking area at the Palenville end of the trail, it may be possible to park in the vicinity of Route 23A and Malden Avenue.

TREMPER MOUNTAIN

*t*remper Mountain towers over the town of Phoenicia, and is just north of Route 28. Tremper makes for a fine day hike. You can climb this mountain from either the north or the south via two different trails that meet at the fire tower on the summit. If you can arrange to have a car left at each end, you will be able to choose from two different styles of approach; one is short and steep and the other is longer but not nearly as steep. (We recommend that you choose the steeper trail for the descent).

Much has been written about rattlesnakes being found on Tremper. (There are also two other areas in the Catskills where these snakes are known to exist: Overlook Mountain and Vernoy Falls on the Long Path south of Sampson Mountain). While hikers should always have their wits about them and be alert for anything unusual, rattlesnakes do not pose a great danger to the average hiker. Although their venom is poisonous, rattlesnakes normally want little to do with people.

As long as you are cautious in rocky areas (such as abandoned quarries, the rock ledges common in the Catskills, and near water sources in dry areas), you need not worry. Never put your hands or feet onto rocky ledges that you cannot see. In any case, we suspect that you have a better chance of being struck by a car or winning Lotto than being bitten by a rattlesnake.

We'll start at the northern approach via the *blue-blazed* **Willow Trail**. To get to the Willow Trail from Route 28, turn north on Route 212. Make a left onto Van Wagner Road and

Tremper Mountain.

another left onto Jessup Road, where blue markers can be seen. Follow Jessup Road for about 1.3 miles until you reach a small clearing on your left with a trail signpost. This is at elevation 1,300 feet. Park here and enter the woods on a wide trail that very shortly starts to climb. The woods here are an attractive mixture of maple, oak, white birch and hemlock. You'll also notice a healthy population of mountain laurel that show off their flowers in early summer.

After an ascent of a few hundred feet, the trail turns sharply to the right and starts a long, steady ascent. On the lower section there are several unmarked side trails and some cleared areas, reminders that this section of trail is not state-owned.

The trail levels off briefly and then continues a slow steady ascent. On your left you'll notice steep rocky areas that might tempt you to explore off trail if you're feeling adventurous. On your right is Hoyt Hollow, and if the leaves are down you'll see mountains as you climb. Even with leaves on the trees, there are a few spots that allow partial views. The large mountain a few miles away is Olderbark Mountain, while the small rocky peak immediately to the left of Olderbark is aptly named Little Rocky.

As you continue to get higher, you'll see **Carl Mountain** off to your right (north). This 2,880-foot mountain is trailless and is attached to the ridge you will reach shortly. It is state-owned and is open to bushwhackers.

About 1.5 miles from the parking area, as you near the 2,400-foot mark, the trail turns left and ascends rather steeply. At this point, you've finished the majority of the climbing. The trail then follows along the north side of an unnamed mountain and actually drops 100 feet or so before starting a slow climb along a ridge line.

There are no clear views here, but the trail follows close to the eastern side of the ridge and one can make out the distinct head of Overlook Mountain to the east and Cooper Lake below. *Cooper Lake*, which supplies water for the city of Kingston, is one of the largest natural lakes in the Catskills. It can be seen from few other mountains because of the hills that surround it.

At 3.65 miles from the parking lot, the trail opens up to a small clearing at the summit where the fire tower juts out above rather tall trees. The sum-

mit, dominated by red oak, is only 2,740 feet high. Near the base of the tower is the ruined foundation of the ranger's cabin that used to stand here.

There is a partial view to the east over the trees here, but the *fire tower* affords the real views. However, the state has closed this fire tower to the public and has removed the bottom row of stairs. Many of the fire towers in the Catskills have been closed to the public in recent years as the DEC now uses aircraft to patrol the forest. If you choose to climb the fire tower (and we don't recommend that you do) you do so at your own risk. No doubt the views are great, but some of these fire towers are getting shaky. The tower on Tremper Mountain has a wooden floor that actually has a hole in one corner!

Tremper Mountain is situated between the high peaks of the Slide Mountain area to the south and the Devil's Path to the north. Looking east, you'll see one round mountain that seems to be

Devil's Path northeast from Tremper Mtn. fire tower.

Mt. Tobias northeast from fire tower.

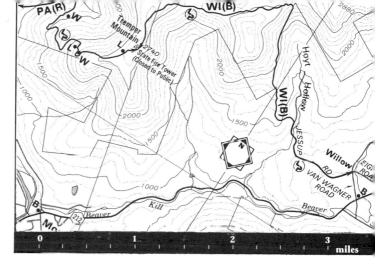

the only thing between you and the Hudson Valley: this is Mt. Tobias. Just down and to the left (north) you'll see the blue specter of Cooper Lake, and just beyond the lake you'll see the distinctive head of Overlook Mountain, which seems to be rearing out toward the Hudson Valley. Coming around to the west, the mountains of the Devil's Path make up the scene. Further to the north, Blackhead and Black Dome are visible through Stony Clove between Plateau and Hunter. Hal-

cott Mountain stands out to the northwest.

Sweeping further south you'll see the scars on Belleayre Mountain, the state-owned ski area. Balsam Mountain stands to the left (south) of Belleayre. Continuing your sweep toward the south, you'll see Panther Mountain with its long ridge line of false summits. Giant Ledge stands to the south of Panther, and you can see Slide Mountain towering above the Burroughs Range to the south. The steeply angled top of

Northwest through Stony Clove from fire tower.

Ashokan Reservoir southeast from tower.

The tower itself...taking it all in!

Wittenberg is the distinctive mountain to the left of Slide. The Ashokan Reservoir can be seen to the east (left) of these southern high peaks, with Ashokan High Peak behind it.

After a lunch at the pleasant shady area near the tower, you'll be ready to head down the *red-blazed* **Phoenicia Trail**, which drops more than 1,900 feet in 2.75 miles. This wide, rocky jeep trail cuts back and forth down the mountainside, maintaining an almost constant grade. You'll be glad if you choose to come down this way rather than up.

When the foliage is full there are no views, but if the trees are leafless, you'll be able to see the village of Phoenicia below tucked into the surrounding mountains.

Just below the summit, you'll pass a **lean-to**. At 0.8 mile, there is a *reliable spring* on your right (north), with a pipe extending from the ground having been placed there to tap the water beneath the surface. A few hundred yards further down the trail, there is a **second lean-to** off to the left. The elevation here is about 2,000 feet. An *abandoned quarry* is on the right at about 1.8 miles. At about 1.9 miles down there is *another spring*, although we had no luck getting water from it in early September.

The trail continues to wind down and passes a register box before ending, 2.75 miles from the summit, on Old Route 28 (now County Route 40) about one mile southeast of Phoenicia.

To begin your hike from this end of the Phoenicia Trail, take Route 28 and turn north onto Route 212. In another 0.6 mile, make a left on County Route 40 and continue for a little over two miles, where you'll see markers on the right for the Phoenicia Trail. An alternative route is to take County Route 40 southeast one mile from the center of Phoenicia to the trailhead. Limited parking is available on the opposite side of the road.

"Off The Beaten Path"

There are several trailless areas in the Northeastern Catskills that might be of interest to experienced hikers who know how to bushwhack. Some are state-owned, but others are on private tracts of land and permission to hike must be obtained.

Olderbark Mountain is one of the most challenging climbs found anywhere in the Catskills. Almost two miles long, it is a long ridge that runs southward off Plateau Mountain. About half the mountain is privately owned, and permission to hike must be obtained.

We approached it from the parking area at the end of Mink Hollow Road to the east of the mountain near the Greene-Ulster County border. The summit of Olderbark Mountain is reached after a climb of just under 2,000 feet in about 1.3 miles. The climb begins moderately through an interesting mix of mountain laurel, hemlock, white birch and beech. The beech trees are of special interest. Many of the larger ones have bear claw markings where black bears have climbed to get at beech nuts in the higher branches. Black bears are good climbers and will not hesitate to climb in pursuit of a good meal.

At approximately 2,300 feet in elevation, the climb steepens for the last 1,100 feet. The entire east face of the mountain is a vir-

Devil's Path from Olderbark summit.

"The entire east face of the mountain is a virtual wall and will test the best hikers any time of the year."

Passing through a grove of white birches in winter on the way to Olderbark.

Mount Tobias across Cooper Lake.

tual wall and will test the best hikers any time of the year. Because of the steep grade, there are several sets of *open ledges* and *views* along this side of the sum-

> **"Cooper Lake, which supplies water for the city of Kingston, is one of the largest natural lakes in the Catskills."**

mit. The northeast view includes a fine look at Sugarloaf, Twin, Indian Head and Plattekill Mountains of the Devil's Path. Overlook Mountain and Mount Guardian are just to the south of these

Exploring a cave on Olderbark.

mountains. Mink Hollow lies at your feet. Looking south you can see Cooper Lake, Mount Tobias, Ticetonyk Mountain and, in the distance, Ashokan High Point. Parts of the Ashokan Reservoir can also be seen.

The summit of Olderbark is very wild and overgrown with red spruce and balsam fir. The western slope is more gradual but is similarly heavily overgrown.

If you are hiking in the area, you should also try to do **Little Rocky Mountain**. It has a drop of only 120 feet towards Olderbark, yet at 3,060 feet its bare rock summit offers a *good view.* It can also be approached from Silver Hollow Road to the west, but this road may be closed in the winter.

You might also want to try climbing 3,000-foot **Silver Hollow Mountain**. Access to this small twin-peaked mountain is easy from Route 214, but you'll have to cross private property, for which you'll need permission. A *fine view* of Stony Clove Notch can be had from its summit.

Another mountain that is mostly state-owned is **Mount Tobias**. East of Tremper Mountain, its summit is only 2,550 feet in elevation. It is an easy climb and ideal for novices wishing to test their skills with a map and compass, but you'll have to obtain permission to cross some private property to reach the state land. South of this are **Ticetonyk** and **Tonshi Mountains**. They are privately owned and permission to hike is necessary. When the leaves are down, the Ashokan Reservoir can be spotted to the south from Ticetonyk.

Another area worth checking out is the state land south of the

---

"Black bears are good climbers and will not hesitate to climb in pursuit of a good meal."

Blackhead Range. This includes **Culgate Lake**, which is now state-owned. **West Stoppel Point** (elevation 3,100 feet) could make an interesting approach to the views of the Escarpment. To the west lie **Onteora Mountain** (elevation 3,220 feet) and the **East Jewett Range** (elevation 3,140 feet), with its evergreen-clad summit. They fill the large valley between the Devil's Path and the Blackhead Range and probably offer views of both.

Both of these mountains are privately owned, and permission to hike them must be sought.

Lastly, for those who don't find the smaller mountains challenging enough, you might try to ascend the wall of the Escarpment from Jones Road in the Hudson Valley up to Blackhead Mountain. The ascent is almost 3,000 feet in a little over two miles, through second-growth woods. Don't try this one unless you're in top shape and accompanied by an experienced hiker. You'll also have to get permission to cross the private property at the end of Jones Road. Good luck!

©1989 OCHMAN

SOUTH CENTRAL CATSKILLS

We Breathed

no sound...
...no wind sparkling
powder
on trees blue
sky
enveloped the land
& the air we breathed...
...we breathed...
...we breathed

*t*he South Central Catskills consist of the area south of Route 28 and east of a line formed by the Dry Brook Ridge, Balsam Lake Mountain and the Neversink-Hardenburgh Trail. (We consider anything west of this line to be in the Western Catskills). There are a number of large wilderness tracts in this area, most notably around Slide Mountain and in the Big Indian-Doubletop region.

The area contains many marked trails, including the trails around Slide Mountain, which are some of the most heavily used trails in the Catskills. But it also includes many lesser traveled and relatively un-spoiled regions. The area is shown on Maps #42 and

#43 of the Trail Conference Catskill Trail Maps. For those who enjoy bushwhacking, this area provides many interesting opportunities for exploration, both on state land and on private land (provided the owner's permission has been obtained).

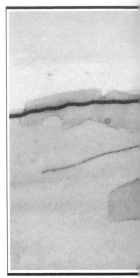

Slide from Table.

SLIDE MOUNTAIN

Today, **Slide Mountain** is the most popular mountain in the Catskills, both by foot and by mouth. It wasn't always that way, though. Slide was relatively unknown until the early 1880's when surveyor Arnold Guyot, who was surveying the Catskill peaks, boldly announced that Slide was the highest peak in the entire area. This did not sit well with the owners of the large hotels in the Northeast Catskills, and they quickly denied it. For years, they had claimed that Kaaterskill High Peak was the tallest, since it rises so high above the Hudson Valley (although it had been determined that Hunter Mountain was taller). The great hotel owners refused to accept the fact that higher mountains were to the south, since they feared a loss of business. In fact, they referred to the Southern Catskills as the Shandaken Mountains, which only further served to isolate them from the "real" Catskills, so well known to the north. Of course, the facts could not be hidden forever.

Writer-naturalist John Burroughs was also responsible for publicizing Slide and the surrounding mountains. Burroughs made many treks up Slide and the nearby peaks and, through his writings (including his well-known essay IN THE HEART OF THE SOUTHERN CATSKILLS), made the public aware of this beautiful area. A plaque commemorating Burroughs and his love for the Catskills has been placed on a large rock just below the summit of Slide.

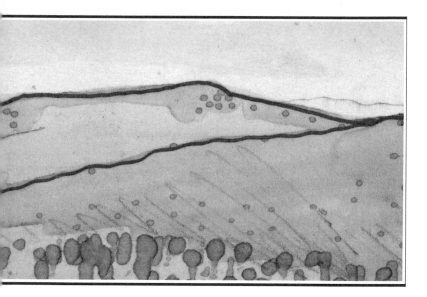

If you make your way up Slide in the "off-season" (late fall to early spring) on a clear day, you can feel the same awe that Burroughs wrote about. It may not be our favorite view of the Catskills but it is certainly one of the most impressive. All of the Catskill Mountains over 3,500 feet in elevation can be seen from different viewpoints on or near Slide's summit. The most difficult to site is Thomas Cole which can be observed with the aid of binoculars just beyond Hunter Mountain to the northeast.

If you're lucky, you'll also be able to see as far south as New Jersey, Pennsylvania and the Hudson Highlands. The Shawangunks, immediately to the south, are more easily seen. You will look down on rolling mountains (which afford great climbs and views themselves) as if they were clumps of earth on a tilled field laid out beneath your feet. Interestingly enough, Slide is not readily seen from any major roadways. This is due to the fact that so many high

> *"All of the Catskill Mountains over 3,500 feet in elevation can be seen from different viewpoints on or near Slide's summit."*

peaks surround Slide and keep it hidden from the view of those in the valleys. Just climb almost any of the other high Catskill peaks and you'll probably be able to spot Slide without much trouble.

To climb Slide in the winter can truly be a memorable experience. We were once on the summit in mid-January after several snowstorms had dumped two feet of powder. The still, cold air zapped our senses as the trees were heaped heavy with sparkles of powder forming white statues against a deep blue sky...a mind-clearing experience!

Any publication describing Slide invariably has to mention the crowds that flock to this mountain. In our society, where many want to be number one, it's natural for those deciding to hike in the Catskills to want to climb the highest peak. All kinds of people (including small children) can be found on Slide almost every day during the most popular hiking months.

Our first trip to the summit was on a beautiful mid-October weekend when we shared the summit with 30 or 40 others. A ranger was stationed there to advise the uninitiated that camping is prohibited at the summit and to ensure that people camped below the 3,500-foot limit. Two lean-tos and a lookout tower once stood on the top, but now only open areas remain. Indeed, the lean-tos were removed, due to abuse by thoughtless campers, even before the 3,500-foot limit for camping was established.

There are three marked trails to the summit. (Of course, experienced hikers could find other routes suitable for bushwhacking). The most popular route is the western section of the Wittenberg-Cornell-Slide Trail that comes up from a parking area just south of Winnisook Lake on the Oliverea-Big Indian Road (County Route 47, also known as Slide Mountain Road). This trail, a former jeep road, is not at all challenging, and indeed is rather uninteresting, but it is the reason why so many people can make it to the

Moon and treescape after snowstorm on summit of Slide.

Trekking, snow and Slide on the Curtis-Ormsbee Trail.

summit. It was built in the late 1800's to enable well-dressed gentlemen and their wide-dressed lady counterparts to go up for some clean country air. We recommend this route for a quick escape in bad weather or growing darkness, and as a return route for a loop day hike from Slide Mountain Road. The Curtis-Ormsbee Trail offers far better views and more varied terrain.

For the most challenging experience, however, one should try the approach via Wittenberg and Cornell from Woodland Valley. We'll describe all three routes in turn, starting with the most popular access route.

"...the trees were heaped heavy with sparkles of powder forming white statues against a deep blue sky..."

WITTENBERG-CORNELL-SLIDE/ CURTIS-ORMSBEE TRAIL

"Slide Mountain is the unmistakable giant..."

*t*o reach the trailhead for the western approaches to Slide, take Route 28 to Big Indian, then turn south onto County Route 47. After about 6.5 miles, you will go around a hairpin turn where the Giant Ledge parking area is located. Continue for another 1.95 miles, passing Winnisook Lake and the Winnisook Club, to the Slide Mountain parking area (designated by a large trail marker sign).

At the parking lot, you will pick up the *yellow-blazed* **Phoenicia-East Branch Trail**, which climbs moderately for 0.4 mile until it turns right onto an old jeep road. In another 0.2 mile, you'll reach a junction with the *red-blazed* **Wittenberg-Cornell-Slide Trail**, which goes off to the left. This trail for the true novice, the easiest route up Slide, climbs moderately on a wide footpath (formerly a jeep trail) 2.0 miles to the summit. There are no views, though (except just below the summit), and little else to recommend on this trail. If you want a more interesting route, we'd suggest taking the Curtis-Ormsbee Trail instead.

To reach this scenic and moderately challenging trail, continue on the yellow-blazed Phoenicia-East Branch trail another 0.8 mile past the junction with the Wittenberg-Cornell-Slide Trail. Here the *blue-blazed* **Curtis-Ormsbee Trail** goes off to the left. This trail, which leads 2.25 miles to the summit of Slide, was laid out by William Curtis and Allen Ormsbee, both of whom were killed by a sudden snow storm on Mt. Washington, New Hampshire in June 1900. A stone monument near the trail junction commemorates this tragic event. Sad stories like this should serve

Relaxing free on Slide's summit——mountain eternal.

as a reminder for others always to be prepared for the unexpected.

About 0.1 mile from the start of the trail, you'll pass through a short, steep area of large rocks. In another half-mile or so, you'll come to a short, steep climb, at the top of which there is an *excellent view westward* (to the left). Many mountains can be seen from here; the tall, prominent one in the distance is Doubletop. You are now at about 3,400 feet in elevation, a fine place to stop and have a bite to eat.

Soon beyond this lookout, you'll come upon an *open view southward* (right) over the valley of the East Branch of the Neversink. Rocky, Lone and the distinctive flat-topped Table Mountain can be seen from here. As the trail continues upward, it goes through a stand of balsam fir and past *another excellent view southward* and, after 1.6 miles, joins the *red-blazed* **Wittenberg-Cornell-Slide Trail**. You've now gone about three miles from the start, and it's another 0.65 mile to the top.

The red-blazed trail climbs slowly for several hundred yards, with a beautiful viewpoint off the trail to the left. This *striking view* is one of the finest anywhere. Particularly impressive is the view down onto Panther Mountain and Giant Ledge.

The latter casts a distinctive shadow in late afternoon due to the steep ledges on its eastern slopes. Soon the trail begins its final climb to the summit, through thick groves of balsam fir. The summit itself provides views to the east.

The red-blazed trail continues very steeply down the east side of Slide and over Cornell and Wittenberg Mountains. We'll describe this part of the trail in the following trail section. You might want to climb down for 0.25 mile (descending about 300 feet in elevation) to a *reliable spring* where you can fill up with water. (There are also excellent views from the trail at the spring).

If you're day-hiking Slide, we suggest that you take the easy western section of the red-blazed trail down to the yellow-blazed Phoenicia-East Branch Trail, then turn right on the yellow trail and follow it back to the parking lot. This route is a little shorter than the Curtis-Ormsbee Trail, about 2.6 miles to the road.

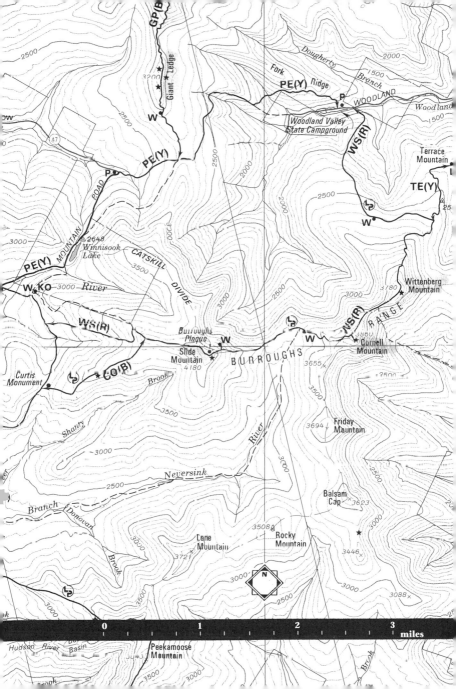

WITTENBERG-CORNELL-SLIDE TRAIL

"...in the summer, watch for wood sorrels and bunchberry growing along the trail..."

*Y*ou will find this route to Slide, via the eastern section of the **Wittenberg-Cornell-Slide Trail** from Woodland Valley, the most challenging. This route passes over Wittenberg and Cornell Mountains (formidable summits in themselves) on the way to Slide, and ascends a total of about 3,500 feet over a distance of 7 miles. It's a much more difficult approach to Slide than the western section of the same trail (which ascends 1,800 feet in 2.6 miles), but it's also far more interesting and rewarding.

To get to the trailhead, turn off Route 28 at the Woodland Val-

The Wittenberg.

ley turnoff, just west of Phoenicia, cross the Esopus Creek on a narrow, old bridge, and turn right onto Woodland Valley Road. (This bridge was damaged during the torrential flooding which followed a 7-inch rainfall in April 1987, but it has since been reopened to traffic). Continue on Woodland Valley Road for about five miles until you come to the Woodland Valley State Campground. A parking lot for hikers is provided on the right side of the road.

During the season (April 1 to the last day of the deer season), there is a charge of $2.50 for parking here, which is payable at the ranger station on the left a little further down the road. The red-blazed Wittenberg-Cornell-Slide Trail begins on the left (south) side of the road just east of the parking area.

After crossing a footbridge over the stream, you'll immediately begin to ascend steeply through an old second-growth forest. The climb soon becomes more gradual, and the trail eventually levels off (and even descends briefly). After 2.5 miles, you'll reach a junction with the *yellow-blazed* **Terrace Mountain Trail**, which leads downhill for 0.9 mile to the **Terrace Mountain Lean-to**. (It should be noted that no water is available at this lean-to). You are now at an elevation of about 2,700 feet, having already climbed over 1,300 feet from Woodland Valley.

Bear right and continue on the red-blazed trail. The trail will remain flat for a short distance, but soon begins to ascend steeply. You'll come to several rock ledges where you'll need to use your hands to help pull yourself up. This part of the hike can be slow and tiring, and the ascent may seem to be longer than it really is. This is especially the case if you do this hike with full backpacks in the summer—as we once did. Our experiences on that hike may have something to do with the respect we developed for The Wittenberg. If you are hiking in the summer, watch for wood sorrels and bunchberry growing along the trail by the steep areas.

As you near the summit, the characteristic summit evergreens begin to appear. Here the trail cuts a narrow path through a dense, virtually impenetrable evergreen growth. Soon, without any forewarning, you'll come out on a large open rock ledge, with a *breathtaking view to the east* of the reservoir. (Hopefully, you've scheduled your hike for a clear day and brought a camera with a wide-angle lens to record the view!). This is the summit of

Overlooking Samuel's Point and the Ashokan Reservoir from The Wittenberg.

South towards Friday and Balsam Cap, with Peekamoose in the distance.

Wittenberg Mountain, which is 3,780 feet high and ranked 14th in elevation. You've gone 3.8 miles and climbed 2,400 feet to get to this point.

The most noticeable feature you'll see is the 12-mile Ashokan Reservoir. Samuels Point is below and a little to the left. Looking to the right (south), the Southeast Catskills meld into a jumble. Picking out the individual mountains by name is a challenge here. Just past neighboring Cornell Mountain is Friday Mountain (note the scar from the large slide on the eastern slope) and then Balsam Cap, with Hanover Mountain behind it. The mountain rising prominently just south of the reservoir is Ashokan High Point. (There are no views to the west, as the firs have grown too thick).

If you go back down the trail for a few hundred feet, you'll find an *unmarked* (but used) *trail* going left (west). Although almost overgrown, this trail leads a short distance to a *small spring* under a rock. You'll have to lean down and dip a cup to get water. We've found this to be a good water source in spring and early summer, but don't rely on it in dry weather.

You'll also want to check out the *cave* below the ledge view on the summit. It is a rock shelter with room for two or three people, and you can climb down to it from just north of the summit ledge. Of course, camping is prohibited here (except in the winter) because it is well over 3,500 feet in elevation. But it does make a nice place to relax and eat your lunch while getting a panoramic view of the valley below you. If you're here between May and October, you'll probably have to share this magnificent view with many others.

After savoring the view and quenching your thirst, you'll continue along the trail towards Cornell Mountain. The trail descends slightly to a level area,

Cornell Mountain from Maltby Hollow.

Weathered spruce trees near Cornell summit.

known on some old maps as "Bruins' Causeway." To the left, an *old unmarked trail*, which should not be attempted except by experienced bushwhackers in excellent shape, descends steeply into Maltby Hollow. The Wittenberg-Cornell-Slide Trail then begins to ascend again. Most of the ascent is not too difficult, but just below the summit of Cornell you'll encounter a very steep rock ledge. If you're wearing anything more than a day pack, you'll probably have to take it off here and hand it up to your partner, while you struggle to find handholds and footholds which enable you to negotiate the sharp climb.

Soon afterwards, you'll reach the overgrown summit of **Cornell Mountain** (elevation 3,860 feet; 4.7 miles from Woodland Valley). You'll know you're there when you see a *short yellow-blazed trail* which goes off to the left (southeast) and leads to a *view east* over the Ashokan Reser-voir towards the Hudson Valley. The view from Cornell is not as all-encompassing as that from Wittenberg.

Returning to the red-blazed trail, you'll begin to descend the western side of Cornell. Soon you'll get a view of Slide Mountain (directly ahead) and the slide (appearing as a steep dropoff) which gives the mountain its name. Now overgrown, it was used as a means of access to the mountain by early enthusiasts, such as John Burroughs. The trail then goes by a *spring* and levels off, passing through a virgin spruce grove protected by the sheltered col. At the low point between Cornell and Slide, an *unmaintained trail* (marked sporadically by red paint blazes) drops off to the left into the valley of the East Branch of the Neversink. It's easy to get lost here, and this wilderness trail is recommended only for experienced hikers.

Now you'll begin the climb

up **Slide Mountain**. The first part of the climb is gradual, but you'll soon begin to climb much more steeply, ascending 900 feet in less than a mile. You'll need both your hands and feet to clamber over several rock ledges, and you'll find yourself taking frequent rests from the strenuous climb. After about 0.65 mile of climbing, you'll reach a *spring* to the right of the trail at about 3,900 feet in elevation. You'll want to pause here to fill your canteens with the clear, cold water and to enjoy the views. Looking back on the trail, you can clearly see Cornell and Wittenberg Mountains, and the mountains of the Devil's Path are visible to the north.

At this point, the trail to Slide from Cornell was rerouted several years ago due to a severe erosion problem. Several flights of wooden steps have been constructed over a very steep area to help prevent further erosion. If you persevere a little longer, you will soon arrive at the rock outcrop on which the plaque in memory of John Burroughs has been placed. Climb up this rock and you're on the summit, with its *magnificent views* detailed in the previous section.

As we have mentioned, it's seven miles from Woodland Valley to Slide. If you're going to make a day hike out of it, we'd suggest that you leave a second car at the Slide Mountain parking area on County Route 47 so that you can hike down the western slope and reach the car in another 2.6 miles. If you only have one car and you're in excellent shape, you might want to hike back to Woodland Valley via the Phoenicia-East Branch Trail.

The return trip on this route is also 7 miles, so you'll have completed a 14-mile round trip by the time you reach your car. This long hike should be attempted in one day only in the summer months, when the days are long. But if you have two days to spare, this circuit hike makes an excellent backpacking trip. You can find good places to camp in the col between Cornell and Slide, and water is usually available nearby.

Finally, if you want to take a day hike from Woodland Valley but don't feel up to doing the full 14-mile loop, the climbs of Wittenberg and Cornell are themselves very rewarding. It's only 4.7 miles to the summit of Cornell, and the 9.4 mile round trip can be done, if you're in reasonably good shape, even on short winter days (as long as you get an early start).

Gazing towards Table Mountain across the valley of the East Branch of the Neversink.

"Off The Beaten Path"
SOUTH OF SLIDE MOUNTAIN

"Closer examination revealed it to be an old beaver meadow."

*t*here are several trailless high peaks (Lone, Rocky, Balsam Cap and Friday) immediately south of the Wittenberg-Cornell-Slide Range (also known as the **Burroughs Range**), and separated from it by the valley of the East Branch of the Neversink. Despite its proximity to Slide, this valley is one of the most remote and untouched places in the Catskills. The valley and these trailless peaks to the south are part of a designated wilderness area, and contain much virgin forest and few signs of human intrusion.

For the experienced hiker, proficient in the use of map and

Beaver! On the East Branch of the Neversink.

compass, this area offers some of the best opportunities to see the Catskills as close to their natural state as possible. One word of caution: Since you will encounter thick conifer growth along the ridge tops, hiking in this area in shorts is not suggested.

All four mountains can be

The beaver did it!

reached by *bushwhacking* from an old, little-used trail, marked for part of the way with red paint blazes, which follows the East Branch of the Neversink from the Denning Lean-to to the col between Slide and Cornell.

One cold, blustery day in mid-April, as we hiked through this valley, we suddenly came to a clearing where all the trees had long-ago been cut down, and the ground was covered with pools of water. Closer examination revealed it to be an old beaver meadow. A few hundred feet further we came to the area where the beavers had taken up residence. There were dams, pools and freshly-cut trees all over. A lodge was built around an old dead tree, giving it the appearance of a chimney.

We could easily have spent the entire day just studying this area! Later that day we found more beaver activity further upstream. Not bad for an animal nearly extinct in New York State at the turn of the century!

Lone Mountain, the first of the four trailless peaks, can be easily approached from the Neversink Valley by following the gentle ridge leading up to the summit from the west. There are *excellent views* in all directions near the register box on the 3,721-foot summit. Among the best views are those of Peekamoose and Table Mountains to the south and of Mombaccus Mountain to the southeast. Lone can also be approached from Table Mountain,

immediately to its south, to which it is connected by a ridge. Finally, you might want to try the eastern approach, which is the most difficult, with multiple levels of steep cascading ledges.

Rocky Mountain, the lowest of all the 3,500-foot peaks (it's only 3,508 feet in elevation), can also be approached by bushwhacking from the valley of the East Branch of the Neversink. Rocky is considered one of the more difficult peaks, as you'll have to find your way through a dense spruce growth on your way to the summit. You can approach Rocky from Lone, immediately to the west, but this area is also very difficult to traverse due to the thick growth of evergreens. From the fairly flat summit of Rocky you can get a partial view of Slide Mountain to the north.

The distance between Rocky and Balsam Cap (elevation 3,623 feet) is only about a mile, but distances here can be deceptive. There are some ledges on the

Cornell and Friday from Lone Mountain, with Devil's Path in the distance.

Peekamoose and Table from Lone Mountain.

eastern slope of Rocky, and you'll have to fight your way through some dense stands of evergreens before you reach the summit of **Balsam Cap**. This area is quite interesting as it receives little use.

Although they can also be reached from the East Branch of the Neversink, Balsam Cap and Friday, its neighbor to the north, are often approached from Moon Haw Road to the east. This approach makes for one of the toughest climbs in the Catskills, since you start at an elevation of only about 1,200 feet, leaving a climb of well over 2,000 feet to the summits. In addition, you can expect to encounter several steep ledges near the tops of these mountains. The eastern approach to Balsam Cap's summit leads you to seemingly endless vertical ledges where hand to-foot climbing can be fun but difficult. You really "earn your wings" on these hikes!

An interesting feature of Friday is *a slide on its eastern face*

that occurred in 1968 after heavy rains. The slide is a steep, 1,700 to 1,800-foot climb in less than a mile. We'd suggest this route only for experienced hikers in top physical condition, but for the special breed of hiker who loves exploring slides, this is one of the best in the Catskills.

The slide can be reached from Moon Haw Road by following a stream that runs between Friday and Cornell. We followed this stream on a cold, foggy day in February to approximately 1,600 feet in elevation, where we reached a huge swath in the woods rising southwest of the stream. From this vantage point, the slide, reaching steeply upwards into the mist, was awesome indeed. But the best part of our climb up this slide was when we climbed out of the fog...and into the sun (at about elevation 3,500 feet).

The temperature was in the 60's as we observed the entire Hudson Valley carpeted in white. In fact, the only things we could

The slide on Friday Mountain.

Ashokan High Point from Balsam Cap Mountain.

Ashokan Reservoir from Balsam Cap.

see sticking out of the clouds were the tops of nearby Cornell, Wittenberg and Slide. Of course, we wouldn't suggest trying this hike in inclement weather. The only reason we did it on that particular day was that the forecast called for sunny skies. They just didn't tell us how high we'd have to go to find them!

> **"...we climbed out of the fog... and into the sun."**

The summit of **Friday** (elevation 3,694 feet) is covered with a thick stand of spruce and fir trees. The summit box, which is located amidst this jumble, can be hard to find. There is a *fine viewpoint* on the northern part of the summit overlooking Cornell and Wittenberg Mountains.

Friday and Balsam Cap are often climbed together. The drop between them is only about 300 feet, but the undergrowth is very thick and the going is slow. We once came across the scattered wreckage of a small airplane in this area. Balsam Cap's top is more open than Friday's; thus, the 3500 Club's summit box is more easily found. With some luck and perseverance, there are *views to be had in all directions* from near the summit of Balsam Cap. The most striking are those of the Ashokan Reservoir and Ashokan High Point to the southeast. The latter view, from the southeastern end of the summit, is due to a recent blowdown of a large spruce tree.

Whichever approach you decide to take to reach these formidable and rugged mountains, you will be rewarded with beautiful views and an opportunity to explore a little-used area which has almost completely escaped the imprint of man.

PEEKAMOOSE-TABLE TRAIL

"...these mountains do not see too much use by hikers."

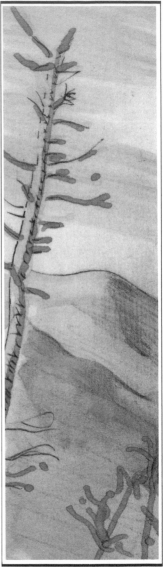

Van Wyck Mtn. from trail on Table Mtn.

*l*ocated across the valley of the East Branch of the Neversink River, south of Slide Mountain lie **Peekamoose** and **Table Mountains**. As a forest ranger once informed us, these mountains do not see too much use by hikers. Most prefer to climb Slide Mountain for its prestige or Giant Ledge because of easy access. Another reason these two mountains are not heavily traveled is that it is a hefty trek to get up on top of either of them. Both mountains, the 10th and 11th highest in the Catskills, afford excellent views. The Long Path follows the entire length of this trail, which is maintained by the Catskill 3500 Club, a member club of the NY-NJ Trail Conference. They have regular trail clean-ups for those interested in combining work with pleasure.

We'll pick up the *blue trail markers* of the **Peekamoose-Table Trail** on the north side of County Route 42 (Peekamoose-Gulf Road). A small parking area will hold a few cars here. The trail will start traveling northeast. You'll pass a register box and follow a wide old road. Within a mile the trail will turn right at a stand of red pine. It will continue to climb through a second-growth hardwood area. After approximately two miles, it will pass over several large rocks with small overhangs and reach a ridge.

The trail now follows the ridge line up towards the summit of Peekamoose Mountain. If the leaves are down, you'll get a glimpse of mountains on either side of the trail, to the east and west. It won't be long before you see stunted trees and a fine *open rock ledge* with *southerly views*. This ledge is at elevation 3,500 feet, and it's 2.75 miles from the start. Notice the Shawangunk Mountains ridge to the south. Samson Mountain (2,812 feet) is the ridge closest to you. If you look ahead on the trail to the north, the top of Peekamoose rises up before you. A short herd path from the trail leads to another open ledge. Just beyond these ledges, you'll pass an old

trail on the right. This trail, marked with faint red paint blazes, drops down to Peekamoose Road, reaching it a few hundred yards east of **Buttermilk Falls**.

Let's continue on the Peekamoose-Table Trail. The trail will remain relatively level for about 0.5 mile, after which you'll reach a short, rather steep uphill stretch which leads to the top of **Peekamoose Mountain** (3,843 feet), 3.4 miles from the start. The trees on top are a mixture of stunted firs with a few yellow birch. It is a small summit with *limited views that can be found* if you scrounge around for them. The day we first climbed Peekamoose it was extremely clear, with the wind chill well below zero as strong gusty winds blasted us from all directions! This kind of weather usually makes for the best visibility.

Just as you start to descend, you'll see the level ridge of Table Mountain nearby. The drop in the saddle between Peekamoose and Table is short, and the trail passes through a beautiful grove of balsam fir. We found this area a fine wind break and a good place to make some much needed hot chocolate.

The climb to the level summit of **Table** is an ascent of only 200 feet. When you finally level

Overlooking Lone, with Wittenberg, Cornell, Friday and Balsam Cap.

off near the top, you will come upon an *unmarked trail* which leads a few hundred feet to the right (north) and comes out on an *excellent lookout* over all the high peaks of the Slide Mountain area. Lone Mountain is closest and directly in front of you. To its right is Rocky Mountain, which is 200 feet shorter than Lone. Standing high beyond Rocky is Balsam Cap, and to its left is Friday Mountain. To the left of Friday is Cornell Mountain, and part of Wittenberg can be seen to the right of Cornell. These last two may appear as one at first glance but binoculars will help separate them. Slide Mountain is the unmistakable giant further to your left (north).

If you return to the trail and continue, you'll eventually come to the canister on Table's summit (elevation 3,847 feet). This is the only summit box the 3500 Club has erected on a mountain with a marked trail to the summit. In winter time, the hiker with snowshoes may be able to get a

good view westward from the west end of the mountain. On another trip in September, we were unable to find this view westward from which we had previously taken some dramatic photos. Obviously, the vegetation was just too overgrown to allow a clear view.

If you have only driven one car to this hike, you may choose to turn back at this point and retrace your steps the full 4.25 miles back to Peekamoose Road. If you have two cars, you may wish to continue 2.5 miles down toward the Denning Lean-to at the base of the north side of Table, at the junction of Deer Shanty Brook and the East Branch of the Neversink. (The lean-to is 1.45 miles from the parking area at the end of Denning Road, where you can leave a second car).

Shortly past the summit box, the trail will start to drop quickly, with *one more fine view* (to the northeast) through a large opening in the trees on your right. The trail descends through a hardwood forest and follows the north side of a spur coming off Table Mountain. At one point, the trail even climbs back up slightly before continuing its descent. There is an *unreliable spring* 0.3 mile from the summit off to the right (north) of

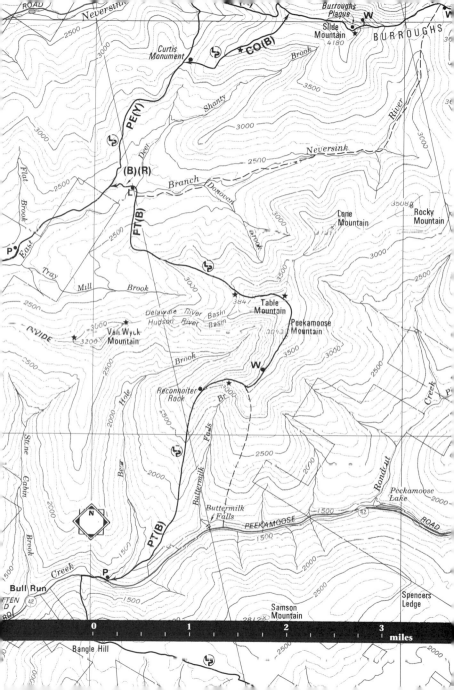

the trail. At 5.1 miles from the start, there are *open ledges* off to the left of the trail with a fine view.

The closest mountain across the valley is Van Wyck Mountain (elevation 3,206 feet). Looking southwest, you can also make out Woodhull Mountain (3,040 feet) and the fire tower on top of Red Hill (2,990 feet). Looking down to your right, you'll see a clearing a few miles off. This is the Denning clearing with the parking area for the Phoenicia-East Branch Trail. If you have a second car, this is where you'll be heading. The trail will continue to drop, sometimes fairly steeply, and then ascend slightly again.

At 6.25 miles, you'll reach the *East Branch of the Neversink River* and the **Denning Lean-to** on the other side of a log crossing. The lean-to is fairly well kept with a fireplace and, of course, plenty of water is available. Be sure to thoroughly boil any water taken from the Neversink! There are often campers in tents nearby. You'll now follow the trail across the tributary *Deer Shanty Brook* and uphill to the junction with the *yellow* **Phoenicia-East Branch Trail** at 7.0 miles. The Denning parking area is 1.1 miles to the left on this trail, an old rocky road. 🅜

THE LONG PATH

South of Peekamoose Road

"In June, the showy pink and white flowers of the mountain laurel light up the otherwise dull forest understory."

*m*aking its way northward from the Roundout Valley, the **Long Path** makes its southern entry into the Catskills via Cherrytown Road, a pleasant, winding country road which it follows north from Kerhonkson. It then turns left onto Upper Cherrytown Road, which it follows for about 3.5 miles until it reaches a parking area on the right. (The *turquoise paint blazes* on the trees will assure you that you're on the right track). For help in following the trail in this area, consult the USGS topo map for Kerhonkson or a local county map.

Opposite the parking area, a trail marker sign indicates that the trail turns left off the road and continues on an old woods road blocked off by a metal gate. You'll pass under a canopy of tall hemlocks and, in 0.25 mile, cross a small brook on a wooden footbridge. In spring and summer, you'll notice a wide variety of plants and wildflowers, including those more commonly found in southerly climates. Most notable is the attractive little fringed polygala (or gaywings). This bright pink, low-growing flower, which can be seen in May and early June, resembles rare orchids that grow in bogs, although it is actually a member of the milkwort family.

The trail then starts to climb, leaving the hemlocks, and makes a sharp right turn as it continues to ascend. It passes through a stand of large white birch trees and thickets of mountain laurel. In June, the showy pink and white flowers of the mountain laurel light up the otherwise dull forest understory. After a while, the old road followed by the trail will level off and cross several wet areas dotted with violets in the spring.

About 1.7 miles from the start, you'll reach **Vernoy Falls**, a fine destination for a short day hike and an excellent spot for a picnic. Just before you reach the falls, you'll see some open areas on the left under tall pines, which could serve as attractive campsites. Vernoy Falls is really a series of cascades in the Vernoy Kill, which tumbles southward towards the Roundout Reservoir. A sturdy footbridge which crosses the creek just south of the falls affords *fine views* of this scenic spot. On the bank just below the bridge, you'll notice an old stone wall, *a remnant of an old mill* once powered by the stream. If you choose to explore further, you'll find other foundations and walls nearby.

If you're in an energetic mood, you might want to follow the *Vernoy Kill* downstream for about half a mile to an area filled with potholes and other interesting remnants from the last Ice Age. Rattlesnakes have been known to inhabit this area, so use extra caution if you choose to explore here. Another option is to continue across the bridge and follow a well worn trail about three-quarters of a mile to *Balsam Swamp.* You'll be able to discover many unique plants there, but make sure you bring insect repellent in warm weather!

From Vernoy Falls, the Long Path turns sharply to the right, continuing to follow the wide road for about half a mile and passing several old stone walls. It then turns left, leaving the road, and proceeds uphill for about 1.5 miles. After descending slightly, the trail turns left and joins another woods road, eventually cresting on 2,350-foot **Bangle Hill**. From here, the trail descends steeply a vertical distance of over 1,200 feet to County Route 42 (Peekamoose-Gulf Road) and the scenic *Roundout Creek*, which it reaches 9.7 miles from the start. A primitive campsite, frequented by local fishermen, is located across the road. The Long Path turns right and follows the road for a short distance before turning off to the left onto the **Peekamoose-Table Trail**.

PHOENICIA-EAST BRANCH TRAIL

*t*he **Phoenicia-East Branch Trail** is a *yellow-blazed trail* which runs from Route 28, just west of Phoenicia, to the village of Claryville on the East Branch of the Neversink River. It is generally used to gain access to other trails which branch off of it, and is rarely hiked in its entirety. At both ends, the trail runs along paved roads, and for the remainder of its route it follows, for the most part, fairly level old woods roads (except for the rather steep climb out of Woodland Valley). For this reason, it is a good *cross-country ski trail* in the winter.

Since most of us have no particular desire to hike along paved roads, we'll begin our description from the parking lot at the Woodland Valley State Campground. We've described how to get to this point in a previous section (pages 204-205). The Phoenicia-East Branch Trail goes into the woods from the parking lot on the right side of the road. After climbing for a while, it begins to descend and, in about a mile, crosses a small bridge over a stream. Soon afterward, the trail turns right (northwest) onto an old road and begins a steady, rather steep climb, paralleling a stream below. It then turns sharply left, crosses the stream, and continues to ascend more moderately. At 2.65 miles (elevation 2,700 feet), it reaches a junction with the *blue-blazed* **Giant Ledge-Panther-Fox Hollow Trail**.

At this point, the trail turns left briefly, then immediately makes a sharp right turn, leaving the old road, and descends to reach County Route 47 (Slide Mountain Road) at the **Giant Ledge Parking Area** by the hairpin turn. This point is 3.4 miles from the start at Woodland Valley. (If you prefer, you can continue straight ahead on the old road, which rejoins the trail in about 1.5 miles, just north of Winnisook Lake. By following this old town road, which is the former route of the trail, you'll save about 400 feet of climbing and avoid a walk along a paved road).

From the junction with County Route 47, the trail turns left and follows the paved road uphill, past Winnisook Lake, then continues along the road as it descends. After about 1.95 miles of road-walking, you'll come to the *Slide Mountain Parking Area* on the left. Here the trail turns left and goes uphill on a footpath (which is not safe to

ski). In another 0.4 mile, you reach an old woods road, and the trail turns right (south) and follows the road, which soon begins a rather gentle climb. The western end of the *red-blazed* **Wittenberg-Cornell-Slide Trail** is passed in another 0.3 mile, and 0.8 mile beyond that the *blue-blazed* **Curtis-Ormsbee Trail** goes off to the left (east). From this point on, the trail begins to descend. About 1.2 miles further, there is a *spring* on the right (west) of the trail.

For the next few miles, the trail is a pleasant stroll through the forest. A junction with the *blue-blazed* **Peekamoose-Table Trail** is reached about a half-mile beyond the spring. This trail descends to the **Denning Lean-to** in 0.25 mile, and continues up Table and Peekamoose Mountains (see description on pages 216-220). The trail continues to descend and, in another 1.2 miles, reaches a parking area in a clearing at the end of Denning Road. This trailhead is 9.8 miles from Woodland Valley and 4.5 miles from the Slide Mountain Parking Area on County Route 47. It is about another 7 miles along Denning Road to the village of Claryville.

GIANT LEDGE-
PANTHER-
FOX HOLLOW
TRAIL

"This is a glacial cirque believed to have held a local glacier long after the Ice Age receded some 14,000 years ago."

*g*reat diversity and challenge await the hiker on this trail. Panther Mountain and Giant Ledge contrast nicely, and the entire trail makes an excellent day hike (with two cars) or backpacking trip at any time of the year. You can choose to start at either end, but we'd suggest starting from Fox Hollow and enjoying the hike as it unfolds. A trail signpost can be seen on the south side of Route 28 at its intersection with Fox Hollow Road

between the towns of Allaben and Shandaken. You can drive up the road for about 1.5 miles to a parking area on your right.

Set out from the parking lot and soon start ascending rather steeply along an old road at a steady pace. Soon you'll pass the sign-in box and be grateful for the break. Shortly after crossing a small brook, a path to the right will take you to the nearby **Fox Hollow Lean-to**, which is about 0.4 mile from the start. There is

Northeast from summit of Panther.

water running from a pipe about 40 feet from the lean-to to the north. The lean-to, which is in relatively good shape, is nestled on a hillside and has a wooden floor. It provides a fine place to camp, especially when the leaves are down and you can catch the last vestiges of sun atop Garfield Mountain across Fox Hollow and enjoy the sun-filled lean-to in the morning.

Back on the trail, you'll continue to head uphill on a rather wide footpath. The trees are very large and mature on this part of the hike. During the winter we've always found this area full of nuthatches, kinglets, woodpeckers and assorted winter birds searching out the trees for wintering insects. The trail will continue to climb steadily for about another mile and then levels off.

This brings us to a disturbing sight we saw near this part of the hike. At one turn in the trail a large old yellow birch had fresh markings on it from someone carving on the trunk. Not only was this very unsightly, but it left this old tree open to parasites and infection. There are better ways to leave your mark in this world than by destroying something that has been growing for hundreds of years and has earned its own niche in the woods. This sort of thing is really looked down upon by us or anyone who really appreciates nature; besides, it's against the law in the Forest Preserve. Leave the trees and wildflowers the way you found them so others can enjoy them too.

After this level stretch, a welcome respite from steady uphill climbing, the trail will begin to ascend more gradually. About 2.5 miles from the beginning of the trail (elevation 3,000 feet), you'll come to a steep, rocky area. If there are no leaves in the trees you'll see what appears to be a summit up ahead, but don't be fooled—this is just the *first false summit* on this deceptive hike. You'll also notice that the trees become smaller and closer together and most of the larger ones disappear. At this point, you're on the ridge line and you'll remain there for quite a while. The trail will pass by a *viewpoint* on the left which looks down over Fox Hollow and northeast towards Hunter and West Kill Mountains. Especially noticeable is the steep drop into the notch between North Dome and West West Kill Mountains.

A little further on you'll reach a *level open area with views* east and west. Ahead of you to the east, you can see another "false summit" and then the real thing—the summit of **Panther Mountain**. This is a good spot to stop for lunch or to set up a campsite nearby.

From here, the trail descends over some large rocks and starts up to the *next false summit*, passing through an area of balsam fir. In late summer there are blueberries all along this section of trail. After a short descent, the

From false summit of Panther with actual summit in the background.

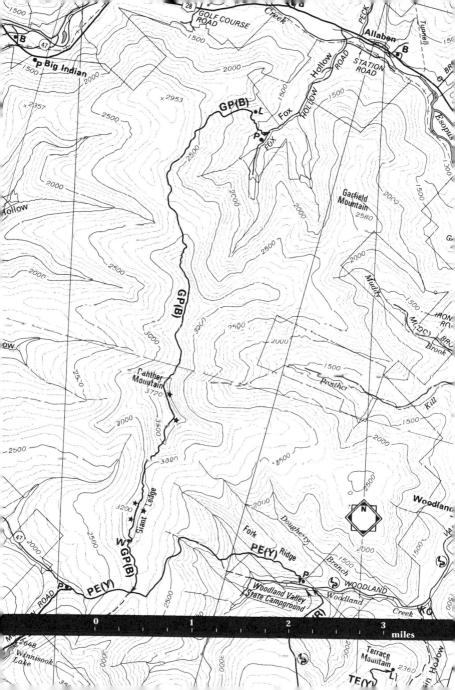

A winter's gate.

trail levels off and passes through a virgin spruce grove atop the ridge. You can feel the height with glimpses through the trees. In winter the mountains provide an excellent backdrop along this section. There is an interesting mixture of spruce and fir, and then the final ascent of Panther starts.

Persevere to the top along a steep section of trail and know that the toughest is now behind you. On the top (4.9 miles), the trail runs along the northeast side of the mountain, providing an *excellent panorama* of the Devil's Path and mountain ranges to the north. The Hudson Valley is off to the far right (east). The summit is dominated by balsam fir, and on days when the air is just

right the fragrance adds to the experience. You will notice a steep drop-off at the summit viewpoint. This is a *glacial cirque* believed to have held a local glacier long after the Ice Age receded some 14,000 years ago. You might also be able to find some faint red paint blazes, remnants of an old trail that starts in an open area and drops off to the west into Little Peck Hollow.

Just before the trail starts its descent, you'll be able to see Slide, Wittenberg and Cornell straight ahead and, down to the right, surprisingly insignificant looking Giant Ledge, your next stop. As you descend, you'll leave the firs on the summit and pass through more varied terrain. After going through a few clearings from which Slide will seem to loom larger and larger, you'll descend a natural narrow steep rocky stairway. A little beyond this (5.4 miles from the start), a sign will point to a *spring* (unreliable) on the left of the trail.

In another quarter of a mile, you'll come to a rock ledge (on the left) with an unheralded but *inspiring view* of Giant Ledge, Wittenberg, Cornell, Slide and Woodland Valley. Continue down the trail, with glimpses of the Hemlock, Spruce and Fir Range off to the southwest (right). You'll probably pass the low point between Panther and Giant Ledge without knowing it, and from there it's a 200-foot climb to the level ridge known as Giant Ledge, which is 6.7 miles from the start. The climb is not particularly difficult, although there are a few rather steep places.

Only 3,200 feet high, **Giant Ledge** is superbly placed between valleys and mountain ranges. The mountain derives its name from a series of open rock ledges facing east with steep drops, providing *great views* over Woodland Valley.

Here you feel right on top of the trees below (unlike the airy feeling you experience on the summit of Panther). The mountain range well to the northeast

> ## "*The mountain derives its name from a series of open rock ledges...*"

is the Devil's Path. There are also a few *enticing views west* towards the Big Indian-Eagle-Balsam Mountain Range.

The sunrises and sunsets you can catch from Giant Ledge are particularly rewarding. One summer night, we stayed up to view the moon inch its way over The Wittenberg, a view worth far more to us than the cost of any movie.

Giant Ledge is a beautiful mountain, with a fine mix of fir and hardwoods, a diversity of spring and summer flowers and plenty of birds to observe. It's not far from Slide Mountain Road, though, and in recent years it has been receiving heavier use from campers, especially those lugging up coolers of beer and radios. *We ask that everyone make an effort to keep it clean and beautiful as it should always be.* On many hikes we've carried out more than we carried in!

As the trail starts to drop between large rocks, you'll pass the site of the former Giant Ledge Lean-to (6.8 miles from Fox Hollow), with an *excellent pipe spring* a few hundred feet to the right (west). This lean-to received heavy use and abuse and was torn down by the DEC in 1984 as it was in a deteriorated condition. At the present time, there are no plans for a replacement.

You'll continue downhill and, in another 0.6 mile, you'll come to a trail junction with the *yellow-blazed* **Phoenicia-East Branch Trail**. To the left it's 2.65 miles to the Woodland Valley State Campground and parking area (see pages 222-223). To the right it's 1.3 miles to County Route 47 and the parking lot at the famous hairpin turn. It's your choice to end this strenuous but enjoyable hike. If you have to go back to your car at Fox Hollow, good luck! It's a long hike back and chances of hitching a ride are slim. ◣

PINE HILL- WEST BRANCH TRAIL

"...the longest stretch of trail through virgin forest in all the Catskills..."

*t*his trail goes over a mountain range that forms the backbone of the Southern Catskills and divides them in half. It proceeds southward from Route 28 in Pine Hill and, after crossing five mountains (three of them over 3,500 feet), terminates on County Route 47 (also known as West Branch Road). The trail includes a 9.9 mile stretch of virgin forest.

This is the longest stretch of trail through virgin forest in all the Catskills beginning at Belleayre Mountain and continuing southward to Biscuit Brook. There are relatively few clear vantage points or open views along the trail, especially when the trees are full of leaves. However, in winter, many fine views "open up."

Several side trails meet the Pine Hill-West Branch Trail in notches between mountains. These side trails drop down into the hollows and provide excellent access for day hiking. They also allow bailouts at several points along the way so you are never more than two hours from a road and civilization.

There are eight lean-tos in the area, with good water near most of them. Backpackers will find many interesting areas to camp off the trail and, other than Balsam Mountain, the area does not receive the constant heavy use that the Slide Mountain area does. All in all, the area offers the opportunity for many excellent day hikes and overnight camping trips.

We'll start at the trail's northern terminus. The *blue blazes* of the **Pine Hill-West Branch Trail** begin on Mill Street in Pine Hill. After passing under a railroad bridge, the road goes uphill, and vehicles can be parked at a point where the road is closed off with a gate. Follow the private road uphill to its end, where the trail goes sharply to the left and proceeds to climb steadily to a junction at 1.4 miles (elevation 2,800 feet) with the *red-blazed* **Lost Clove Trail**.

The Lost Clove Trail drops down 1,200 feet in 1.3 miles to a parking area on Lost Clove Road. Route 28 is about another 2 miles further on. (The bridge over the Esopus Creek which formerly led to County Route 47 was washed

"...a remnant of the once-great stands of hemlock that filled the shady cloves and hollows of the Catskills."

away in a flood during the spring of 1987, and it's unlikely to be replaced in the near future). Although strenuous, this side trail, which runs along the north side of Lost Clove, provides good access for day hikers.

Returning to the Pine Hill-West Branch Trail, the **Belleayre Mountain Lean-to** is reached after 1.6 miles, at about 3,000 feet in elevation. There is a *spring* about 100 feet down a short side trail to the right of the lean-to. From here the trail continues up another 375 feet in elevation and reaches the ridge of **Belleayre Mountain**, elevation 3,375 feet, at 2.05 miles. The fire tower which formerly stood here was recently removed by the DEC.

Belleayre Mountain is a ridge which runs east-west for about two miles. It is interesting to note that the top of Belleayre is covered with hardwoods, with none of the characteristic evergreens seen on peaks to the east. The *red-blazed* **Belleayre Ridge Trail**

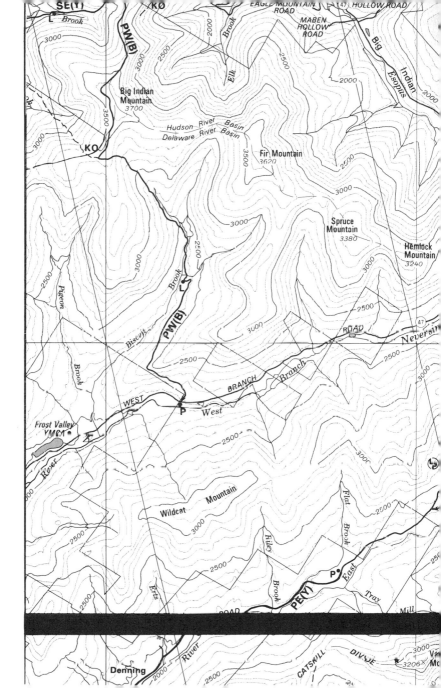

runs westward along the ridge from the fire tower site. In 0.25 mile it passes the *blue-blazed* **Cathedral Glen Trail** (which follows a ski trail down part of its length and ends 1.7 miles down in the village of Pine Hill). In another 0.2 mile, it reaches a wooden **lean-to** at the top of a chairlift for the ski area. *Fine views* over Pine Hill can be had here. The ski area itself has been a target of controversy among those concerned with the use of the land that is supposed to be "forever wild" (not to be altered or abused in any way).

The Belleayre Ridge Trail ends at the top of a chairlift, one mile from its start. The true summit of the mountain (elevation 3,420 feet) is at the west end of the ridge. The trail used to drop down to a hamlet named Hanley Corners to the west, but this portion of the trail is no longer open to hikers.

Let's return to the Pine Hill-West Branch Trail. The trail drops off into the gap between Belleayre and Balsam Mountains, where it levels off for a while. While on a backpacking trip with his wife, one of us found this col a fine area to pitch a tent off the trail.

At 2.95 miles (elevation 2,800 feet), the *yellow-blazed* **Mine Hollow Trail** goes off to the right (west). This short one-mile trail drops into Mine Hollow and ends at a junction with the Oliverea-Mapledale Trail in Rider Hollow. There is a **lean-to** near this junction, with **another lean-to** about 0.15 mile to the south (left) on the Oliverea-Mapledale Trail.

Of particular interest along this trail are the narrow well-trodden deer paths along slopes, perpendicular to the trail. These are regularly used by deer to get from one area to another. At about elevation 2,400 feet, the Mine Hollow Trail passes through a virgin hemlock grove, a remnant of the once-great stands of hemlock that filled the shady cloves and hollows of the Catskills.

From its junction with the Mine Hollow Trail, the Pine Hill-West Branch Trail continues southward through the woods. In a couple of hundred yards it starts a steep 700-foot ascent up **Balsam Mountain**. At first, you'll have to clamber around some large rocks. As you ascend, you'll see a change from mature tall trees to smaller summit trees such as mountain ash and red cherry. Just before you start to level off, there is a *view* back toward Belleayre Mountain.

Soon you'll reach the level summit, about 0.3 mile long, covered by a healthy mixture of balsam fir which gives the mountain its name. After passing through several clearings, you'll come upon an *excellent viewpoint* off to the left, facing east. This is a good place to take a break. It is one of the finest views from the entire Pine Hill-West Branch Trail. Directly below is the Lost Clove and beyond it lies the village of Big Indian. Route 28 can be seen as it snakes its way eastward. Amongst the collage of mountains, Plateau, Hunter and West Kill Mountains can easily be picked out.

On a balmy 40-degree day in January, we saw fresh signs of snowshoe hare all over the summit. Balsam Mountain is one of the required winter peaks for the Catskill 3500 Club.

Proceeding southward along the summit, at 4.3 miles you'll reach a small bare rock area just before you start to descend. A partial view westward over the fir trees reveals Dry Brook Ridge several miles off. From here the trail drops more than 400 feet into a col at elevation 3,030 feet, where it intersects with the *red-blazed* **Oliverea-Mapledale Trail**, 5.0 miles from the start. This trail drops off in both directions and provides good access for day hikers. *There are lean-tos with ample water supply near each end of the trail.*

Balsam Mountain overlooking village of Big Indian.

To the left (southeast), the Oliverea-Mapledale Trail drops rather steeply along the side of a steep rocky ravine into McKenley Hollow, with split log steps and handrails in the steeper sections. You'll reach a **lean-to** in 1.15 mile, and in another 0.3 mile there is a **second lean-to**. Both lie alongside *a brook* that the trail crosses and recrosses. These lean-tos receive heavy use (because of easy access) but appear to be well maintained. At 1.85 miles the trail ends near a building, the former Mountain Gate Lodge of the Appalachian Mountain Club. From here, it's one mile along a paved road to County Route 47 in Oliverea. The village of Big Indian and Route 28 are about 3 miles further to the north.

You also have the option of taking the Oliverea-Mapledale Trail down to the right (north-west). In about 150 feet, you'll pass a *spring* 60 feet to the left of the trail. This branch of the trail then drops, sometimes steeply, into Rider Hollow. In about 0.8 mile, you'll cross a brook and go through a clearing. You'll reach a **lean-to** after 1.25 miles and, in another 0.15 mile, arrive at a junction with the *yellow-blazed* **Mine Hollow Trail** (described above). Just beyond this junction, you'll come to a **second lean-to**, *which faces a brook.*

In late summer, look for the beautiful red flowered bee balm alongside the brook. Tasty raspberries also grow in this area. At 1.75 miles you'll reach a small parking area at the end of Rider Hollow Road. This dirt road leads to roads going to Arkville (left) or Fleischmanns (right).

Let's return to the blue-blazed Pine Hill-West Branch Trail. The trail climbs moderately for 0.7 mile to the summit of **Haynes Mountain** (elevation 3,420 feet) at 5.75 miles. You'll notice a few scattered fir trees that appear to be struggling for existence amongst the dominant hardwoods. These are remnants of the boreal (evergreen) forest that dominated this area after the last Ice Age receded some 14,000 years ago. You'll hardly realize you're on top of Haynes when you'll start to descend. Just before you start to drop off, you may catch a glimpse of Slide Mountain between the trees, looking southeast. The distinctive steep dropoff from the huge slide that gives Slide Mountain its name is the key to identifying it from here. You will also be able to look ahead and get a glimpse of the ridge of Eagle Mountain, the next mountain you'll climb.

From Haynes, the trail drops a mere 180 feet onto the ridge connecting it to Eagle. It levels off for a short while and then starts an easy climb of about 330 feet up to the top of Eagle. There are no views from this mountain, as it is overgrown with tall trees. At 7.15 miles the trail passes just below the true summit of **Eagle Mountain**. A *short bushwhack* of a few hundred feet to the right (west) will bring you to an area of fir trees which is the vicinity of the true summit (elevation 3,600 feet). We flushed out no less than 11 ruffed grouse early one September morning in this area!

The trail then makes an easy, steady descent of Eagle. When you reach an elevation of 3,200 feet, you'll pass through an area of sugar maple in the midst of a ridge hardwoods-fir slope. This is a rather unusual phenomenon.

As noted by Michael Kudish, there are only a few isolated spots in the Catskills where, while ascending or descending a peak, one passes from the northern hardwoods forest into the spruce-fir forest usually associated with summits and then back into the hardwoods forest. This interesting situation, which goes against the rule of thumb for distribution of these types of trees, is attributed to the volume of flowing soil water, soil depth, availability of light and exposure to wind.

At 8.25 miles, you'll reach a junction with the *yellow blazed* **Seager-Big Indian Trail**, which drops off to the right (west) and runs alongside *Shandaken Brook*, reaching the **Shandaken Brook Lean-to** in 0.9 mile (elevation 2,600 feet). It continues down and crosses *Dry Brook* at 1.75 miles, reaching a parking area near a covered bridge in remote Seager at 3.0 miles.

Just south of this junction, an unmarked, difficult-to-follow trail drops off to the left (east) towards Oliverea and Esopus Creek. It crosses private property all the way down, and permission to hike must be obtained. The Pine Hill-West Branch Trail continues southward and starts to climb up the north side of Big Indian Mountain.

Big Indian Mountain got its name from a local legend about a seven-foot tall Indian named Winnisook, who fell in love with a white woman around 1800. According to one legend, he was supposedly killed by a jealous settler and his body stuffed in a large tree near the village of Big Indian.

At about 9.65 miles, the trail reaches the western ridge of **Big Indian Mountain**. A *bushwhack* of a few hundred yards to the east will lead to the 3,700-foot summit, with a canister of the 3500 Club. In summer and early fall, there are virtually no views from the summit, since the mountain is covered with a dense mixture of hardwoods and fir trees. The absence of views is disappointing, considering the mountain's height and location. However, in winter, when there are no leaves on the trees, you can get good views of Doubletop and

---

"The hillsides are steep and water is abundant as it gushes across the trail…"

Graham Mountains to the west.

About half a mile after the trail starts to descend off the ridge, an old unmarked side trail goes off to the right. This trail, which leads to Seager, passes through private property, and permission to hike must be obtained. The Pine Hill-West Branch Trail makes a sharp left at this point and goes down a steep, eroded area that has recently been supported to prevent further erosion. It continues down through a mature virgin forest area of large trees, and eventually levels off, following the *Biscuit Brook*. The mountain that appears up to your left (east) is Fir Mountain. The pleasant murmur of the water is a welcome change.
The hillsides are steep as you are enclosed on all sides of a seemingly remote and primal mini valley. Water is abundant as it fills the air and gushes across the trail in several places in the springtime.

At 12.2 miles, a short side trail to the right leads to the **Biscuit Brook Lean-to**. The lean-to is on the east bank of the Biscuit Brook and makes a nice place to camp. The trail straightens out past the lean-to and climbs a small spur before coming down to County Route 47 (West Branch Road) at 14.1 miles. The Biscuit Brook parking area across the road is a good place to leave a second car or to start a hike of this trail in the opposite direction. If you are hiking without a car at this end, you should note that there are no towns of any size for almost 13 miles. Your chances of hitching a ride from here aren't too good!

FIR MOUNTAIN

"The two mountains have similar summits that cause some to believe they are on Big Indian when they are in fact on Fir Mountain."

*f*ir Mountain (3,620 feet) is a trailless peak with a summit box maintained by the Catskill 3500 Club. It offers good bushwhacking from almost any direction. The most challenging route is from Slide Mountain Road over Hemlock (3,240 feet) and Spruce (3,380 feet) Mountains (see page 266). Many hikers reach Fir from the summit of Big Indian Mountain to the west. They are connected by a spur; the climbing is not difficult. It is also possible to approach Fir from the south by following the Pine Hill-West Branch Trail to just beyond the Biscuit Brook Lean-to and then taking a compass bearing to the summit. There are no clear views from the summit, which is covered with a mixture of balsam fir and summit hardwoods, although you may be able to get glimpses of the Slide Mountain area and adjacent high peaks to the east. There is *one fine view* to the west, a 15 minute bushwhack northwest of the summit.

Although the mountain is not in a remote area, and the distance to it is relatively short, many hikers we've talked to have told us that they have had difficulty finding the true summit. This might be because of the mountain's fairly flat top, the thick foliage and its proximity to Big Indian Mountain. The two mountains have similar summits that cause some to believe they are on Big Indian when they are in fact on Fir Mountain. Keep in mind that Slide Mountain Road is not very far from the summit of Fir.

NEVERSINK HARDEN- BURGH TRAIL

"Level, peaceful and relaxing, it is enjoyable at any time of the year."

*t*his trail offers the opportunity for a long stroll through beautiful woodlands with minimal climbing. Following country roads at each end, the trail cuts through the mountains and never reaches any ridgeline. Its northern half crosses several tributaries of the famous *Beaver Kill trout stream*, while the southern half of the trail crosses tributaries of *Fall Brook*, which runs into the *West Branch of the Neversink River*. This trail allows one to feel close to the earth and the running waters that are so much part of the Catskills.

Level, peaceful and relaxing, it is enjoyable at any time of the year. It is an *excellent cross-country ski trail* in winter. Despite the many hunter's cabins it passes, a good deal of the trail treks through untouched wilderness areas of the Forest Preserve. It should be noted that both ends of the trail are fairly remote. The drive from one end to the other on back roads can take the better part of an hour. This should be taken into account if you plan on using two cars.

The trail can be started from either end without difficulty. We'll begin at the trail's southern approach. *Yellow trail markers* can be found at the junction of West Branch Road and Denning Road in Claryville. Follow West Branch Road northward across the East Branch and then the West Branch of the Neversink River, and continue along the West Branch. After 1.3 miles, bear left and head uphill on Round Pond Road, which will pass privately owned Round Pond. Just past the pond at 1.9 miles, bear right on unpaved Willowemoc Road. At 2.1 miles you'll pass the *red-blazed* **Long Pond-Beaverkill Ridge Trail** that goes off to the left on Basily Road.

The Neversink-Hardenburgh Trail continues uphill through private land, passing a hunter's club at 3.3 miles, with *excellent*

views to the southeast towards Wildcat Mountain and Red Hill. This is the only clear view on the trail. Continuing a gradual climb, you'll come to a clearing on the right (on state land) at 5.1 miles, where cars may be parked. The many hunter's cabins you've passed on the trail should tell you this is big game country; deer are very prevalent in the area due to the ideal mixture of clearings and woods.

Neversink-Hardenburgh Trail.

The trail soon returns briefly onto private land, passing another hunter's clubhouse, and then continues on state land, crossing a few pleasant tributaries of *Fall Brook*. The grade of the land slopes off to your right (east) but rises rather steeply on the left. After crossing another tributary in a narrow gully, you'll reach the **Fall Brook Lean-to**, with *running water nearby*, at 6.65 miles. The lean-to is about 100 feet to the left (west) of the trail.

The trail continues and crosses several tributaries through beautiful woods. If the leaves are down, Doubletop Mountain can be spotted to the right (northeast) through the trees. At 7.75 miles, there is a large beaver dam to the right of the trail which has created a pond with many dead trees. Soon afterwards, you'll cross the headwaters of the Beaver Kill and start to descend slowly, paralleling the stream for the rest of the way.

At about 8.2 miles, you might want to *bushwhack* to **Tunis Pond**, which lies 100 feet above and 0.25 mile north of the trail. The pond, which has a great diversity of wildlife, makes an excellent secluded camping area. Make sure you've got a compass and a good map before you try to find this pond, though.

Continuing on the trail, you'll cross more stream tributaries and, at approximately 9.35 miles, the outlet stream of **Vly Pond**. Shortly thereafter, you'll pass a private house and cross the *Gulf of Mexico Brook*. At 10.75 miles the trail crosses *Black Brook*, and it ends, 11.0 miles from the start, at Quaker Clearing on Beaver Kill Road.

The Beaverkill with freshly fallen snow.

DRY BROOK RIDGE TRAIL

"Clear ledges facing west are uncommon in the Catskills, and these are among the finest we've found."

*t*his trail runs generally north to south and is 13.65 miles long. Starting just south of Route 28 and ending at Quaker Clearing near the Beaver Kill, a famous trout stream, this trail can actually be separated into two completely different hikes.

The first nine miles traverse the Dry Brook Ridge, from Route 28 to Mill Brook Road. South of this point the trail follows a wide jeep road to Balsam Lake Mountain and Beaver Kill Road. The first part over Dry Brook Ridge makes for good backpacking and does not see much use by hikers. The more popular Balsam Lake Mountain section makes a relatively easy day hike (despite the

mountain's 3,720-foot elevation) and offers *superb views* from the state *fire tower* on the mountain's summit.

Dry Brook Ridge Section

Dry Brook Ridge is a true ridge in the full sense of the word. Long and narrow, it is almost nine miles long and is very prominent when seen from Arkville on Route 28. To reach the trailhead, make a turn south off Route 28 at the Agway Store 0.5 mile west of the junction with Route 30 in Margaretville. Take the first left and look for the trailhead marker sign on your right in a few hundred feet.

At elevation 1,380 feet, this *blue-blazed trail* begins its climb into the woods. It soon joins an old logging road and makes small cuts back and forth along the grade of the mountain, passing through second-growth hardwoods.

At elevation 1,950 feet, it levels off for about 0.4 mile as it cuts across the grain of the mountain to the southwest. The trail then switches back to the left (east) and starts to climb again. After another series of switchbacks the trail levels off, 1.8

Old homestead just off southern end of Dry Brook Ridge Trail, near Balsam Lake Mtn.

miles from the start, at the top of **Pakatakan Mountain** (elevation 2,500 feet).

Pakatakan Mountain is actually just another name for the northern spur of Dry Brook Ridge. At this point the trail runs along the western slope of the ridge, with *limited views* to the west (best with the leaves down) towards the Pepacton Reservoir.

From here on, the trail ascends at a much slower rate (except for a few steep sections where it climbs 100 feet or so in a short span).

At about 2.6 miles (elevation 2,790 feet), you'll reach a junction with the *yellow-blazed* **German Hollow Trail**, which drops down to the left (east) into German Hollow. The German Hollow Trail passes a *reliable spring* in about 0.3 mile, and in 0.75 mile it reaches the **German Hollow Lean-to** (elevation 2,000 feet).

This lean-to is located on the mountainside overlooking Reservoir Hollow and is especially nice when there are no leaves in the trees and the Dry Brook Valley can be seen to the east.

The German Hollow Trail continues down and ends, 1.5 miles from its start, on Soderlind Road south of Arkville. To reach Arkville from this point, continue on Soderlind Road, bear left when it merges into Dry Brook Road, and turn right when you reach Route 28 just west of the village. This trail provides a shorter alternative to get to the top of Dry Brook Ridge and makes a pleasant hike.

From the junction, the Dry Brook Ridge Trail climbs moderately a few hundred feet, and then actually drops a little to the eastern side of the mountain, before coming back up to the middle of the ridge line. We saw animal droppings, unmistakably those of a black bear, in this area.

At about elevation 3,000 feet, you'll see a change in vegetation. While there are hardwoods for the entire length of the ridge, the trees become noticeably smaller and scrubby above 3,000 feet, and the characteristic ridge hardwoods such as beech, yellow birch, black cherry and red maple begin to predominate.

It is interesting to note that, while (according to research gathered by Michael Kudish) the state purchased the majority of Dry Brook Ridge between 1877-1885, an official trail was not cut through this section of virgin forest between Pakatakan Mountain and Mill Brook Road until 1936.

The majority of climbing is over for some time now. At approximately elevation 3,100 feet,

Balsam Lake Mountain from Dry Brook Ridge Trail.

as the trail travels westward for a short distance, there is a small open area on the left containing a *sphagnum moss bog*. While this unique environment is probably a great place to observe wildlife in summer, it was dormant on our early November hike to the area.

From here the trail continues in a generally southerly direction and at 4.1 miles passes an old unmarked trail that drops off to the right (west) into Cold Spring Hollow. In another half-mile or so the trail climbs a little and comes out along a series of excellent *open rock ledges* facing west. Clear ledges facing west are uncommon in the Catskills, and these are among the finest we've found.

If a campsite can be found nearby, this would be a superb place to watch a sunset. The views include Mill Brook Ridge to the south and Cold Spring Hollow to the west. Separating the mountains to the west is a difficult task due to their nearly identical height. The prominent mountain to your right (north) is 3,345-foot Mount Pisgah. You can also look back on the northern portion of Dry Brook Ridge itself. We enjoyed this view on a rare 70-degree day in November, and it's on our list to visit in summertime when cool breezes can lap the open ledges above the valley.

After a series of these ledges, the trail heads back towards the middle of the ridge. The true summit, elevation 3,460 feet, is just to the east of the trail at this point, 7.15 miles from the trailhead. There is another *fine view* to the west here.

For the next mile, the trail will drop down a bit and then climb slightly in two spots before starting a steep descent and bearing off to the right (west). Along the way here, you'll unceremoniously cross from Delaware County into Ulster County. You'll reach the **Dry Brook Lean-to** at 8.2 miles (elevation 2,720 feet). *A fine spring* nearby marks the source of Mill Brook, while a fence designates private land closed to hikers. (The spring, although open to public use, is actually on private land, so extra care should be taken when using it to ensure that it remains open in the future). The trail then climbs gradually, cresting at elevation 3,040 feet (8.9 miles), and then starts a steady descent past a tree plantation to reach Mill Brook Road at 9.6 miles (elevation 2,620 feet). Limited parking is available here.

If you turn right (west), and follow Mill Brook Road for about a mile, you'll reach a *yellow-blazed trail* on the right side of the road which leads a few hundred yards north to the **Mill Brook Lean-to**. This lean-to, which is on state land, provides the opportunity for a hiker to arrive late in the day, set up camp and get an early start on the trail the next morning.

From Mill Brook Road south, the Dry Brook Ridge Trail offers a very different type of hike that we'll describe next.

Balsam Lake Mountain Section

This section of the trail is a continuation of the *blue-blazed trail* that runs the length of Dry Brook Ridge. The first 2.15 miles go through private land, so please respect the rights of the landowner. This entire section follows a road wide enough for a four-wheel drive vehicle, which is used by the DEC fire tower observer on Balsam Lake Mountain. Of course, this makes for easy hiking and helps explain the heavy use the trail receives in summer. In any event, the views from the fire tower are worth it. We'll give you mileage starting from Mill Brook Road and occasionally give mileage from the trail's beginning near Route 28, 9.6 miles to the north.

From the road (elevation 2,620 feet) the trail goes uphill

moderately and makes one noticeable turn to the left before continuing uphill in a southerly direction. Walking is never too difficult as the wide road is in pretty
good condition. The trail levels
off briefly, with a *good spring*
located some 30 yards to the
right of the trail at 1.0 mile
(elevation 3,100 feet). From here
the road climbs a little and then
levels off for more than half a
mile. At 2.05 miles, an unmarked
private road goes off to the left.
This is the Old Tappan Road, constructed in the 1800's, which eventually runs down Turner Hollow
and into Seager. This old road
also gives easy access to an unmarked trail that climbs Graham
Mountain (see pages 254-256).

Continuing on the blue-
blazed trail, you'll see the tall
crown of Balsam Lake Mountain
on your right. At 2.15 miles
(11.75 miles from the start of the
Dry Brook Ridge Trail) a junction
is reached with the *red-blazed*
Balsam Lake Mountain Trail.
The elevation here is about 3,320
feet. This trail forms a loop that
will reconnect to the blue-blazed
trail 0.95 mile further on.

By all means take the rather
steep red trail up a distance of
0.75 mile, climbing the final 400
feet to the 3,720-foot summit of
Balsam Lake Mountain. Here
there is a clearing with a cabin

*"There are mountains
spread out in all
directions, and we feel
this may possibly be the
finest view from any
of the fire towers
in the Catskills."*

for the use of the forest fire
observer. Just southwest of the
tower, there's a partial view to
the west (cleared because of a
severe blowdown) over the multi-
tude of balsam fir that gives the
mountain its name.

The real view is from the *fire
tower*. The present steel tower
has been standing since 1919 and
replaced a wooden one that had

been there since 1905. The original tower at this location was the first fire observation station in the state. A spectacle awaits you from the top of the tower. There are mountains spread out in all directions, and we feel this may possibly be the finest view from any of the fire towers in the Catskills.

On one of our trips there, we were graced with one of those rare dry, pleasant blue sky days in July. The view from the fire tower prompted one of the members of our party to reaffirm his belief in God. Due to the location of Balsam Lake Mountain, and the fact that no mountains over 3,500 feet stand west of it, the mountain towers over its neighbors to the west and allows views as far as the eye can see.

Looking west, Mill Brook Ridge extends away from you for a few miles. Dry Brook Ridge is nearest to the north, with Mount Pisgah in the distance to its left. On a clear day, Mt. Utsayantha may be visible far beyond Dry Brook Ridge to the north. Binoculars may be needed to make out the fire tower on its summit. Swinging around to the east, you'll see Graham Mountain, with twin-topped Doubletop behind and to the right. Between the two is the distinctive head of Slide Mountain which can be seen from so many places in different sections of these mountains.

If you have binoculars, swing to the south from Slide, and due southeast you'll see the fire tower on Red Hill. The moun-

Slide is visible between Graham and Doubletop east of Balsam Lake Mountain fire tower.

tains directly to your south comprise the Beaver Kill Range. If the forest fire observer is in the tower, he'll be able to help you pick out any peaks you can't find and probably throw in a story like the one he told us about the bobcat that ran out in front of his jeep one morning. The observers are always helpful and welcome any questions you might have.

When you return to solid ground, another surprise awaits you. A few hundred yards north-northwest of the tower (at elevation 3,700 feet), is a 15-acre *sphagnum bog*, formed due to poor drainage. Between the tower and cabin, a faint path goes off in the direction of the bog. Keep an eye on your compass, as the path is hard to follow at points. According to a topo map, it lies approximately 20 feet lower than the summit.

Please be careful of the fragile plants that grow along the path. The bog is thick with balsam fir, and the edges make an interesting place to study the unique life found in the atypical bog environment. Sphagnum moss, wild raisin and the beautiful cinnamon fern are a few of the plants found in a bog environment. *A bog of this size is rare enough*, but especially odd at this elevation. Explore!

> *"The bog is thick with balsam fir, and the edges make an interesting place to study the unique life found in the atypical bog environment."*

From the summit, you can either retrace your steps back down or proceed on the red trail to the south. If you choose the latter, you'll remain relatively level for about 0.35 mile, where you'll pass a *reliable spring* on the trail and the two **Balsam Lake Mountain Lean-tos** nearby. With leaves down, the views southward towards Balsam Lake make for a picturesque setting. The trail drops rather steeply after the lean-tos, but footing is firm.

At 0.85 miles from the summit, the junction with the *blue-blazed* **Dry Brook Ridge Trail** is reached. To the left (north), Mill Brook Road is 3.1 miles. To the right (south), the trail follows this wide jeep road for less than a mile on a gradual descent through the woods and passes an old homestead to your right. Just beyond this homestead you'll pass a dirt road on your right (west) which leads to Balsam Lake in 0.3 mile. You won't be able to see it in summer. An elite group of fishermen owns the Balsam Lake Club. In seconds, you'll pass a meadow and reach a parking area in a clearing, with a *view* eastward toward Doubletop, Graham and the Beaver Kill Range. Cars may be driven to this point.

After another mile, you'll reach a small parking area, which marks the terminus of the trail. This point, known as *Quaker Clearing*, is 5.0 miles from Mill Brook Road and a full 14.6 miles from the trail's beginning near Route 28. The *yellow-blazed* **Neversink-Hardenburgh Trail** begins here, while the trailhead for the *blue-blazed* **Mongaup-Hardenburgh Trail** is 0.7 mile further west along the road. (We'd also like to note that Balsam Lake Mountain can be easily reached in 2.75 miles from the parking area near the Balsam Lake Club entrance. However, auto access from Beaver Kill Road may be difficult in wet weather. ◣◢

GRAHAM MOUNTAIN

"Near the top, a stunning view northward of Dry Brook Ridge contrasting with the nearby valley makes all the effort worthwhile."

*L*ying east of Balsam Lake Mountain is **Graham Mountain**. At 3,868 feet, it is prominent and provides excellent views from the top. The highest privately owned peak in the Catskills, it is the property of the Gould family (direct descendants of railroad magnate Jay Gould) who own large tracts of land in this area of the Catskills. Permission to hike here must be obtained from the landowner.

One route you can take to the summit starts by following the **Dry Brook Ridge Trail** 1.8 miles south from Mill Brook Road. At this point, turn left (east) onto the wide **Old Tappan Road**, which actually drops slightly before leveling off. You may catch a glimpse of the summit of Graham well ahead of you. The distinctive structure that rises from the top is an abandoned television relay station. In less than a mile, you'll pass the spot where the Old Tappan Road goes off to the left down into Turner Hollow. (In about two miles it meets Dry Brook Road in Seager. This road, which dates back to the 1800's, was reused in the 1960's for logging purposes.) Dry Brook Road can also be used to provide access to Graham. In this case you would park on Dry Brook Road and begin your hike up Graham on the unmarked Old Tappan Road going through Turner Hollow. After about two miles, turn left at the junction. This route is the shorter, yet steeper of the two.

Continue walking ahead straight on a private road which was built about 1960 to install the television relay tower on top of Graham. It is overgrown in some areas but still allows good footing for hikers. After being relatively level for some time, the road starts a moderate climb up the last 600 feet to the summit. As you ascend, the vegetation changes to smaller, scrubbier summit hardwoods.

Just below the summit, there are some balsam fir trees, not unusual for this height. What is unusual is the fact that none exist on the summit itself. While mountain ash, yellow birch and even beech are found on the top, no summit evergreens are to be found on this 3,868-foot mountain.

If you scrounge off the trail to the right (southwest) just below the summit, you will find *open rock ledges with wide views south and west.* Near the top, a *stunning view northward* of Dry Brook Ridge contrasting with the nearby valley makes all the effort worthwhile. On the north side of the mountain, wires are still visible on the poles that brought power to the building once run by Educational Radio for TV relay. The building has a solid concrete shell and will probably stand for a long time.

On our November hike, the wires to the building and all the trees were glazed from the night before. Due to the frost, the ferns near the summit were dying and had a distinctive unpleasant smell. Scrounging around the summit, we found excellent views toward Doubletop Mountain and the Dry Brook Valley to the east. Big Indian, Eagle and Fir Mountains are also close neighbors easily visible. To the west, Balsam Lake Mountain is the most prominent peak to be seen.

After having our lunch we were ready to head down the mountain. Although it was a sunny day, we watched the dark foaming waves of clouds rolling towards us, from beyond West Kill and Hunter Mountains, engulfing the land. We decided it was time for us to go. Hopefully, Graham Mountain will stay open to hikers for years to come, showcasing a fine contrast of valley and mountain.

The challenge of the bushwhack.

DOUBLETOP MOUNTAIN

*d*oubletop is the highest trailless peak in the Catskills and one of the most formidable hikes for those willing to *bushwhack* to its distinctive twin-peaked summit. *It is filled with all kinds of wildlife that will surprise even the least perceptive hiker.* There are no roads that run close to it and no towns to speak of in the area. This isolated setting, plus *awe-inspiring views from the top*, help make it a sought-after prize for die-hard Catskill trekkers. The northern or true summit is privately owned.

We've approached this mountain from both the north and south routes. (It's also possible to approach Doubletop from the west by following the Beaver Kill up from its junction with the Neversink-Hardenburgh Trail). We first tried the southern approach, via the High Falls Brook Valley, in mid-June. The hike turned into an endurance test due to heavy ground cover and vegeta-

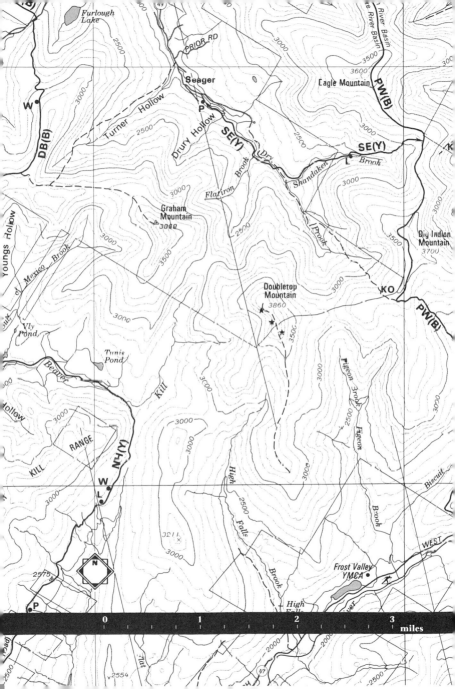

> *"Despite a 42-degree chill, light rain and deteriorating weather conditions, we arrived at the summit only to be happily greeted by a ruby-throated hummingbird."*

tion.

Just when we were feeling discouraged, the summit became visible through the trees. We pulled our strength together for the final march. Despite a 42-degree chill, light rain and deteriorating weather conditions, we arrived at the summit only to be happily greeted by a ruby-throated hummingbird. We also saw a large common raven, rarely seen in the northeast, near the top. Because of superstitions linking it with evil, the raven has been persecuted and has consequently become very rare in the northeast, except in remote mountain areas.

On another visit to Doubletop, we approached it from the north and found some steep 30-foot rock ledges that unexpectedly rose out of the forest. They made for some challenging and tough climbing.

It was the final climb for the 3500 Club for one of us, and the mountain was dressed in its best. Wildflowers such as goldthread, star flower and yellow clintonia were sprinkled all over the summit. In some clearings, low-growing bunchberry gave the scene a fantasy-like appearance. A couple of hundred feet below and east of the south summit, we found the grim remains of a small plane that had crashed into the mountainside. After inspecting it and the nearby downed trees, we surmised that it was a fairly recent crash.

The real reward for hiking this mountain is the *superb westward view* from the north summit. Doubletop towers over all the mountains to the west and southwest, providing open views for great distances in those directions. To the northwest, Balsam Lake Mountain's fire tower can be seen. The Beaver Kill Range is straight ahead and below you. If you look to the right of this range (north), you can see a large clearing, which is near the Balsam Lake Club. *The famous Beaver Kill Creek*, which actually has its origins on the western slopes of Doubletop, runs past it and out to the west.

As challenging as it is, Doubletop has a frail environment on its summit. There is a fragile yet healthy growth of balsam fir on top. For this rea-

Open rock views west from Doubletop.

son, we ask that hikers stay on the distinct "herd path" between the two summits as much as possible to avoid damage to the many small wildflowers and herbs growing on the forest floor.

One last note: In Pigeon Notch, between Doubletop and Big Indian Mountains, is a virgin spruce grove and bog growing in a sheltered location. Red spruce are uncommon this far west in the Catskills. If you choose to visit this unique area, which makes for an interesting excursion, give yourself ample time.

Whichever way you choose to climb Doubletop, make sure you have at least one person familiar with the use of map and compass. As mentioned before, *surprises await you on this hike.*

HIGH POINT & VICINITY

"In the late 1800's, this area was repeatedly burned by berry pickers to encourage the profuse growth of berry bushes."

Ashokan Reservoir from High Point.

*S*ituated at the eastern end of the Southern Catskills, **High Point**, also known as **Ashokan High Point**, stands tall like a guardian over the southwestern part of the Ashokan Reservoir. This mountain, which is almost entirely on state land, offers *superb views in all directions*. Although it is only 3,080 feet in elevation, it rises over 2,000 feet above the reservoir. High Point makes an excellent day hike or backpacking trip, and should not be neglected because of its comparatively low elevation. Although the *trail is unmarked*, its route is very clear at all times, as it parallels the Kanape Brook most of the way.

It is possible to approach High Point from the south, via Freeman Avery Road (which goes off Upper Samsonville Road). However, the southern part of this route passes through private lands, and the landowner at the

Ashokan High Point from a pasture in the valley.

end of the road has closed the property to hikers. A longer but more enchanting route approaches High Point from the northwest, following the valley of the Kanape Brook. The trail from Peekamoose Road to Freeman Avery Road is actually an old carriage road that cut the traveling time in the old days considerably.

To get to the starting point of the northwest approach, take County Route 42 (Peekamoose

Road) to the beginning of the Kanape Brook valley. You can see the Kanape southeast of the roadside. The trail begins just beyond a large open grassy area—on the other side of a wooden bridge. Proceed southeast along the brook. In the late 1800's, this area was repeatedly burned by berry pickers to encourage the profuse growth of berry bushes.

This walk is extremely easy going for the first two miles as it parallels the babbling Kanape Brook, passing through a beautiful hardwoods forest. However, you will find a formidable stand of evergreens just beyond where the trail crosses the Kanape Brook. We have found this area a great place to relax and take it all in. Following this wide trail, in less than a mile and an ascent of about 500 feet you'll reach the height of land between Mombaccus Mountain and High Point (elevation 2,050 feet). Here, an unmarked trail starts up High Point. On the way up, you may get glimpses of Mombaccus Mountain through the trees. The climb becomes steeper at about elevation 2,600 feet, and at elevation 2,800 feet the trees suddenly become stunted and smaller.

Most of High Point, including the summit, is dominated by various types of hardwoods.

You'll find various types of oak trees all the way up to the top, which is rather unusual for the Catskills. We even found some healthy but stunted American chestnut trees in the valley and at about 2,800 feet. Once a common tree in eastern United States, the chestnut was devastated by a disease introduced into this country in the early part of this century. It is now rare and sickly, struggling for survival.

A number of species, including chestnut oak and blackgum, are found at higher elevations on High Point than elsewhere in the Catskills. This may be due to the mountain's proximity to the Hudson Valley.

At about elevation 2,900 feet, you'll pass a *rock overhang* to the left of the trail which could provide shelter for one or two people. You'll soon reach the summit, about 3.5 miles from the start, coming out on a large rock with *excellent views south and east*. You should be able to see the Shawangunks, which form a distinct ridge to the southeast. The tower you see on the ridge is the Sky Top Tower of the Mohonk Mountain House.

On a clear day you can see down the Hudson Valley to Schunemunk Mountain, Harriman State Park and the Hudson Highlands. In the distance to the east, you may be able to make out the Taconic Mountains of Connecticut and Massachusetts. Directly below you, through the trees, you can see the 12-mile long Ashokan Reservoir. If the leaves are down, you may be able to get a good shot of the reservoir if you scrounge northward along

"...views from this spot, while unheralded, are among the best in the Catskills."

Panorama of high peaks from a meadow on Ashokan High Point.

the eastern edge of the summit.

From this open rock, a distinctive herd path leads to the western side of the level summit. You'll come to two beautiful clearings, with *excellent views* west towards Mombaccus Mountain (elevation 2,840 feet) and Lit-

tle Rocky (elevation 3,015 feet).

Continue on the herd path past blueberry bushes (great in late summer!) and you'll come to a large grassy meadow, with *a great panorama* of the high peaks around Slide Mountain. You can see nine peaks over 3,500 feet in

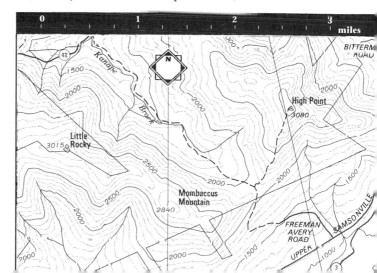

elevation. These mountains appear to be much higher than they really are, and seem to resemble the Rockies as viewed from an alpine meadow. We think that the views from this spot are among the best unheralded views in the Catskills.

Even wider views can be had from an open spur about 0.35 mile east-southeast of High Point. A short tricky downhill bushwhack leads to a mini-gorge about 325 feet below the summit. After climbing up and out of this gorge, hand-to-foot in spots, you will continue east-southeast gently climbing uphill through a sparsely wooded area leading to an open field overgrown with knee-high blueberry bushes and stunted trees. You are now at 2,800 feet, about 300 feet below the summit. The views from the ledges at the end of this spur are similar to but much wider than those from High Point itself. You are afforded a superb 270-degree panorama (with High Point obscuring a full 360-degree view). From these ledges you feel as if you might just reach out and wet your hand in the Ashokan. Most noteworthy is the view of the mountains of the Devil's Path to the north.

On one of our visits to the spur we bushwhacked northwest back along the spur to High

Typical open areas found on southeast slope of Ashokan High Point.

Point. From here we encircled it, heading west at an elevation of approximately 2,700 feet, until we met up with the trail. The going was difficult, as the angle of High Point's slope is quite steep. Along this bushwhack we came across many open areas that seemed to appear from nowhere.

"Off The Beaten Path"

The South Central Catskills have many *trailless areas* available to hikers seeking out unique views or wishing to explore areas not visited by most hikers. Most of these areas lie on state land inside the Forest Preserve.

West of High Point, there is a range of mountains which includes **Mombaccus Mountain**, **Little Rocky**, **Spencers Ledge** (elevation 2,700 feet) and **Samson Mountain** (elevation 2,812 feet).

Most of these mountains are on state land, and can be approached by *bushwhacking* from Peekamoose Road to the north. (The summit of Little Rocky is on private land, and permission to hike must be obtained). These mountains will provide an interesting and challenging adventure for experienced bushwhackers.

South of Route 28 and east of Woodland Valley lies a ridge beginning with **Romer Mountain** (2,160 feet) and continuing southward to **Mount Pleasant** (2,800 feet). **Cross Mountain** (2,500 feet) runs southwest off Mount Pleasant and connects to a spur off the eastern slope of The Wittenberg. On the eastern end of this spur rises **Samuels Point** (elevation 2,885 feet). All the summits of this ridge are state-owned. Although the areas were previously burned over, they are now covered with second-growth hardwoods. Once access is gained to the ridge line the going is relatively easy. Ledges on the northeastern face of Romer Mountain (about one-third the way down the slope) offer *fine views* of Route 28 and Tremper Mountain. Samuels Point is an especially difficult *bushwhack* due to its steep rise from surrounding roads, but it affords *excellent views* to those who explore its summit.

Balsam Swamp lies south of Samson Mountain on the southern fringes of the Catskills. It makes for interesting exploring (watch out for rattlesnakes!) and is a definite contrast to mountain hiking. Swamps were once thought of as waste areas useless to man, but we now realize how important these areas are to the life cycles of many species of plants and animals. Today, swamps are studied and appreciated for their amazing diversity of life, and measures are being taken to preserve them. Anyone exploring Balsam Swamp should be accompanied by an experienced hiker, have a topo map and know how to use a compass. Be prepared to get wet and dirty!

Another area worth checking out is trailless **Van Wyck Mountain** (3,206 feet). Lying just west of Table Mountain, it has *fine views* from around its summit. Many brooks drain from its slopes southward into Roundout Creek.

To the northwest of Van Wyck, across the valley of the East Branch of the Neversink River, is the ridge known as **Wildcat Mountain**. Running roughly east-west for several miles, this ridge, which separates the watersheds of the East and West Branches of the Neversink,

> **"In early June the fragrant and colorful mountain azalea will fire up your senses."**

Table from Wildcat Mountain.

attains elevations of 3,160 feet on its western summit and 3,340 feet on its eastern summit. Although few hikers venture up this mountain, it makes a fine hike, especially in winter when the foliage is gone. On the ridge line we found two *sphagnum bogs* with interesting plants such as wild raisin, skunk currant, cinnamon fern and two species of mountain holly. There are *views along the ridge* to the south towards Table and Van Wyck Mountains. In early June the fragrant and colorful mountain azalea will fire up your senses.

North of Wildcat are **Hemlock** (3,240 feet) and **Spruce** (3,380 feet) **Mountains**. They provide an interesting approach to Fir Mountain to the

northwest. We've found *open rock ledges* with fine views on the south side of the eastern ridge leading up to Hemlock Mountain. Bushwhackers wishing to climb Hemlock will find access from the nearby Slide Mountain Parking Area.

For hikers interested in exploring the Southern Catskills further, there are a few peaks over 3,000 feet near the Ulster County-Sullivan County border. The 3,040-foot **Woodhull Mountain** has two summits. The true summit is privately owned, although state land reaches the 3,000-foot mark on the north side. Dirt roads get within 0.3 mile of the summit on the privately-owned side of the mountain, but permission to hike here must be obtained. Southwest of Woodhull Mountain is **Red Hill** (2,990 feet). There is a state *fire tower on the summit with beautiful views*. For years a trail followed the jeep road to the summit, making the short enjoyable hike very popular. Unfortunately, the land the road passes through changed hands and it is now completely off limits to hikers. However, a tract of state land runs up the north slope of Red Hill from unpaved Coons Road. This road was washed out by flooding on our visit to the area. For those still wishing to enjoy the view from the fire tower, it's a one mile bushwhack and a 1,000-foot climb on the state land approach.

Southwest of Red Hill lies **Denman Mountain**. At 3,053 feet, it is the highest point in Sullivan County and the only mountain in that county higher than 3,000 feet. The state owns tracts of land around the mountain but not the summit itself, so you'll need to seek permission to hike it.

There are many other tracts of state land available to those wishing to explore the forest and find true solitude. A good example of this is the **Fork Ridge** and the area west of Woodland Valley at the base of Giant Ledge. One can wander around this area for days without running into another soul. There is a beautiful virgin forest of large spruce, hemlock and various northern hardwoods in this valley. Another area worth exploring is **Garfield Mountain** (2,580 feet), to the northeast of Panther Mountain. As you can see, the hiking possibilities are unlimited in the South Central Catskills.

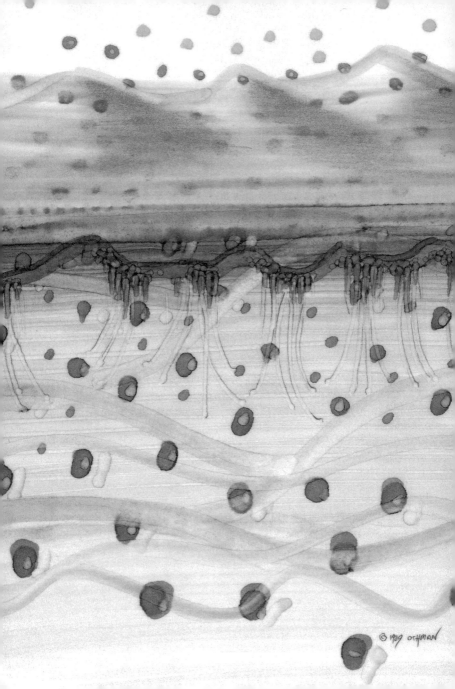

© 1989 OTHMAN

NORTH CENTRAL CATSKILLS

Shadows of Smiles

she only shadows of smiles
on her face
only shadows
in the sunlight
we darken the day
under shadows of smiles
on our face

We've designated the North Central area of the Catskills as the land north of Route 28 and west of the gorge located between North Dome and West West Kill Mountain. A good deal of this area lies outside the "Blue Line" that marks the Catskill Forest Preserve, with most of the land in northern Delaware County and western Greene County. Parts of the area are state-owned, including two large tracts on the north and south sides of Spruceton Valley, and most of Halcott Mountain. North Dome, Sherrill and Halcott Mountains are on Map #42 of the Trail Conference Catskill Maps, but you'll need other maps for the areas to the north. The North Central area includes several towns, Roxbury, Prattsville and Stamford, which are of historic significance. Many visitors are drawn to the region not only because of its natural beauty, but also to visit these places of historical interest.

The North Central Catskills offer many excellent hikes on private land that few hikers would think of trying because so little has been written about them in the past. We've found that in almost every case the courteous hiker is granted permission by the landowner, who is generally glad to take a few minutes out to chat. This is a great way to get to know the people of the Catskills and experience their true hospitality.

You'll find more farms and high clearings when hiking on private land outside the Forest Preserve than you will inside the Blue Line. These private farmlands are probably a good representation of what the Catskills looked like in the late 1800's when much of the land was cleared for farming and logging. Hiking up through a sprawling open pasture nearly 3,000 feet in elevation is an exhilarating experience that few hikers get the chance to enjoy. The wide views of open distant valleys form a patchwork of farms and stage the backdrop to many a tall wildflower. Areas with this type of landscape include Ashland, Roxbury, Stamford and Andes. It helps to use a USGS topo map, not just for the planned hike, but to assist you in negotiating the unpaved and unmarked roads which lead to your desired starting point.

———

"It is not always our line
of sight that proves to be
the shortest distance
between two points!"

———

NORTH DOME-SHERRILL AREA

"This area can be a real challenge for the experienced bushwhacker."

*t*hese two mountains, North Dome and Sherrill, are located in a large state-owned tract of land west of the Devil's Path which has been designated as a wilderness area. The area shows little evidence of man and almost appears to look as it might have a thousand years ago. At one time there was some talk of pushing the Devil's Path on past its present end and over North Dome and Sherrill but, fortunately, this has never been done.

North Dome and Sherrill make an excellent *bushwhack*; you're not likely to run into other hikers here. Water sources are rare at the higher elevations, so bring plenty of fluids. As with all bushwhacks, the routes you could choose to reach your destination are practically limitless.

The most popular route up **North Dome** is an old trail that goes up the south side of the mountain from Timber Lake Camp, which is located in Broadstreet Hollow. However permission to hike must be obtained from the owner of the camp, and the trail is closed in the summer. We once received a report of a hiker who had his car towed away when he parked there illegally! This route has many excellent views, and we suggest that you try to get the owner's permission if you wish to enjoy them.

In the summer, you may want to climb North Dome from Mink Hollow (not the same as the one between Sugarloaf and Plateau Mountains to the east), the col between West West Kill and North Dome Mountains. This route is steep but rewarding. Take the Devil's Path from a small parking lot on Spruceton Road at the trail's western end about 3.25 miles east of West Kill Village and Route 42. When you reach the col, you will come to a small swampy clearing on the right (west) directly below the steep, rocky face of North Dome. Leave the trail at this point, pass the outlet of the swamp and head west, working your way up through the very steep, rocky ledges. At about 3,400 feet, the mountain begins to level off.

Before you continue on to the summit, you may want to spend some time exploring this area, as *many views* can be found from these ledges to the north, or to the south from the head of the trail coming up from Timber Lake Camp. Directly to the east and across the deep col is the 3,420-foot peak known as West West Kill or St. Anne's Peak. Hunter Mountain is further to the east, while Rusk Mountain is to the northeast, across the Sprucoton Valley. From the southern viewpoint, you can also see the many peaks of the Southern Catskills.

From these ledges, you'll now have to set your compass west for the 3,610-foot summit of North Dome with a register box put up by the Catskill 3500 Club. Near the top, the forest turns into a thick grove of balsam fir trees. We saw evidence of weasel and snowshoe hare near the summit.

After you've signed in, you'll want to take another compass reading to reach **Mount Sherrill**. As you proceed west, you will come to a fir grove so thick that you will be forced to go around it. The descent off North Dome westward is gradual, and

after a drop of 550 feet or so you'll reach the col between North Dome and Mount Sherrill. A short scramble that traverses a few steep rocky areas takes you up about 500 feet to the top of Mount Sherrill (elevation 3,540 feet). You'll find the summit has some fir trees mixed in with the predominant hardwoods. Steep ledges near the top give a *fine view* to the southeast. Of course, there is also a Catskill 3500 Club summit box to sign on Sherrill.

Keep an eye on your compass for your return trip. The truly adventurous might want to leave a car near Route 42 and proceed down over a ridge known as

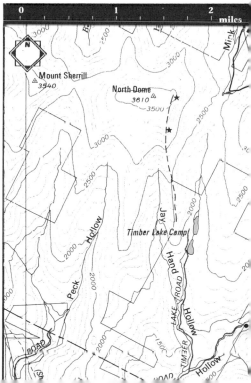

Balsam Mountain (not to be confused with Balsam Mountain on the Pine Hill-West Branch Trail). Since the difference in elevation between Balsam and Sherrill is only 120 feet, Balsam cannot really be considered a separate mountain. From Balsam, the drop into Deep Notch and Route 42 is 1,300 feet in 0.6 mile. This area can be a real challenge for the experienced bushwhacker.

An alternative (and much easier) route is to follow another ridge southwest off Sherrill that leads to a Forest Preserve parking area off Route 42 in the vicinity of the Catskill Aqueduct.

NORTH OF SPRUCETON VALLEY

The North Dome Range runs along the south side of Spruceton Valley, but the north side of this valley also provides *excellent bushwhacking* opportunities for hikers looking for *solitude and good views*. Just west of Rusk Mountain is **Evergreen Mountain** (elevation 3,360 feet), with fine ledges on the south side of its level summit allowing a close-up view of Spruceton Valley and the North Dome Range.

Attached to Evergreen and further west are two smaller peaks known as **Pine Island** (3,140 feet) and **Packsaddle Mountains** (3,100 feet). The state owns most of the land along the ridge line but most of the lower land is privately owned. You should carefully check your map for the best access routes to avoid private land.

The romantic Schoharie Creek is north of Spruceton Valley.

HALCOTT MOUNTAIN

---

*"One of which
had settled into
the landscape,
radiating
an intense
mysterious aura—
a photographer's
delight."*

*h*alcott Mountain
stands west of Route 42 and can
be climbed from several different starting points. *Trailless, it
makes a pleasant bushwhack* for
the day hiker, with a canister
placed by the Catskill 3500 Club
marking the summit. Halcott is
connected by a ridge to a 3,408-
foot peak shown on some maps
as **Northeast Halcott Mountain**, which could also make an
interesting bushwhack. The state
owns the areas around both summits and down to Route 42 on
the eastern slopes. It is also possible to approach Halcott from the
south or west, but these approaches involve crossing private
land, and permission from the
landowners must be obtained.

The summit of Halcott has
few if any views. It is dominated
by black cheery trees and other
slope hardwoods. However, we
did find an *open ledge with views
southwest* at an elevation of approximately 3,000 feet, south of

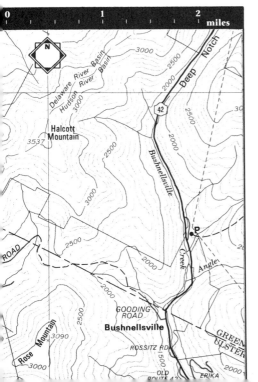

On the way up Halcott Mountain.

the summit at the edge of state land. On a visit there in summer, one of us almost stepped on the nest of a hermit thrush—the mother didn't fly away until we were about three feet away! Naturally, we left the delicate blue-green eggs alone, and we hope that the mother returned to raise her family.

Once, on an overcast winter day, as we slowly snowshoed our way to the summit of Halcott, we came upon some interesting stone buildings. One of which had settled into the landscape, radiating an intense mysterious aura—a photographer's delight Nearby we watched a flock of bright yellow evening grosbeaks feeding against the backdrop of a hemlock grove.

You may well be surprised by an unexpected view or some trace of early Catskill history while hiking Halcott. *This is a beautiful area worth exploring!*

VLY & BEARPEN MOUNTAINS

Turk Hollow and Vly Mountain from Vly Creek.

*V*ly and Bearpen stand out above the surrounding area and offer *fine panoramas of the countryside*. Both of these peaks are privately owned and permission to hike them must be obtained. Although on the required list of peaks for membership in the Catskill 3500 Club, these mountains are actually outside of the Catskill Park and do not appear on the Catskill Trails map set published by the New York-New Jersey Trail Conference. They are found on the USGS topo maps for West Kill and Prattsville.

Vly Mountain lies to the north of Halcott Mountain and may be reached by a number of routes. The easiest is via the old *Halcott Mountain Road*, which runs between Bearpen and Vly. This road is a remnant of an old turnpike that ran through the mountains from the valley to the south. According to Michael Kudish, this road dates back prior to 1856 and was one of five turnpikes that crossed the range between Halcott and Roundtop (also known as Onteora Mountain) in the 19th century.

Although we chose to hike Vly and Bearpen separately and at different times of the year, many hikers elect to do them together.

We approached Vly from Halcott Mountain Road, at the end of a beautiful valley west of the mountain, on a very windy day in early March. After obtaining permission from the landowner, we made a short, steep ascent that led us to partial views over Johnson Hollow. We continued up to the level summit (elevation 3,529 feet) which is dominated by a mixture of hardwoods such as black cherry, mountain ash and beech.

There is a summit box on top that was put up by the Catskill 3500 Club so that you can register your accomplishment. On this visit, the trees were glazed with up to an inch of ice

Huntersfield Range at the horizon from old abandoned ski slope on Bearpen Mountain.

due to an ice storm the night before. We found several *views looking southward* toward the peak attached to Vly known as **South Vly** (elevation 3,360 feet). There are also *open views from the north side* overlooking Bearpen Mountain and the Schoharie Valley, through which Route 23A runs. Vly is a delightful summit in an area not often visited by most hikers.

Just south of Vly, there is a state-maintained **lean-to** in *Turk Hollow*, east of County Route 3 which leads into Johnson Hollow. Designated as the **Halcott Lean-to**, it is unusual because it is located far from any marked trails and in an area that is definitely off the beaten path. Our research suggests it is probably one of the remaining lean-tos built by the Civilian Conservation Corps in the 1930's.

To reach this lean-to, drive up Turk Hollow to a point where the road becomes rough and unpaved. There is a house here (on your left) and you'll see many "posted" signs. You'll need to get permission to park here. From this point, walk up the road (part of an old turnpike dating back to the early 1800's) for about 15 minutes, passing private lands. A sign will soon point to the lean-to, located to the right in open woods at about elevation 2,200 feet.

The lean-to has three fireplaces, a nearby outhouse, a sturdy wooden floor and *running water nearby* (the water may not be reliable during the dry season). This lean-to gives easy access for those wishing to bushwhack up South Vly or Northeast Halcott and, because of its seclusion, it also makes an excellent choice for those who just wish to spend a quiet night in the woods.

Bearpen is northwest of Vly in an area that shows much evidence of prior use by man. Hikers and residents of neighboring valleys have been going there for years to enjoy the *view north over*

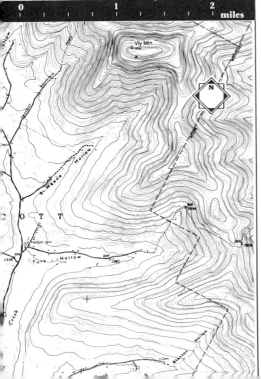

the Schoharie Valley. An old jeep road goes all the way to the top of this mountain. We hiked it on a cool, clear day in late October, picking up the jeep trail at the end of Ski Run Road, which is a dirt road north of the summit. This jeep trail is actually another of the old turnpikes that traversed this range of mountains in the 1800's.

Our hike was a long horseshoe-shaped walk from the valley to the summit. Although the hike was nearly 3.5 miles each way, we found it to be quite easy. The lower part of the road passes through a state-owned reforestation area that has been logged. After passing the 3,440-foot summit of Roundtop Mountain (also known as Ontcora Mountain), a branch of the road forks to the left and leads to the top of Bearpen. (The right fork heads down to the valley on the other side of the mountain).

Bearpen is the farthest northwest of all the 3,500-foot peaks; therefore, it offers *unique views.* As you round the valley and approach the summit, you'll enter a clearing in front of a low abandoned concrete building that is, of all colors, pink. This structure, which has not been used for over twenty years, was once a small ski lodge. The clearing is one of three old ski

On the way to Bearpen Mountain.

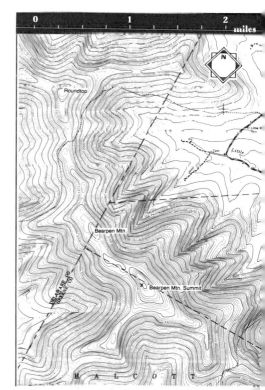

slopes that are still visible on the northern side of the mountain.

On a clear day there are excellent views from the top of these open slopes. Part of the Schoharie Reservoir can be seen to the north, and the Huntersfield Mountain Range stands out distinctly to the northeast.

The true summit is a short but steep scamper of 120 feet just beyond the abandoned ski house, and the views are even more impressive from it. A pleasant surprise is the *view west* toward the quiet valley and farmlands around Roxbury. Despite being 3,600 feet in elevation, the summit of Bearpen is covered only with hardwoods. It should also be noted that there is no summit box on the top of this mountain.

Bearpen is attached by a ridge to **South Bearpen** (elevation 3,410 feet), which would make an *interesting bushwhack.*

HIKING WEST OF BEARPEN

"*Mount Utsayantha…is named for an Indian princess who, according to legend, took her life in despair over a forbidden love affair with a white settler.*"

*W*est of Bearpen, the range of mountains continues with **Roundtop** (3,440 feet), **Shultice** (3,280 feet) and **Irish** (3,060 feet) **Mountains**, then crosses Route 30 and continues on as the **Moresville Range**, which reaches an elevation of 3,160 feet. The range ends with **McGregor Mountain** (3,180 feet) and **Mount Utsayantha** (3,214 feet). All these mountains traverse private property, but with permission from the landowners you can put together an interesting and extensive hike.

Mount Utsayantha is located near Route 23 and the West Branch of the Delaware River. It is named for an Indian princess who, according to legend, took

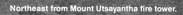
Northeast from Mount Utsayantha fire tower.

her life in despair over a forbidden love affair with a white settler. A trail leads up the mountain's north side, and a dirt and gravel road (passable by car) surmounts the summit from the south. The "grave" of Utsayantha lies beside this road about halfway up the mountain. On the top, there are several small buildings and a fire tower still operated by the state.

Mount Utsayantha is well worth a visit for its *excellent views*, it being the highest mountain in the area. There are wooden tables on the summit, making this a great place for a family picnic. To the west, the mountains begin to round off and gradually lead into rolling dairy and farm country. This becomes evident as you view the scene from the *fire tower* and see a patchwork of fields, lakes and woods dotted with farm silos. From this vantage point, you get the impression that you are looking at a plateau to the north and west.

Churchill Mountain (3,060 feet) stands out to the southwest. Looking southeast over nearby McGregor Mountain, you can count the peaks all the way to Bearpen Mountain. Binoculars will help you see the old ski area on Bearpen's northern slope. The higher peaks of the Central Catskills can be seen in the background. Glancing east, you can see the entire Schoharie Reservoir and the Huntersfield Range beyond it.

Don't overlook the lovely town of Stamford lying at the base of Mount Utsayantha to the west. The founding settlers of this community were from Stamford, Connecticut. Today, the town still has an air of New England about it. There are many hiking trails around Stamford that go through farmland and over hills, and provide an interesting way to see the area.

Known as the **Utsayantha Trail System**, these trails are laid out on private land with the cooperation of the landowners. For more information, call the Western Catskills Community Revitalization Council, Inc. at (607) 652-2823. Maps can be obtained in the town of Stamford or at the DEC regional sub-office on Jefferson Road north of town.

There may also be some rewarding hiking near Route 30 in the Roxbury area, especially **White Man Mountain** (3,140 feet) and its surrounding area. Some of the mountains on the east side of Route 30 have clearings on or near their summits which offer excellent views. Note that they are all on private land, so permission to hike must be obtained.

Of special interest in the Roxbury area is the *John Burroughs Memorial Field* and "boyhood rock" site. On the side of Old Clump Mountain northwest of Roxbury lies the rock where John Burroughs used to sit and ponder his future. Burroughs is buried just in front of this rock.

One of the first true naturalists and nature writers in this country, John Burroughs introduced Slide Mountain to the world and was a true lover of the simple things in life. The open field in front of the rock, full of wildflowers, and the wall of mountains to the east call to mind his concerns and insights into the mystery of life through his unmistakable Zen like powers of observation and intuition. A line from his poem "Waiting," which is inscribed on the rock, speaks for itself: *"I stand amid eternal ways and what is mine shall know my face."*

THE HUNTERS FIELD RANGE

"If you're adventurous, you'll enjoy the challenge of exploring 'off the beaten path' and discovering something new in the back roads and high hills surrounded by farms and pastures."

for the hiker who wants to see the mountains from a different perspective, the **Huntersfield Range** is a very interesting area. Located northeast of Bearpen (and north of Route 23), this range is dominated by **Huntersfield Mountain** (elevation 3,423 feet). Other mountains include **Ashland Pinnacle** (3,060 feet), **Richmond Mountain** (3,220 feet), **Rictmyer Peak** (2,950 feet) and **Mount Pisgah**. Although there is much private land surrounding these mountains, the state owns the ridge lines as reforestation or multiple use areas, and woods roads abound. This is the most northerly Catskill range, with peaks over 3,000 feet in elevation.

Our hike up Huntersfield Mountain is a good example of what to expect in this area. Permission was easy to get from the farmer who owned the land on the route we chose (although he couldn't figure out why we'd want to hike up a mountain on a cloudy and windy January day). The farm pasture rising high up on the mountainside afforded *views of the Catskills from an unusual perspective* rarely enjoyed by hikers. Once in the forest, the walking was easy under the hardwood canopy. Although the climbing was continuous, we found no severely steep areas to negotiate. We noticed state land markers as we ascended. The summit was shrouded in clouds on our hike, but it's likely that good views could be found (especially when the leaves are down) if you're willing to look for them.

Huntersfield stands out from all the nearby mountains, espec-ially those to the north and west. A forest ranger once told us that a marker was set in the ground on the summit to designate the boundary between Schoharie and Greene Counties. We were unable to locate it due to the snow cover, but it would be an interesting goal in warmer seasons. As is normally the case in this area, the summit is covered with hardwoods.

Hikes like these await all of you "ramblers" who want to see another side of the Catskills. If you're adventurous, you'll enjoy the challenge of exploring off the beaten path and discovering something new in the back roads and high hills surrounded by farms and pastures.

"Off The Beaten Path"

West of Black Dome Valley and south of Route 23 there is a range of mountains that runs east to west. **Cave Mountain** (3,100 feet) is large enough to allow the hiker to explore the state land on its south and east slopes without ever seeing the Windham Ski Area that runs down the north side of the mountain. Several clearings on the south side of this mountain afford *fine views* of the mountains to the south. To the west of Cave is 2,960-foot **Tower Mountain**. Attached to Tower Mountain is the **Patterson Ridge** (2,860 feet), which is several miles long. Although this range is on private land, with the owner's permission a fine hike can be planned here.

Other areas to explore are **Rose Mountain** (3,090 feet), which is a privately owned peak between Route 28 and Halcott Mountain just south of the northern border of Ulster County. To its west is small, 2,486-foot **Monka Hill**, on which the huge Grand Hotel once stood. Today, the same view of Slide Mountain that the hotel guests once enjoyed can be obtained by the hiker. Many used the hotel as a starting point from which to set out and explore the Southern Catskills, visible from the piazza of the hotel.

One interesting note is that the Grand Hotel was built with the boundary between the towns of Shandaken and Middletown dividing it. At different points in time the towns went dry and outlawed liquor, causing the hotel's bar to shift from one end of the huge building to the other more than once. This kept the liquor flowing and was a big attraction in its time.

Another area to explore is 2,220-foot **Sheridan Mountain** just west of Route 214. Although this mountain is on private land, the area to its north, which is state-owned, has several ridges that run up toward West Kill Mountain which would be well worth exploring.

To the west of Route 30 and just south of Roxbury is the Plat-

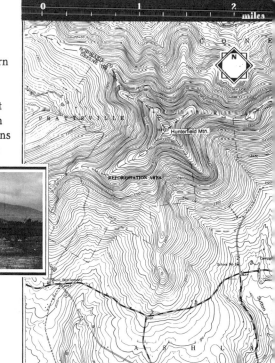

ROAD CLASSIFICATION

Heavy duty —————— Light duty ——————
Medium duty —————— Unimproved dirt ========

*"The farm pasture
rising high up on
the mountainside
afforded views of
the Catskills from an
unusual perspective rarely
enjoyed by hikers."*

Photos from Huntersfield.

tekill Ski Area. It is surrounded by state land high on ridges around **North** (3,340 feet) and **South** (3,260 feet) **Plattekill Mountains**. *Good views west* can be obtained from the higher elevations of North Plattekill and the summit north of it. You can gain access to the state land from Roses Brook Road on the north side of the ridge line. You can also enter via the Plattekill Ski Area at the end of Meeker Hollow. The USGS topo map for Hobart should help you find your way (make sure you have the latest revision, dated 1983). To the west lies **Mt. Pisgah** (3,343 feet). Standing above the surrounding land, it also has a ski area on it. The entire area is privately owned, but it is worth the effort to obtain permission to hike it.

We'd also like to mention that there is *fine hiking in Schoharie County*, although the area does not contain the high elevations and steepness found further south in the Catskills. There is one marked trail that runs from West Kill Road (just west of North Blenheim) to a parking area near Rossman Valley Road, a few miles south of Cobleskill. This enjoyable 11.6-mile trail runs roughly north-south and parallels Route 30, which is to the east. It has moderate grades and passes through a fine mixture of farm lands and woods. It also surmounts **Looking Glass Mountain**, which is barely over the 2,000-foot level. In the winter, *this trail offers fine cross-country skiing*, despite the fact that it crosses several roads. For further information and a rough map of the trail, contact the DEC office in Stamford.

Winter's walk on Huntersfield.

©1989 OCHMAN

WESTERN CATSKILLS

Windless Leaves

walking fields...through
windless leaves
on wing from above

sky the mackerel blue
beyond summers' breeze
of colors we love

walking fields...through
windless leaves
of color color color
feather down from
sunlit trees &
feather down
beneath windless leaves
of color color color

 s the Catskills stretch westward, they drop off in height. None of the mountains in the Western Catskills exceeds 3,500 feet in elevation, and they lack the sheer rock ledges of the higher mountains to the east. Moreover, as you go farther west the summits become more heavily wooded and lack the evergreen tops characteristic of the eastern summits. The summits of the Western Catskills are topped with such species as red and chestnut oak, and in this respect they resemble the more southerly Pocono Mountains of Pennsylvania. (In the Eastern Catskills, such summit vegetation is found only on parts of the eastern ridge of mountains rising from the Hudson Valley).

The heavy cover of hardwoods limits the views available from the higher elevations, but it also makes for colorful fall hiking. In winter and spring, when the leaves are down, you'll be able to find additional views. Wildflowers proliferate on the forest floor in the spring. Another delight that awaits the explorer in the Western Catskills is the many small ponds and lakes that dot the area.

In the early 1980's, there was a serious defoliation problem in the Catskills, with the Western Catskills being affected most severely. The problem was caused by a combination of pests which attacked the trees in the area, including the forest tent caterpillar, the gypsy moth and the saddled prominent. While some trees were killed by the defoliation, in most cases the leaves regenerated once the pests became dormant. As a result of the unusual amount of sunlight which reached the forest floor because of the defoliation, large areas of underbrush have sprouted and spread in the last few years.

In some areas, the ground cover (such as the sticky blackberry) has nearly obscured the trails. The DEC is aware of the situation and is taking remedial action, but it will take time to clear all the trails, especially since some of the tenacious plants have gotten a strong foothold in many areas.

The roads in the area are hilly, winding and often unpaved. However, trail access is well marked, and the inaccessibility of some roads adds to the rural flavor of the area. Most of the land in the valleys and along the roads is privately owned, while the state owns large tracts of land on the ridgetops. There are many cabins and trailer homes in the area, owned mainly by people who reside elsewhere and use them as summer homes or as hunter's lodges during the fall big game season.

For those willing to forsake wide panoramas in favor of solitude, the Western Catskills offer fine hiking opportunities. The open fields that fill with deer

"The open fields that fill with deer in the evenings add to the feeling of 'backwoods Appalachia' that you experience here."

Covered bridge over the Beaverkill.

in the evenings (except during hunting season) add to the feeling of "backwoods Appalachia" that you experience here. Camping is permitted anywhere on state land (except where specifically prohibited); you need not worry about the 3,500-foot rule because no mountains in the area attain that elevation. The Western Catskills are a prime habitat of the wild turkey, which travels in flocks all winter, and we've also seen signs of bobcats and coyotes throughout the area.

"For those willing to forsake wide panoramas in favor of solitude, the Western Catskills offer fine hiking opportunities."

We've defined the Western Catskills as the area west of the Dry Brook Ridge Trail and the Neversink-Hardenburgh Trail and south of Route 28. (Since the mountains taper off into the Appalachian Plateau, it is very difficult to designate a definite western boundary for the Catskills). **The Western Catskills can in turn be subdivided into two trail systems.** *The eastern trail system, in Ulster and Sullivan Counties,* includes the Long Pond-Beaverkill Trail, the Mongaup-Hardenburgh Trail and the Mongaup-Willowemoc Trail. Together with the Neversink-Hardenburgh Trail, which we've included as part of the South Central Catskills (see pages 240-242), these trails, which are shown on Map #43 of the Trail Conference Catskill Trail Maps, make a large loop which would make a nice two or three-day backpacking trip. Although portions of the trails follow drivable roads, these roads are little used and provide enjoyable hiking. You can also use these trails for day hikes, but it would help to have two cars so you won't have to retrace your steps.

The western trail system, located in Delaware County, is composed of several interconnecting trails which primarily run in an east-west direction. These trails follow the ridges which lie south of the Pepacton Reservoir (which is really the dammed East Branch of the Delaware River); thus, this trail system is often referred to as the Delaware Ridge System. These trails are shown on Map #44 of the Trail Conference Catskill Trail Maps. Many of these trails (especially those west of Holiday and Berry Brook Road) were originally designed for snowmobiles. By following all or portions of six different trails, you can make up a 22.2-mile hike, suitable for a two or three-day backpacking trip. Or you can choose to use these trails for enjoyable day hikes. Again, it will probably be best if you can leave a car at each end of the hike (although there are short loops possible at the eastern and western ends of the trail system).

The DEC has plans to connect the Delaware County trail system with Balsam Lake Mountain by constructing a new trail along the Mill Brook Ridge, which is presently trailless. At present, however, the Delaware Ridge System does not connect with the remainder of the Catskill trail system.

*Ulster &
Sullivan Counties*

LONG POND-
BEAVERKILL
RIDGE TRAIL

**Northeast toward the Beaverkill Range
from the outlet of Long Pond.**

*t*his *red-blazed* trail takes you through varied terrain as it traverses country roads and forests and eventually climbs up a spur of the Beaver Kill Ridge, where it terminates at a junction with the Mongaup-Hardenburgh Trail. The **Long Pond-Beaverkill Trail** is 7.6 miles long, and links up with four other trails.

The trail begins at the junction of Basily Road and Willowemoc Road, 0.3 mile north of Round Pond. Trail marker signs indicate that the *yellow-*

blazed **Neversink-Hardenburgh Trail** continues ahead on Willowemoc Road, while the **Long Pond-Beaverkill Ridge Trail** goes left onto Basily Road, an unpaved road which is impassable by car in the winter. You will also notice *large orange disc markers designating a snowmobile trail* which follows the route of the Long Pond-Beaverkill Ridge Trail.

In the winter, the snowmobile tracks pack down the snow and make it possible to hike over the snow even without snowshoes. These tracks can also be used for *cross-country skiing.* One of us once cross-country skied into Long Pond with his wife and we were afforded an excellent day of exercise (and excitement— when snowmobilers came rumbling along behind us).

The first mile of the trail is moderately uphill, with the trail climbing about 300 feet. The trail then briefly leaves the Forest Preserve and passes a cabin and open clearing to the left, which provides a view to the south. The prominent ridge in the foreground is a part of Blue Hill. The trail then returns to state land and begins to descend. After 2.4 miles, the trail turns left and leaves the road. Cars can be driven to this point in good weather.

Continuing on the trail, you'll pass several small hemlock groves which may be remnants of the virgin forest which escaped the tanners (although we've been unable to verify this). In any case, they provide a nice contrast to the surrounding hardwoods and offer good protection from wind and snow in winter.

You'll cross over from Ulster County to Sullivan County and, 3.8 miles from the start, you'll reach a junction with a short red-blazed spur trail to the left which leads in 0.2 mile to the **Long Pond Lean-to**. The lean-to, which looks out over Long Pond, has a wood floor and is in good condition. There is a register box at the trail junction, which enables you to check on how much the lean-to has been used lately. You'll probably find that it's been used rather lightly.

One afternoon, while we enjoyed some hot chocolate at the lean-to, we met some beaver trappers dressed in 18th century garb. Despite the near-zero degree weather that night, they were going to rough it under the stars with wool blankets and animal hides!

Long Pond is secluded and offers a primitive wilderness experience. You'll want to explore the beaver lodges and dams near the outlet at the southern end of the pond. From here, you'll also find a *view to the northeast* towards the Beaver Kill Range.

The Long Pond-Beaverkill Ridge Trail then proceeds northward, away from the pond, and descends steeply to cross Willowemoc Creek on a small bridge. At 4.25 miles it reaches Flugertown Road, with the hamlet of Willowemoc a few miles to the left (south). The trail follows the road to the right (north) for about 0.1 mile, then turns left and re-enters the woods. At this point, the trail is joined by the *yellow-blazed* **Mongaup-Willowemoc Trail**, and both trails follow the same route for 0.5 mile. The trail begins to climb, briefly crossing back into Ulster County and then re-entering Sullivan County. At 5.0 miles, the Mongaup-Willowemoc Trail goes left, eventually reaching Mongaup Pond in 3.1 miles.

Continue on the *red-blazed* trail, which soon crosses back in-

---

"Despite the near-zero degree weather that night, they were going to rough it under the stars with wool blankets and animal hides."

Time to drink...time to rest...time to breathe.

to Ulster County. After a level stretch, the trail begins a rather steep climb of a spur of the Beaver Kill Ridge, ascending about 400 feet in 0.5 mile. At 6.1 miles, you'll reach the ridge line (elevation 2,754 feet), and the trail will remain relatively level for about another mile. There are no worthwhile views from this spur; even when the leaves are down you can see only undiscer-nible parts of mountains through the trees to the right (east). After a gradual climb of about 250 feet, you'll reach a junction with the *blue-blazed* **Mongaup-Hardenburgh Trail**, 7.35 miles from the start (elevation 3,062 feet). To the left, it's 3.2 miles to Mongaup Pond, while to the right it's the same distance to Beaver Kill Road.

*Ulster &
Sullivan Counties*

MONGAUP HARDEN-BURGH TRAIL

"The deep powder made the going rough, but the beauty of this winter wonderland made it all worthwhile."

*t*his *blue-blazed* 6.4-mile trail, completed in 1977, is not heavily used and offers solitude year-round. Although the tall hardwoods along the trail preclude any wide views (except possibly off the trail when the leaves are down), it makes a good backpacking trip, since there are several undisturbed level areas on and between the peaks traversed by the trail. There are also interesting bog areas to explore in the cols.

We'll start from the northern end of the trail, which begins on the south side of Beaver Kill Road about 6.8 miles east of the Turnwood junction (which is just south of the road to the Little

A pristine snowy morning on the Beaverkill Ridge.

Pond State Campsite and a few miles north of the hamlet of Lew Beach). A small parking area is located at the trailhead. After passing a register box, the trail descends to cross the legendary *Beaver Kill* on a shaky footbridge.

We once hiked this trail on a cold, beautiful day, with fresh snow clinging to the trees. The deep powder made the going rough (even with snowshoes), but the beauty of this winter wonderland made it all worthwhile.

After crossing the stream, the trail begins a steady ascent of about 1,000 feet in 1.5 miles, *one of the most arduous climbs in the Western Catskills.* If the leaves are down, you might be able to pick out Woodpecker Ridge and Mill Brook Ridge to the north as you climb. You'll finally reach the highest and first summit of the **Beaver Kill Ridge** (elevation 3,224 feet).

After dropping over 300 feet into a col, you'll begin a fairly steep ascent to the second summit (elevation 3,062 feet), which is 3.0 miles from the start. There are partial views to the left (southeast) as the trail comes close to the side of the ridge. After dropping about 150 feet, you'll reach a junction with the *red-blazed* **Long Pond-Beaverkill Ridge Trail**, which

drops southward to Flugertown Road and Long Pond. You've now gone 3.2 miles from the start.

From here, the trail continues along the ridge and then climbs about 100 feet, cresting on the first summit of Mongaup Mountain (elevation 2,928 feet), 3.7 miles from the start. After dropping into a col, you'll start a fairly steep climb of about 400 feet to the middle summit of Mongaup Mountain (elevation 2,989 feet), which is 4.8 miles from the beginning of the trail. The true summit of Mongaup Mountain (elevation 3,177 feet), is about 1.5 miles to the west. This summit is trailless, but it makes an *interesting bushwhack* for those experienced enough to leave the beaten path.

Continuing on the trail from the middle summit, you'll descend steadily, dropping 700 feet and reaching the Mongaup Pond State Campsite 6.4 miles from the start. (Of course, two cars are essential if you want to make this a one-way day hike, as we've described it). ◣◢

Suspension bridge over the Beaverkill on Mongaup-Hardenburgh Trail.

*Ulster &
Sullivan Counties*

MONGAUP-WILLOWEMOC TRAIL

"*The best time to enjoy this trail is in the spring, when the brooks are at their fullest, the wildflowers are blooming on the forest floor and trail usage is at its lowest.*"

*a*n easy walk, with some gentle climbs, this *yellow-blazed* trail is four miles long. It is an ideal hike for beginners who wish to take a nature walk or for those who wish to get in shape for more strenuous hikes. In the winter, it is used as a snowmobile trail. While this packs the snow down and makes walking easy, don't expect much peace and quiet on winter weekends.

The best time to enjoy this trail is the spring, when the brooks are at their fullest, the wildflowers are blooming on the forest floor and trail usage is at its lowest.

We'll begin at the southeast end of the **Mongaup Pond State Campsite**, which is heavily used in the summer months. The trail heads eastward, gradually ascending 300 feet and reaching a ridge in about a mile. It then begins a descent of about 400 feet, crossing a small stream, and reaches *Butternut Brook* (the low point of the hike) at 2.1 miles. The brook is lined with hemlocks and is cool in the summer, making this a pleasant place to stop and rest.

After crossing the brook on a wooden bridge, the trail continues through tall hardwoods and crosses a dirt road at 2.9 miles. To the right, this road leads to Flugertown Road; to the left, it leads to privately-owned Sand Pond. The trail then crosses another brook and, 3.2 miles from the start, joins the *red-blazed* **Long Pond-Beaverkill Trail**, which comes in from the left. Both trails descend along the same route, and you'll reach Flugertown Road (the end of the Mongaup-Willowemoc Trail) 3.6 miles from the start.

"Off The Beaten Path"

There are many other places in the area that are worth exploring. Much of the land is state-owned, and *there are a surprising number of small ponds and lakes throughout the area,* many of which show signs of beaver activity. These ponds and lakes contain a great diversity of life, and provide an excellent opportunity to study the many plants and animals found in the area.

One trailless area which you might want to visit is the **Beaver Kill Range**, south of Balsam Lake Mountain, which separates the watersheds of the Beaver Kill on the north from those of the West Branch of the Neversink and Willowemoc Creek on the south. (The Beaver Kill Range should not be confused with the Beaver Kill Ridge, farther to the west, which is traversed by the Mongaup-Hardenburgh Trail).

This range reaches an elevation of 3,377 feet, and the summits contain areas of virgin balsam fir, the farthest west such trees are found on the summits of Catskill peaks. Situated in a

Morning fog over dry swamp beneath Mill Brook Ridge.

designated wilderness area, the Beaver Kill Range sees little use and offers the experienced hiker an opportunity for strenuous backpacking, with occasional views of the surrounding mountains. The best access to the area is provided by the Neversink-Hardenburgh Trail.

The state once had plans to run a trail across the ridge from the Fall Brook Lean-to, but these plans have apparently been shelved, leaving a trailless wilderness area for those who wish to venture out on their own. We're glad to see that this area will remain trailless in the future.

Those wanting a less strenuous hike might want to explore the headwaters of *Willowemoc Creek*. The state owns most of the land surrounding the creek. A famous trout stream in its own right, the creek harbors a wealth of wildlife, making it a great place to observe mink, otter and a great variety of birds far away from roads or other people.

Another trailless area worth exploring is the **Mill Brook Ridge**, which can be accessed either from the west via Alder Lake or from the east via Balsam Lake Mountain. A beautiful area dominated by mature virgin hardwoods, Mill Brook Ridge is more than four miles long, with

several summits. The entire ridge is above 3,000 feet in elevation, but the maximum elevation reached is 3,480 feet. The views from the ridge are limited, but when the leaves are down you can see northward towards Margaretville and get a glimpse of Balsam Lake Mountain to the east or Alder Lake to the west.

One warm, peaceful April day, while resting at a viewpoint overlooking Alder Lake, we heard but could not see a flock of wild turkeys. Their clucking grew louder, then disappeared as suddenly as it came. As many a hunter has discovered, wild turkeys are wary birds, and we suspect that the bright red shirt one of us was wearing gave us away.

Shoulder high ferns in an open glade atop Mill Brook Ridge.

Alder Lake baby bye-bye.

There are two ridges just south of Mill Brook Ridge which are worth exploring. **Wood pecker Ridge** (elevation 3,460 feet) runs south from Mill Brook Ridge, while **Cradle Rock Ridge** (elevation 3,160 feet) is south of Alder Lake.

Alder Lake, one of the more recent land acquisitions by the state, is an area worth exploring in itself. We spotted a fine looking beaver lodge along its shore on our visit. During the warmer seasons, spotted newts can be seen swimming in the shallow areas near the shore, bats fly around at night, and yellow-bellied sap suckers rattle the trees on the slopes around the lake. Alder Lake makes a fine place for beginners to explore the Catskills for a day.

Another area that is an excellent place for a day hike or overnight trip is **Kelly Hollow**, north of Mill Brook Ridge. Although there are no designated hiking trails in this area, there is a *snowmobile trail* which makes a loop from two parking lots on Mill Brook Road (only a few hundred yards apart). This trail follows an old woods road and leads to a **lean-to** by a beaver pond nestled at the base of the ridge. Little used (except during the hunting season), this area offers a real sense of wilderness. The loop trail can be hiked in a few hours (allowing ample time for exploring), or you may choose to stay overnight at the lean-to.

LITTLE POND & TOUCH-ME-NOT TRAILS

"...you'll see apple trees and piles of rock laboriously put there by the farmer who once worked this land."

*L*ittle Pond Trail and Touch-Me-Not Trail are the most easterly trails of the *Delaware Ridge Trail System*. Completed in 1973, they both begin at the **Little Pond State Campground** (elevation 2,000 feet). While you could begin your hike with either trail, we'll start with the Little Pond Trail.

From the parking lot at the southeastern tip of Little Pond (where you'll see a sign for the red-blazed Touch-Me-Not Trail),

Morning fog on Little Pond.

proceed north along the eastern side of the pond. You'll notice some *yellow blazes*, which mark the start of the **Little Pond Trail**. At the northern end of the lake, the trail turns left, then crosses the inlet of the pond (which may be dry in the summer) and turns right (north). It begins a gradual ascent and parallels the inlet stream, which lies below and to

Frosted Touchmenot Mountain and deer tracks.

the right. You'll pass a swampy meadow to your right and continue uphill to some old farm clearings, where you'll see apple trees and piles of rock laboriously put there by the farmer who once worked this land. Soon afterwards, you'll pass a mature stand of spruce obviously planted as a windbreak. Notice how the area under these trees seems so dark and lifeless. In winter, grouse, deer and a number of other animals will seek shelter here from the wind and snow.

The trail then continues uphill, passing a small pond, and,

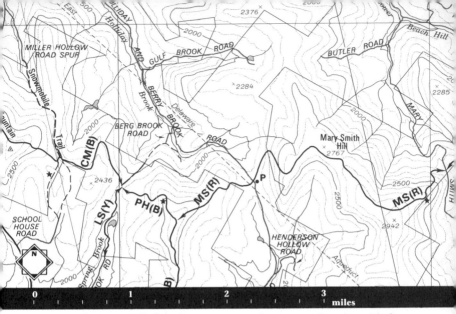

about one mile from its start, comes out in a large clearing. You can see the ruins of an outhouse past the pond on your left, with the foundation of the farmhouse visible nearby.

When we were there, the grass in this large rolling field was straw-colored, and the lack of trees gave the area a look similar to the Pentland Hills of northern Scotland.

Shortly beyond, you'll come to a weathered hilly outcrop, with a *fine view southward*. Touchmenot Mountain is prominent immediately to the southeast. From here, the trail heads uphill, re-entering the woods, and terminates 1.6 miles from the start at a junction with the *red-blazed* **Touch-Me-Not Trail** (elevation 2,400 feet).

At this point, you have the option of turning either right (east) or left (west) on the Touch-Me-Not Trail. If you choose to turn right, you'll begin an ascent of several hundred feet up the northwest ridge of **Touchmenot Mountain**. If there are no leaves on the trees, you'll be able to look back towards the farm clearing as you're ascending. You'll soon reach the 2,760-foot summit of the mountain. From the top, you'll descend steadily and seemingly forever through a hardwoods forest, with many white ash and black cherry trees, and

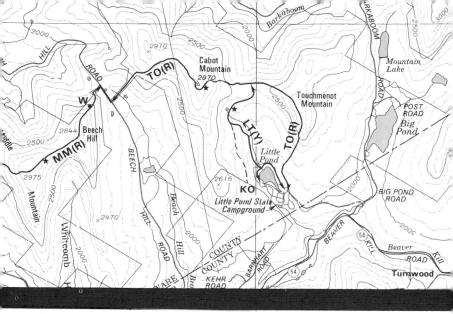

reach the parking lot of the Little Pond State Campground 1.25 miles from the junction.

If you plan on hiking over to Middle Mountain further to the west you should turn left at the junction of the Little Pond and Touch-Me-Not Trails, you'll begin to climb Cabot Mountain, first moderately and then rather steeply. There is much loose rock on the trail, and you'll have to use your hands to help pull yourself up in a few places.

After passing a *large rock overhang* to the left of the trail (which would make a good shelter in bad weather), you'll reach an *excellent viewpoint facing southward* near the top of Cabot Mountain. From this ledge, which stands out above the nearby trees, you should be able to pick out Mill Brook Ridge and Cradle Rock Ridge to the east. Balsam Lake Mountain can be seen in the background, and on a clear day you can make out Doubletop Mountain, a hump barely above the horizon. Continuing on the trail, you'll soon reach the short but level top of **Cabot Mountain** (elevation 2,970 feet), which should provide areas suitable for pitching a tent. You've now gone 1.25 miles from the trail junction.

From the summit, you'll descend gently for a short distance and then follow a ridge line, climbing briefly onto a spur. Here we passed an area that was heavily overgrown with ferns and blackberries, as we flushed out no less than six grouse. Although these birds normally prefer woods edges and clearings, in this case they obviously found the forest open enough, with the heavy ground cover providing sufficient protection from predators. The trail then starts to descend moderately, as it comes out alongside open meadows on the left (southeast). There is a wire fence and "posted" signs to warn you that this is private land. You'll soon reach Beech Hill Road, having traveled 2.75 miles from the trail junction. Looking back, you can see Cabot Mountain and the ridge which

Clearings on Little Pond Trail.

you just followed. To continue westward, turn right and follow the road 0.25 mile to the beginning of the **Middle Mountain Trail.**

Stark hawthorns in autumn's arms on Little Pond Trail.

Delaware County

MIDDLE
MOUNTAIN
TRAIL

*t*his two-mile *red-blazed* trail links the Touch-Me-Not Trail on the east with the Mary Smith Trail on the west. You'll notice a trail marker on the west side of Beech Hill Road about 0.25 mile north of the terminus of the Touch-Me-Not Trail. (Parking for a few cars is available on a wide section of the road a little further north).

The trail begins to ascend on a wide jeep road, but soon leaves the road and continues to ascend moderately. (The jeep road continues straight ahead onto private property). You'll notice blackberries, which make an enjoyable snack in late summer, growing along the trail. There is supposed to be a *small spring* just off the trail 0.3 mile from the start, but

Snow-capped Middle Mountain.

we couldn't locate it due to the leaf cover and the dryness of the season. After about half a mile, you'll reach the top of 2,844-foot **Beech Hill**, and then drop down about 140 feet.

We hiked this area in mid-October under a "yellow ceiling" aglow from the changing leaves of the maple-beech forest. Soon you'll begin a moderate climb of about 275 feet up Middle Mountain, passing through areas overgrown with blackberries. At about 0.9 mile, you'll reach a *viewpoint* over the Beaver Kill Valley to the southeast from a rock ledge (known as *Middle Mountain Vista*). We found this to be an ideal place to stop for lunch, and we enjoyed watching a tiny shrew scurry around in search for food on the ground some ten feet below us.

From this vista, the trail climbs gently to the summit of heavily-wooded **Middle Mountain** (elevation 2,975 feet). The summit is covered primarily with a beech-maple and black cherry forest, and there are areas suitable for camping nearby. After passing an open area to the right with some dead trees, you'll start to descend rather steeply. You can see Mary Smith Hill in the distance ahead as the trail zigzags down the mountainside.

If you climb onto one of the large rocks off the trail, you'll be able to get a partial view of the valley below. After a while, the descent becomes more gradual as you enter a mature forest with a tall canopy of trees. At 1.8 miles you'll see an old stone wall and "posted" signs, and at 2.0 miles you'll reach unpaved Mary Smith Hill Road, the end of the trail.

You'll notice a nice open field with a small lake on private property just to the left (south), and, looking back from the road, you'll be able to get a good view of Middle Mountain. There is room to park a few cars along the side of the road here. To the south, the road eventually becomes paved and reaches the hamlet of Lew Beach in about 3 miles.

We wouldn't suggest trying to negotiate this primitive dirt road in wet or snowy weather (except with a four-wheel drive vehicle). If you wish to continue farther west, the **Mary Smith Trail** begins straight across the road.

Delaware County

MARY SMITH TRAIL

f*our and one-half miles long,* this *red-blazed trail* connects the Middle Mountain and Pelnor Hollow Trails. It begins on Mary Smith Hill Road opposite the western end of the Middle Mountain Trail (elevation 2,250 feet), and, after passing through a stand of red pines, begins a fairly steep ascent of about 500 feet through a yellow birch forest. Near the top of this climb there is an area of dead and dying trees, with a profuse growth of ground cover. In about half a mile, the trail reaches a *fine viewpoint southward* down the valley. The trail levels off, then begins to ascend gently along a ridge line. In this area, we've noticed many signs of deer and wild turkeys, which are so prevalent in the Western Catskills.

The trail passes near the summit of an *unnamed 2,942-foot mountain* and then descends gradually along the ridge line, eventually passing close to the 2,767-foot summit of **Mary Smith Hill**. From here, the trail descends rather steeply, passing several level areas between the steep sections. At 3.3 miles, you'll come out onto a clearing and reach Holiday and Berry Brook Road (named after the two brooks which it follows at each end). The road is referred to by one or both names, depending on where you are (or which sign you happen to see). To the left, there is a parking area which will accommodate several cars.

The trail continues across the road on private land, passing through open areas and under power lines. Soon it re-enters the forest and proceeds uphill on state land, climbing about 500 feet to an unnamed summit, where it junctions with the *blue-blazed* **Pelnor Hollow Trail**. This junction is 1.2 miles from Holiday and Berry Brook Road and 4.5 miles from the start of the trail on Mary Smith Hill Road. If there are no leaves on the trees, you'll be able to get a good view of Mary Smith Hill from near the summit. You have the option of turning right and continuing west on the **Pelnor Hollow Trail,** or turning left and proceeding south.

It is not always our line of sight that proves to be the shortest distance between two points. From Mary Smith Hill.

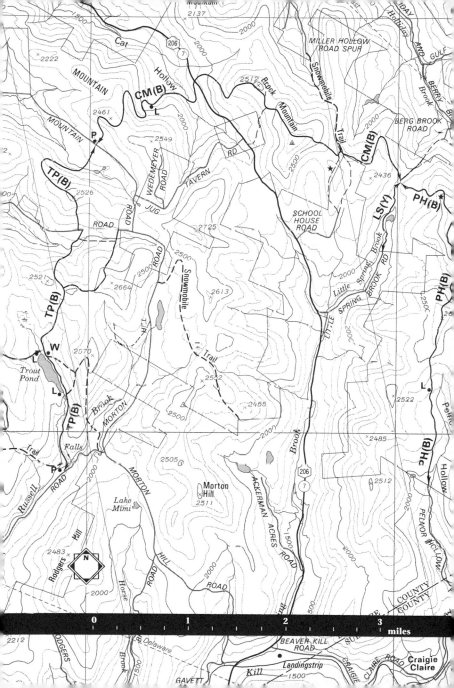

Delaware County

PELNOR HOLLOW TRAIL

"The resulting wet meadow makes a great place to take pictures of wildflowers…"

*b*lue-blazed, this trail is four miles long, offers the hiker good diversity and makes an excellent introductory backpacking trip for the novice.

We'll start from the southern end of the trail, which can be reached by turning up Pelnor Hollow Road (which goes north off Berry Brook Road) and following it for about 1.5 miles, until the road becomes very bumpy and unpaved. You'll pass several small cabins, most of which are vacation homes or hunting lodges owned by people from other parts of the state, particularly the New York metropolitan area. This area of the Western Catskills is dotted with these getaway homes.

You'll probably find it difficult to park near the trailhead because the road is quite narrow and the surrounding land is privately owned. Your best bet is to ask permission to leave your car next to one of the nearby cabins.

The trail continues along the road, which remains wide for about another quarter mile, climbing gently. This stretch of Pelnor Hollow is very enjoyable, with meadows on each side of the trail broken up by small wooded areas, and ridges in the background which give the area its cozy yet remote aura. The clearings also support a wealth of wildlife. We observed ruffed grouse bursting out from hiding alongside the trail and other birds swooping for flies.

After about 0.6 mile, you'll enter the woods, continuing to ascend gradually, and you'll reach the **Pelnor Hollow Lean-to** at 0.9 mile. Although not far from the road, the lean-to pro-

Pelnor Hollow lean-to.

vides an enchanted and isolated feeling. While part of the floor had been hacked up, overall we found the lean-to to be in fairly good condition. There is *a spring* a few hundred feet in front of the lean-to and down the hill. Here, a brook feeds into a large clearing resulting from recent beaver activity. A fair sized pond (not shown on any map) has formed, framed by the trunks of large dead trees. The resulting wet meadow makes a great place to take pictures of wildflowers and to observe the many warblers and flycatchers which come to feed on the numerous insects that hatch here. We observed a flock of cedar wax wings flying over the pond.

Continuing past the lean-to,

the trail climbs moderately, finally leveling off on a 2,672-foot peak, the highest point on this trail. From here, the trail drops down about 300 feet and again starts to climb up to a ridge, passing an *unmarked trail* at about elevation 2,420 feet. At 3.2 miles (elevation 2,663 feet), a junction is reached with the *red-blazed* **Mary Smith Trail**, which descends 1.2 miles to the right (east) to Holiday and Berry Brook Road.

From this junction, the trail descends and, in a few hundred feet, passes some *overhanging rocks* to the left which can provide shelter in bad weather. Nearby, there is an *open viewpoint* northward towards Brock Mountain. The trail continues to descend rather steeply. At 4.0 miles (elevation 2,100 feet), the trail ends at a junction with the Little Spring Brook and Campbell Mountain Trails. The *yellow-blazed* **Little Spring Brook Trail** goes off to the left (south), passing a small pond and reaching Little Spring Brook Road in 0.6 mile. This road in turn leads to State Route 206 in another 1.1 miles.

The Little Spring Brook Trail provides a good way to end this hike. If you prefer, however, you may choose to take the right fork and continue westward on the **Campbell Mountain Trail.**

Delaware County

CAMPBELL MOUNTAIN TRAIL

*t*he *blue-blazed* **Campbell Mountain Trail**, 5.5 miles long, begins in a saddle between two ridges (elevation 2,100 feet) at the junction of the Pelnor Hollow and Little Spring Brook Trails. This point can most easily be reached by following the **Little Spring Brook Trail** north for 0.6 mile (see above). The Campbell Mountain Trail ascends very gently for about half a mile. It then turns left and climbs moderately up an unnamed mountain, reaching an elevation of about 2,320 feet. From there it turns right (west), and drops off slightly, soon crossing an old access road which is used mainly by hunters and snowmobilers in season.

In summer, the road is almost obscured by the heavy ground cover on the forest floor. To the left (south), this road passes through private land and eventually leads to State Route 206. About a quarter mile down the road, to the west, there is a *small abandoned quarry* filled with bluestone, a sedimentary rock. It is one of several such abandoned quarries in the area. (The topo map for Downsville will assist you in locating these abandoned quarries).

Continuing on the trail, you'll soon cross another old woods road and start a 400-foot climb up 2,760-foot **Brock**

Mountain. From the wooded summit (2.1 miles from the start), a portion of the Pepacton Reservoir may be visible to the northwest on a clear day if the leaves are down. The trail descends gradually and then briefly ascends to just below the 2,512-foot north summit of Brock.

If the leaves are down, you should be able to see the outline of Campbell Mountain ahead through the trees. The trail then descends steadily, reaching Route 206 (also known as Cat Hollow Road) in **Cat Hollow** (where there is room to park a few cars). You've now gone 3.1 miles.

The trail crosses the road and descends moderately for about 0.3 mile, where it crosses a brook on a bridge. From here it climbs moderately to the **Campbell Mountain Lean-to** (elevation 1,900 feet), which it reaches 1.3 miles from the road (4.4 miles from the start). *The water supply near this lean-to is not reliable*, so plan on bringing your own water if you want to stay here. The trail continues to ascend on switchbacks, finally reaching one of the six small peaks of the long ridge known as **Campbell Mountain** at elevation 2,461 feet. It then descends moderately and ends at unpaved Campbell Mountain

Road, 5.5 miles from the start. Parking is available here. If you wish to continue westward, the **Trout Pond Trail** begins just across the road.

Delaware County

TROUT POND & MUD POND TRAILS

---

*t*hese *blue-blazed* trails are the most western trails of the Catskill trail system. They can make up part of a longer hike, or you may use the trails for a pleasant day hike around Trout Pond.

The **Trout Pond Trail** begins in a rural setting on Campbell Mountain Road, opposite the terminus of the Campbell Mountain Trail. The trail skirts a large clearing while descending slowly, and soon crosses a stream, with two ponds about 0.3 mile to your left (east). It then enters the woods and turns sharply to the right, climbing a steep slope at an angle. The trail cuts back to the left and continues up to the top

of an unnamed 2,526-foot peak. Because the ridges on this trail are heavily wooded, there are no open viewpoints. From here, the trail descends steadily to Campbell Brook Road, which it reaches at 2.1 miles. It then briefly follows the road to the left. Leaving the road, it descends slightly to cross a stream, then climbs about 400 feet, cresting on a ridge 2,500 feet in elevation. The trail then descends again and reaches the northern end of Trout Pond at a junction with the **Mud Pond Trail** (also *blue-blazed*), 4.0 miles from the start. A **lean-to** is located near the trail junction, with a *good spring* just east of the lean-to.

The Mud Pond Trail, which goes off to the right, climbs up a side of **Cherry Ridge**, leveling off in about 0.75 mile at elevation 2,500 feet. It then descends along a stream and, about 1.4 miles from its start, crosses the stream and skirts the north and west sides of a clearing. It terminates, 1.75 miles from the start, on a wide jeep road that is a designated *snowmobile trail.* To the right, this road leads in 0.25 mile to Mud Pond. To the left, the road leads for one mile to a parking area on Russell Brook Road.

Returning to the trail junction at the north end of Trout Pond, the Trout Pond Trail

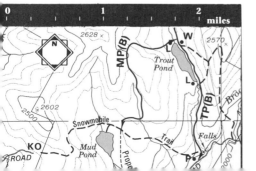

follows the eastern shore of this narrow pond for 0.5 mile to the south end of the pond. There is another **lean-to** here near a dam.

Trout Pond (formerly known as Cables Pond, which name still appears on the topo map) receives heavy use during summer months, largely because of its easy access from the road, and garbage clean-up is a serious problem faced by the DEC. In the off-season, however, the pond is a lovely place, and it makes for excellent fishing (of course, a fishing permit is required).

From the southern end of Trout Pond, the trail leads southward 0.9 mile to a parking area on Russell Brook Road, 5.4 miles from the start of the trail. **Russell Brook Falls**, just to the north below the road, makes a fine place to rest and refresh yourself before leaving the area. To the south, Russell Brook Road leads to State Route 17 (the main highway in the area) in about 3.5 miles. To the north, Russell Brook Road junctions in 0.5 mile with Morton Hill Road, which leads (to the right) to State Route 206.

It is also possible to use the Trout Pond and Mud Pond Trails to make a short loop day hike. Take the Trout Pond Trail north from Russell Brook Road to its junction with the Mud Pond Trail at the north end of Trout Pond. Continue west and south on the Mud Pond Trail, then turn right on the snowmobile trail and follow it back to the parking area on Russell Brook Road.

"Off The Beaten Path"

In the Delaware County portion of the Western Catskills, large tracts of state land await the hiker prepared with map and compass. With the aid of a topo map, you might be able to find old abandoned quarries or overgrown clearings high on a hillside.

One interesting area is **Huggins Lake,** south of Mary Smith Hill. An old four-wheel drive road which leads to the lake from Holiday and Berry Brook Road provides access to the area, which offers the opportunity for a moderately strenuous day of exploring. This road starts up near a *fine pipe spring* on the east side of the road. It should be noted that the DEC has proposed draining this secluded lake because of the possibility of the dam breaking, but this shouldn't deter you from checking out this interesting area.

The areas north and south of the Pepacton Reservoir are also of interest to those hikers who wish to explore trailless areas. Many of the ridges which rise south of the reservoir are on state land and, when the trees are bare, these ridges offer impressive glimpses of this huge body of water that snakes through the countryside.

North of the reservoir (and outside of the boundary of the Catskill Park), **Murphy Hill State Forest** and **Wolf Hollow Wildlife Management Area**, both of which can be found on the Andes topo map, provide interesting opportunities for hiking. Although most of this area is comprised of private lands, and permission to hike on these lands must be obtained, we've found that landowners in the area often grant consent to courteous hikers to traverse their property. The farms and cleared hollows make this area a pleasure to drive through, and the old dirt roads which lace the hills make access for hikers relatively easy.

One location of specific interest is **Dingle Hill**, a rather average looking set of hills a few miles south of the village of Andes. In the mid-1800's, this area was the site of the so-called "Anti-Rent War." Beginning with the Hardenburgh patent, the land had always been leased to tenant farmers who toiled hard on the land but were deprived of the opportunity to own it.

An almost feudal type of system developed, under which rich landowners would issue "three life" leases. These leases provided that a family would have the land for three generations, after which it would revert to the previous owner. Thus, tenants rarely had the opportunity to purchase the land that their fathers and grandfathers had worked, and the result was great animosity towards the wealthy landowners who were profiting at the expense of the tenants.

The tenants organized themselves and met to plan methods to counteract the power possessed by the landlords, including a boycott of all rents due to the wealthy landlords. The tenants dressed as "Calico Indians" in furs and skins and wore face masks to avoid being identified by the authorities.

Finally, the rebellion came to a head on August 7, 1845 with the death by shooting of a sheriff who came to collect rent from a tenant who was participating in the "rent strike." This event, which occurred on Dingle Hill, resulted in a massive law-enforcement effort which put an end to the "Anti-Rent War," but hostile feelings remained long afterwards.

Today, the gowns and masks of "Calico Indians" found in museums are all that remain of the Anti-Rent Wars.

Another area of note is the **Bear Spring Mountain State Wildlife Management Area**, off Route 206 west of the village of Downsville. This area, which contains a variety of terrain and abundant wildlife, has about *12 to 15 miles of horse trails and six miles of marked hiking trails*. Those interested in hiking in this area should contact the DEC office in Stamford for additional information or consult a map (such as the Delaware County map) which shows state-owned land.

On the trail again!

APPENDIX

THE FIFTY HIGHEST PEAKS

Mountain	*Elevation*	*County*
1. Slide	4180	Ulster
2. Hunter	4040	Greene
3. Black Dome	3980	Greene
4. Blackhead	3940	Greene
5. Thomas Cole	3940	Greene
6. West Kill	3880	Greene
7. Graham●	3868	Ulster
8. Doubletop●□	3860	Ulster
9. Cornell	3860	Ulster
10. Table□	3847	Ulster
11. Peekamoose	3843	Ulster
12. Plateau	3840	Greene
13. Sugarloaf	3800	Greene
14. Wittenberg	3780	Ulster
15. Southwest Hunter●□	3740	Greene
16. Balsam Lake	3723	Ulster
17. Lone●□	3721	Ulster
18. Panther	3720	Ulster
19. Big Indian●□	3700	Ulster
20. Friday●□	3694	Ulster
21. Rusk●□	3680	Greene
22. Kaaterskill High Peak●	3655	Greene
23. Twin	3640	Greene
24. Balsam Cap●□	3623	Ulster
25. Fir●□	3620	Ulster
26. North Dome●□	3610	Greene
27. Eagle	3600	Ulster
28. Balsam	3600	Ulster
29. Bearpen●	3600	Greene
30. Indian Head	3573	Greene
31. Sherrill●□	3540	Greene
32. Vly●□	3529	Greene
33. Windham High Peak	3524	Greene
34. Halcott●□	3520	Greene

35. Rocky•□	3508	Ulster
36. Mill Brook Ridge•	3480	Ulster
37. Dry Brook Ridge	3460	Delaware
38. Woodpecker Ridge•	3460	Ulster
39. Olderbark•	3440	Greene
40. Roundtop•	3440	Greene
41. Roundtop (Onteora)•	3440	Delaware
42. Huntersfield•	3423	Greene/ Schoharie
43. Belleayre	3420	Ulster
44. Stoppel Point	3420	Greene
45. W. West Kill (St. Anne's)	3420	Greene
46. South Bearpen•	3410	Greene
47. Northeast Halcott•	3408	Greene
48. Spruce•	3380	Ulster
49. Beaver Kill Range•	3377	Ulster
50. South Vly•	3360	Greene

• Without maintained trail to summit
□ Catskill 3500 Club summit canister

TRAIL MILEAGES

These trail mileages, arranged according to the chapters of this book, are taken from the backs of the Catskill Trails map set published by the New York-New Jersey Trail Conference. The letters in brackets at the beginning of each trail are the abbreviated trail names, used to designate the trail on the maps. Following the trail names are the trail marker blaze colors, coordinates for the grid locations of the trail heads, map numbers and *Hiking the Catskills* page numbers.

NORTHEASTERN CATSKILLS

[BK]   **Batavia Kill Trail**   128-29
        Yellow [O2] Map #41
0.00   Start of trail at junction with Escarpment
        Trail, 1.0m north of Blackhead Mountain
        summit.
0.25   Batavia Kill Lean-to.
0.90   Trail ends. Left on red-marked Black Dome
        Range Trail 1.85m to Black Dome Mountain
        or right 0.6m to parking area at end of Big
        Hollow Road.

[BH]   **Becker Hollow Trail**   151
        Blue [M4] Map #41

0.00   Start of trail on Rt. 214, 1.2m south of junc-
        tion with Rt. 23A.
2.00   Pass yellow spur trail going right to spring
        (250′) and Hunter tower (0.3m).
2.30   Trail ends. Left on yellow Hunter Mountain
        Trail to Devil's Acre Lean-to and Devil's
        Path (1.35m). Right on blue Spruceton Trail
        to summit of Hunter and tower (0.25m).

[BD]   **Black Dome Range Trail**   134-40
        Red [N2/O2] Map #41

(Also known as Blackhead Range Trail)

0.00	Marked trail starts on Elmer Barnum Road at its junction with County Rt. 40. Proceed easterly along Barnum Road (driveable).
0.65	Cars may be driven to this point. Leave road to left, following red markers.
3.55	Summit of Thomas Cole Mountain (3940').
4.30	Summit of Black Dome Mountain (3980'). View to the south.
4.90	Pass yellow Blackhead Mountain Trail. Continue left steeply downgrade.
5.30	Spring to right of trail.
6.05	Pass yellow Batavia Kill Trail going right to lean-to (0.65m).
6.65	Reach parking area on Big Hollow Road. Trail turns right.
7.00	Cross stream.
7.65	Trail ends at junction with blue Escarpment Trail between Burnt Knob and Acra Point.

[BM] **Blackhead Mountain Trail**   138
Yellow [02] Map #41

0.00	Summit of Blackhead Mountain at junction with Escarpment Trail. Proceed west along summit.
0.20	Steep descent begins with fine views.
0.60	Blackhead-Black Dome col and junction with red Black Dome Range Trail. Ahead to Black Dome Mountain (0.6m) or right to Big Hollow Road (1.75m).

[CL] **Colgate Lake Trail**   124-25
Yellow [03] Map #41

0.00	Start of trail at parking lot east of Colgate Lake. Follow markers north.
2.25	Join old road from Lake Capra. Go left past beaver area.
4.25	Junction with Escarpment and Dutcher Notch Trails. Left on blue 2.45m to Black-

head Mountain or right 6.4m to North Lake State Campground. Ahead goes down 0.35m to spring.

[CC]	**Colonel's Chair Trail**	154

Yellow [M3] Map #41
(Also known as the Shanty Hollow Trail)

0.00   Junction with blue Spruceton Trail, 0.1m above John Robb Lean-to. Follow yellow markers north to ski area trails and service road.

1.00   Top of Colonel's Chair at end of chairlift. Snack bar in season.

[DP]	**Devil's Path** *Red* [O4/K3] Map #41	**140-59**

(Also known as the Indian Head-Hunter-West Kill Range Trail)

0.00   Platte Clove Road (County Rt. 16) 0.5m west of N.Y.C. Police Camp (Indian Head Lodge). Turn south following Prediger Road.

0.40   Limited parking at end of road.

0.90   Trail forks; take left fork (red). Right fork (blue) is Jimmy Dolan Notch Trail.

2.30   Trail joins old road going from Platte Clove to Overlook Mountain.

2.35   Turn right at trail junction, leaving old road. Overlook Trail (blue) ahead leads to Devil's Kitchen Lean-to (0.1m) and Overlook Mountain.

4.10   Spectacular lookout after steep ascent.

4.80   Summit of Indian Head Mountain (3573′).

6.00   Jimmy Dolan Notch. Trail junction; north on blue markers goes 2.45m back to Platte Clove Road. Continue ahead on red.

6.45   East peak of Twin Mountain.

7.05   Summit of Twin Mountain (3640′).

7.70   Pecoy Notch. Pass blue trail going right 1.9m to Platte Clove Road (County Rt. 16).

8.90   Summit of Sugarloaf Mountain (3800′).

9.85	Pass blue Mink Hollow Trail. Right goes to spring (0.25m) and towards Tannersville. Left goes to lean-to (250′) and Lake Hill (5.9m).
10.20	Excellent spring.
11.05	Summit of Plateau Mountain (3840′).
13.10	Fine view to north. Begin steep descent.
14.15	Rt. 214 at Stony Clove Notch. Devil's Tombstone State Campground. Cross road and stream south of dam, continuing on red markers.
16.30	Pass yellow Hunter Mountain Trail leading right towards Hunter Mountain.
16.40	Devil's Acre Lean-to and spring.
17.10	Lookout to south and southwest.
18.65	Diamond Notch Falls. Blue trail to right leads to Spruceton Road (1.0m). Continue left on red across bridge and right along stream. Blue trail (left) goes on to Diamond Notch Lean-to (0.5m) and Lanesville.
19.40	Spring.
19.90	Top of West Kill's east ridge.
20.10	Good rock ledge for getting out of the rain.
21.05	Buck Ridge Lookout. Good views to the north, south, and east.
21.15	Summit of West Kill Mountain (3880′).
23.20	Summit of western peak (West West Kill Mountain).
24.35	Swamp in Mink Hollow, between North Dome and West Kill Mountains. Spring on right side of trail.
25.85	End of trail on Spruceton Road (County Rt. 6) about 3.25m east of West Kill village.

[DN]	**Diamond Notch Trail** *Blue* [L4] Map #41	**155-56**
0.00	Bridge at Lanesville on Rt. 214. Turn north on Diamond Notch Road.	
1.50	Road ends. Trail indicated by sign.	
2.60	Spring.	

3.00	Diamond Notch Lean-to to right of trail.
3.50	Trail junction with Devil's Path (red markers): left for West Kill Mountain. Cross bridge. Devil's Path now goes right to Hunter. Continue left on blue markers. Diamond Notch Falls under bridge.
4.50	Trail ends on Spruceton Road (County Rt. 6) at junction with Spruceton Trail, also blue.

[DU] **Dutcher Notch Trail** *Yellow* [03/P2]   **124-25**
      Map #41

0.00	Junction with Escarpment Trail in Dutcher Notch between Stoppel Point and Blackhead Mountain.
0.35	Spring.
2.40	End of trail. To get here from Round Top village, go southeast to end of Maple Lawn Road. Then left onto Floyd Hawver Road and quick right onto Storks Nest Road.

[EL] **Echo Lake Trail** *Yellow* [O5] Map #41   **170**

0.00	Junction with Overlook Trail, 2.25m south of Devil's Kitchen Lean-to.
0.60	Echo Lake and lean-to. Camping permitted only at designated sites.

[ER] **Elm Ridge Trail** *Yellow* [N2] Map #41   **133**

0.00	Parking at end of Peck Road about 1.5m north of Maplecrest.
0.65	Spring.
0.85	Trail end and junction with blue Escarpment Trail. Ahead on blue 1.1m to parking area on Rt. 23 or right 30 yds. to Elm Ridge Lean-to.

[ES] **Escarpment Trail** *Blue* [O3/M1]   **106-33**
      Maps #40 & 41

0.00	Start of trail at parking area on Schutt Road, just south of North Lake State Campground gatehouse.
0.55	Trail junction. Left on red (Schutt Road Trail)

	leads to junction with Escarpment Trail near Hotel Kaaterskill site in 1.0m. Turn right and continue on blue markers.
0.75	Pass near top of Kaaterskill Falls, which are to the right.
1.25	Layman Monument.
1.70	Trail junction. Left on yellow leads to Schutt Road Trail (0.35m). Continue on blue markers.
1.80	Sunset Rock.
1.95	Inspiration Point.
2.70	Trail joins old Kaaterskill Road and follows it to the right 200′ to junction. Turn sharp left up grade along laurel-bordered road. Road to right, a part of the Sleepy Hollow Horse Trail network and the Long Path, leads to Palenville.
3.20	Pass red Schutt Road Trail leading left to Hotel Kaaterskill site and North Lake Road. Follow blue trail to right.
3.80	Trail junction. Red trail to left shortcuts to site of Catskill Mountain House. Keep right on blue-marked trail along ledges.
4.00	Boulder Rock. Lookout towards Palenville and Hudson Valley.
4.10	Trail junction. Red trail to left cuts back to Escarpment Trail. Continue on blue.
4.50	Catskill Mountain House site and historical marker.
4.75	Parking lot at North Lake State Campground. Continue on blue markers along cliff edge.
5.15	Artist's Rock. Excellent view of the Hudson Valley.
5.60	Stiff climb begins.
5.65	Pass yellow spur going 0.1m to Lookout Rock and 0.25m to Sunset Rock.
5.85	Newman's Ledge. Excellent view of the Hudson Valley.

6.40	Badman Cave and junction with yellow Rock Shelter Trail to Mary's Glen Trail and North Lake State Campground. Continue on blue.
7.05	Pass red Mary's Glen Trail going left to Rock Shelter Trail (0.8m) and campground (1.4m). This is last junction for turnaround to North Lake. Continue right on blue markers, a stiff scramble.
7.20	North Point (3000'). Spectacular views.
7.65	North Mountain (3180').
8.90	Stoppel Point (3420').
10.00	Start moderate descent from top.
11.15	Pass yellow Dutcher Notch and Colgate Lake Trails leading right to spring and to Floyd Hawver Road and left to East Jewett.
13.65	Summit of Blackhead Mountain (3940'). Trail junction. Left on yellow Blackhead Mountain Trail leads to Black Dome and Thomas Cole Mountains. Continue right on blue. Steep downgrade.
14.65	Pass yellow Batavia Kill Trail leading left to lean-to 0.25m and Big Hollow Road 1.5m.
16.45	Acra Point (3100').
17.15	Pass red Black Dome Range Trail leading left to Big Hollow Road 1.1m.
17.40	Burnt Knob. Views.
19.85	Summit of Windham High Peak (3524').
22.00	Elm Ridge Lean-to.
22.05	Pass yellow Elm Ridge Trail going left 0.2m to spring and 0.85m to end of Peck Road.
23.15	Terminus on Rt. 23; 3.0m west of East Windham. Extension (of Long Path) planned.

[HU]	**Hunter Mountain Trail** *Yellow* [M4] **151**
	Map #41
0.00	Junction with Becker Hollow and Spruceton Trails, 0.25m south of Hunter Mountain Tower.

1.35	Trail ends at junction with Devil's Path (red). Devil's Acre Lean-to 0.1m to right.	
[JD]	**Jimmy Dolan Notch Trail** *Blue* [O5/O4] Map #41	**146**
0.00	Trail junction with Devil's Path in Jimmy Dolan Notch between Indian Head and Twin Mountains. Follow blue markers downhill.	
1.00	Join old log road and turn right.	
1.55	Second junction with red Devil's Path: right leads to Indian Head Mountain and Overlook Trail or left to trailhead on Prediger Road (0.5m).	
[KF]	**Kaaterskill Falls Trail** *Yellow* [O3] Map #40	**112-13**
0.00	Junction of Rt. 23A and Kaaterskill Creek. Parking just west of this point. Trail leaves north side of highway and follows up stream through mixed hardwoods and high hemlocks.	
0.40	Lower falls.	
[MG]	**Mary's Glen Trail** *Red* [P3] Map #40	**118**
0.00	Starts on Escarpment Trail below North Point.	
0.80	Pass yellow Rock Shelter Trail.	
1.40	North Lake State Campground.	
[MK]	**Mink Hollow Trail** *Blue* [N5/N4] Map #41	**160-62**
0.00	Lake Hill, on Rt. 212. Follow blue markers north on Mink Hollow Road.	
2.85	Cars can be driven to this point. Bear right and follow stream.	
5.85	Height of land and Mink Hollow Lean-to.	
5.90	Junction: red Devil's Path goes right to Sugarloaf, Twin and Indian Head Mountains, or left to Plateau Mountain. Continue ahead on blue.	
6.15	Spring 300' to left.	

| 7.15 | Cars can be driven to this point from Elka Park Road. |
| 8.60 | Elka Park Road: left for Tannersville or right for Platte Clove. |

[OL]   **Overlook Trail** *Blue* [O5] Map #41   **170-71**

0.00	Start of trail at junction with Devil's Path, 1.95m from its trailhead on Prediger Road.
0.10	Devil's Kitchen Lean-to.
1.45	Skunk Springs; water except in dry seasons.
2.35	Pass yellow Echo Lake Trail to lake and lean-to (0.6m), with camping only at designated sites.
3.20	Spring.
3.75	Trail ends (spring nearby). Overlook Spur Trail (red) goes left 0.4m to Overlook Tower or right 2.0m to Meads.

[OS]   **Overlook Spur Trail** *Red* [O5] Map #41   **166-70**

0.00	Start of trail on Meads Mountain Road at parking area about 2.0m north of Woodstock.
0.50	Spring on north side of trail.
2.00	Pass blue Overlook Trail which provides access to Echo Lake (2.0m) and Devil's Kitchen Lean-to (3.65m).
2.40	Summit of Overlook Mountain (3140') and tower.

[PN]   **Pecoy Notch Trail** *Blue* [N4] Map #41   **147**

0.00	Platte Clove Road (County Rt. 16) at turn to Twin Mountain House. Proceed up Dale Lane.
0.45	Road forks. Right fork, across bridge, leads to start of Mink Hollow Trail. Take left fork.
0.75	Leave road where it bends sharply to left and follow blue markers.
1.90	Pecoy Notch: junction with red Devil's Path. Right for Sugarloaf Mountain or left for Twin Mountain.

[PA]	**Phoenicia Trail** *Red* [L5] Map #41	**184-85**

0.00	Start of trail on County Rt. 40 (old Rt. 28), 1.4m east of Phoenicia.
0.85	Spring on left.
0.95	Pass quarry on left.
1.90	Baldwin Memorial Lean-to.
1.95	Pipe spring 50' left of trail.
2.70	Tremper Mountain Lean-to.
2.75	Summit of Tremper Mountain (2740') and junction with blue Willow Trail.

[RS]	**Rock Shelter Trail** *Yellow* [P3] Map #40	**118**

0.00	Start of trail near North Lake State Campground gatehouse
1.30	Junction with Mary's Glen Trail. Left on red leads to North Point or right to Mary's Glen and North Lake Campground. Continue ahead.
1.75	Trail ends at junction with Escarpment Trail at Badman Cave. Left 0.8m to North Point or right 0.55m to Newman's Ledge.

[SC]	**Schutt Road Trail** *Red* [O3/P3] Map #40	**108**

0.00	Start of trail on Schutt Road near North Lake State Campground gatehouse.
0.50	Cross blue Escarpment Trail.
0.80	Pass yellow spur trail leading 0.35m to Escarpment Trail near Sunset Rock.
1.50	Trail ends at junction with blue Escarpment Trail near Hotel Kaaterskill site.

[SP]	**Spruceton Trail** *Blue* [L4/M4] Map #41	**151-54**

0.00	Junction of trail and Spruceton Road (County Rt. 6) about 6.5m east of West Kill village. Follow blue markers to left on jeep trail, which is barred to vehicles. Road, continuing ahead with blue markers, is Diamond Notch Trail.

1.70	Height of land. Turn right off old Hunter Road.
2.10	Spring 300′ to right of trail on yellow spur.
2.30	John Robb Lean-to on left.
2.40	Pass yellow Colonel's Chair Trail going left to chairlift (1.0m).
3.35	Hunter Mountain Observatory Tower (4040′).
3.60	Trail ends. Blue-marked Becker Hollow Trail goes left to Devil's Tombstone State Campground (2.3m). Ahead on yellow Hunter Mountain Trail leads to Devil's Acre Lean-to (1.45m).

[WI]	**Willow Trail** *Blue* [M5/L5] Map #41	**180-82**

0.00	Crossroads just west of Willow Post Office. Follow blue markers on Jessup Road running west.
1.25	Turn left off dirt road through clearing to woods and begin climb.
4.90	Summit of Tremper Mountain and junction with Phoenicia Trail (red).

SOUTH CENTRAL CATSKILLS

[BL]	**Balsam Lake Mountain Trail** *Red* [G6] Maps #42 & 43	**251-53**

0.00	Start of trail at junction with blue Dry Brook Ridge Trail, 2.2m south of Mill Brook Road. Bear right on red markers.
0.75	Summit of Balsam Lake Mountain (3723′) and tower.
1.10	Balsam Lake Mountain Lean-tos. Spring to left of trail at foot of ledge.
1.60	End of trail at second junction with Dry Brook Ridge Trail. Left 3.15m to Mill Brook Road or right 1.9m to Quaker Clearing.

[BR] **Belleayre Ridge Trail** *Red* [H4/I5] Map #42 **231-34**

0.00 Top #1 chairlift and summit shelter.
0.55 Hirschland Lean-to on left, at top of ski trail.
0.75 Pass blue Cathedral Glen Trail.
1.00 Belleayre Mountain (3375'). Tower removed. Junction with blue Pine Hill-West Branch Trail. Left to Belleayre Lean-to and spring (0.45m) or right to Rider Hollow Lean-tos (1.9m) and Balsam Mountain.

[CG] **Cathedral Glen Trail** *Blue* [I4/H5] Map #42 **234**
(From junction of Rt. 28 and Main Street in Pine Hill, turn west on Bonnie View Road; next left on Mill Street going under railroad bridge. Old station site on right. Reach trailhead by following railroad right-of-way west from site of old station; about 0.5m.)

0.00 Start of trail at old railroad near Belleayre Ski Center snowmaking reservoir. Trail ascends moderately along east side of Cathedral Brook through hemlock and hardwoods.
1.15 Junction with ski trail. Unmarked road to right leads to Belleayre Ski Center. Climb steeply following ski trail.
1.50 Turn left off ski trail onto foot trail.
1.70 Junction with Belleayre Ridge Trail (red). Left to summit (0.25m) or right to Hirschland Lean-to (0.2m) and chairlift (0.75m).

[CO] **Curtis-Ormsbee Trail** *Blue* [J6/J7] Map #43 **200-02**
Named after William Curtis and Allen Ormsbee who laid out this scenic route. Both died in June 1900 in a snowstorm on Mt. Washington.

0.00 Trail starts at junction with Wittenberg-Cornell-Slide Trail, 0.65m east of summit of Slide Mountain (4180').

0.95	Flat rock ledge and lookout to left of trail. View towards Lone, Table and Rocky Mtns.
1.60	Junction with yellow Phoenicia-East Branch Trail: left 2.95m to Denning parking area or right 1.5m to Slide Mountain parking area.

[DB]	**Dry Brook Ridge Trail** *Blue* [F4/G6] Map #42 (Also known as the Pakatakan-Dry Brook Ridge-Beaverkill Trail)	**244-54**

0.00	To get to trailhead, turn south from the Agway Farm Store on Rt. 28 in Margaretville and take the first left (dead end). Follow this 0.15m to start of trail on right. Follow blue markers uphill, steeply in places.
1.80	Top of Pakatakan Mountain (2500').
2.65	Pass yellow German Hollow trail to lean-to and Dry Brook Road.
3.80	Summit.
4.70	Several overlooks west.
5.20	Trail skirts top of Dry Brook Ridge at 3400' with fine views to west. Summit (3460') is just east of the trail.
7.15	Summit.
8.25	Dry Brook Lean-to and spring. Start climb.
9.60	Mill Brook Road. Left on road goes to Dry Brook Road and Arkville or right to Mill Brook Lean-to. Continue across road.
10.80	Spring to right.
11.80	Pass red Balsam Lake Mountain Trail leading to summit (0.75m).
12.75	Second junction with Balsam Lake Mountain Trail. Right on red leads to lean-to (0.5m) and summit (0.85m). Continue on blue.
13.65	Junction with road to Balsam Lake Club (private). Turn left on road. Parking.
14.65	Trail ends at Quaker Clearing. Neversink-Hardenburgh Trail (yellow) goes left to

Round Pond and Claryville. Blue trail leads
right to Mongaup Pond.

| [GH] | **German Hollow Trail** *Yellow* [F4/G4]
Map #42 | **248** |

0.00	Start of trail at junction with blue-marked Dry Brook Ridge Trail, 2.65m from its trailhead near Margaretville.
0.75	German Hollow Lean-to. Trail continues to left (north) of lean-to and down between German Hollow and Reservoir Hollow Brooks.
1.50	Trail ends on Soderlind Road, which con- nects with Dry Brook Road 1.0m from Rt. 28 in Arkville.

| [GP] | **Giant Ledge-Panther-Fox Hollow Trail**
Blue [J6] Map #42 | **224-30** |

0.00	Trailhead on Fox Hollow Road, 1.5m south of intersection with Rt. 28 in Allaben. Parking.
0.40	Fox Hollow Lean-to.
4.90	Moderate climb to summit of Panther Mountain (3720′) with a fine lookout to east.
5.45	Seasonal spring.
5.65	Lookout towards Slide and Wittenberg Mountains as trail goes down to Panther- Giant Ledge col.
6.70	Giant Ledge (3200′): views both east & west.
6.85	Spring (former lean-to site).
7.45	Trail ends at junction with yellow Phoenicia- East Branch Trail. Right 0.75m downhill to parking area at hairpin turn on County Rt. 47. Left 2.65m to Woodland Valley.

| [LC] | **Lost Clove Trail** *Red* [I5] Map #42 | **231** |

| 0.00 | Parking area. To get here from Big Indian
village, go west on Rt. 28 to Lasher Road.
Turn left (south) and go for about 0.5m to |

Lost Clove Road. Turn right and proceed for about 1.2m up road. Trail leaves road, bearing right.

1.30   Trail joins blue Pine Hill-West Branch Trail after climb up ridge of Belleayre Mountain. Evidence of recent lumbering apparent. Left on blue 0.2m to lean-to and 0.65m to summit.

[MN]   **Mine Hollow Trail** *Yellow* [I5/H5] Map #42   **234**

0.00   Beginning of trail at junction with Pine Hill-West Branch Trail (blue), 0.9m south of Belleayre summit. Trail heads down (south then east) through Mine Hollow, paralleling stream's north bank.

0.45   Trail bends right in hemlock grove.

1.00   Trail ends between lean-tos in Rider Hollow at junction with red Oliverea-Mapledale Trail.

[NH]   **Neversink-Hardenburgh Trail** *Yellow*   **240-42**
        [G8/G6] Map #43
        (First five miles follow driveable roads)

0.00   Bridge over East Branch of the Neversink at Claryville. Follow yellow markers across bridge and along County Rt. 47.

1.30   Bear left on Round Pond Road.

1.90   Bear right on Willowemoc Road. Round Pond on left.

2.10   Pass red Long Pond-Beaverkill Ridge Trail leading left to Long Pond Lean-to (4.0m).

5.10   Parking area on right.

6.65   Fall Brook Lean-to on left.

7.75   Cross headwaters of Beaver Kill and follow down north side of stream.

9.10   State land boundary. Stream private below this point.

11.00   Trail ends at Quaker Clearing. Blue-marked Dry Brook Trail to right leads to Balsam

Lake Mountain. Ahead, also blue-marked, is the Mongaup-Hardenburgh Trail, 7.1m to Mongaup Pond.

[OM] **Oliverea-Mapledale Trail** *Red* [I5/H5] 235-36
Map #42
(Markers start in Oliverea at junction of County Rt. 47 and McKenley Hollow Road. Drive up McKenley Hollow 1.0m.)

0.00 Parking area near Mountain Gate Lodge. Follow red markers up hollow.
0.40 McKenley Hollow Lean-to No. 1.
0.70 McKenley Hollow Lean-to No. 2.
1.85 Height of land and junction with Pine Hill-West Branch Trail. Blue markers lead right to Balsam and Belleayre Mountains or to left for Haynes and Eagle Mountains. Continue on red.
1.95 Spring 60' left of trail.
2.65 Cross stream at forks and enter clearing.
3.10 Rider Hollow Lean-to No. 2.
3.25 Pass yellow Mine Hollow Trail leading right to Belleayre Mountain.
3.30 Rider Hollow Lean-to No. 1.
3.60 Parking area. Red markers, on road, continue to Dry Brook Road.

[PT] **Peekamoose-Table Trail** *Blue* [J7/J8] 216-20
Map #43

0.00 Trail begins at parking area on Peekamoose Road about 3.5 miles west of Peekamoose Lake. Proceed north at moderate grade with a few steep pitches.
1.90 Pass Reconnoiter Rock. Nice view.
2.35 Fine view is reached after short pitch.
2.45 Pass old red-paint-blazed trail on right, leading to Peekamoose Road. Not maintained.
2.75 Spring to left of trail. Fails in dry weather.

3.35	Summit of Peekamoose Mountain (3843').
3.70	Saddle between mountains after 150' drop.
4.30	Summit of Table Mountain (3847') with Catskill 3500 Club canister. Please sign.
4.60	Small spring to right of trail. Fails in dry weather.
6.80	Denning Lean-to. Stream crossing can be difficult here after snow melt or heavy rain.
7.15	Junction with Phoenicia-East Branch Trail (yellow). Parking area at end of Denning Road is 1.2m left; Curtis-Ormsbee Trail 1.75m right.

[PE]   **Phoenicia-East Branch Trail** *Yellow* [K6/J6]   **222-23**
Map #43
(Trail is reached by going south 5.4m on Woodland Valley Road (0.5m west of Phoenicia on Rt. 28.) Highway has occasional yellow trail markers.)

0.00	Woodland Valley State Campground. Parking fee in season. Wittenberg-Cornell-Slide Trail (red) leaves road opposite parking area. Follow yellow markers to right (north) up steps from parking area.
1.00	Cross footbridge over tributary of Woodland Creek in ravine.
1.20	Trail turns right, following old road.
1.75	Seasonal spring.
2.65	Height of land and junction with blue Giant Ledge-Panther-Fox Hollow Trail. Turn right off old road and descend.
3.40	Meet County Rt. 47 and parking area. Turn left up hill, following road. Right on road leads to Oliverea.
4.45	Winnisook Lake. Continue on road past lake.
5.35	Trail turns left off road into parking area. Road continues to Claryville. Begin climb.
5.75	Meet old road and turn right.

6.05	Pass red Wittenberg-Cornell-Slide Trail going left to Slide Mountain summit (2.0m).
6.55	Spring on left.
6.85	Pass blue Curtis-Ormsbee Trail leading left to Slide Mountain (2.25m). Continue ahead.
7.75	Cross bridge.
8.05	Spring to right of trail.
8.60	Pass blue-marked Peekamoose-Table Trail going left 0.25m to Denning Lean-to.
9.80	Enter clearing at end of Denning Road. Cars can be driven to this point from Claryville.

[PW]	**Pine Hill-West Branch Trail** *Blue* [I4/I6] Maps #42 & 43	**230-38**

0.00	Road junction at Rt. 28 and Main Street in Pine Hill. Turn west on Bonnie View Road; next left on Mill Street.
0.25	Pass under railroad bridge. Old Pine Hill Station site to right.
0.80	Road gated, becomes private road. Cars can be driven to this point.
1.20	Turn right off private dirt road.
2.20	Pass red Lost Clove Trail, which leads left to Lost Clove Road (1.3m) and Big Indian village.
2.40	Belleayre Mountain Lean-to and spring.
2.85	Belleayre Mountain (fire tower removed) and trail junction. Belleayre Ridge Trail (red) to right leads to Cathedral Glen Trail (0.25m), lean-to (0.45m) and ski lift (1.0m). Continue ahead on blue.
3.75	Pass yellow Mine Hollow Trail to right for Rider Hollow Lean-tos and Mapledale.
5.05	Summit of Balsam Mountain (3600').
5.80	Pass red Oliverea-Mapledale Trail leading left to Oliverea or right to spring (100'), Rider Hollow Lean-tos and Mapledale.
6.55	Summit of Haynes Mountain (3420').
7.95	Eagle Mountain (3600').

9.05	Pass yellow Seager-Big Indian Trail leading right, downhill, to Shandaken Creek Lean-to (0.9m), Seager and Dry Brook Road.
10.45	Big Indian Mountain (3700'). Actual peak is about 0.25m east of trail.
10.90	Meet old trail and turn sharply east.
13.00	Biscuit Brook Lean-to.
14.90	Trail ends at County Rt. 47. Right 8.0m to Claryville or left 12.8m to Big Indian village.

[SE]   **Seager-Big Indian Trail** *Yellow* [H6/I6]   **237**
      Maps #42 & 43

0.00	Trail begins at covered bridge near Seager, 8.8m from Arkville via Dry Brook Road. Parking area 150' past (not over) bridge. Trail, following old road, goes upstream.
1.25	Cross Dry Brook and follow along Shandaken Brook.
2.15	Shandaken Brook Lean-to.
3.05	Trail ends at junction with Pine Hill-West Branch Trail (blue).

[TE]   **Terrace Mountain Trail** *Yellow* [K6]   **205**
      Map #43

0.00	Start of trail on red Wittenberg-Cornell-Slide Trail, 2.6m from its trailhead at Woodland Valley State Campground.
0.30	Cross rock terraces.
0.90	Terrace Lean-to (no water).

[WS]   **Wittenberg-Cornell-Slide Trail** *Red* [K6/J6]   **194-208**
      Map #43
      (May be renamed The Burroughs Range Trail)

| 0.00 | Start of trail at Woodland Valley State Campground. Turn left on red markers, crossing Woodland Creek on footbridge. Cars can be driven here from Phoenicia. Parking area to the right; fee in season. |

1.45	Spring 300′ right of trail.
2.60	Pass yellow Terrace Mountain Trail going left to lean-to, 0.9m. No water at lean-to.
3.90	Summit of Wittenberg Mountain (3780′) with fine views.
4.25	Pass unmaintained red-paint-blazed path to Moon Haw Road. *Very steep!*
4.70	Blue spur trail to left (0.1m) to summit of Cornell Mountain (3860′).
6.15	Lowest point between mountains. Spring 400′ left of trail. Unmaintained path, with faint paint blazes, goes south along East Branch of the Neversink.
6.80	Fine spring to right of trail on spur.
7.05	Summit of Slide Mountain (4180′).
7.70	Pass blue Curtis-Ormsbee Trail leading to East Branch of the Neversink.
7.85	Pass unmarked trail on right leading towards Winnisook Lake over private land.
9.05	Trail ends at junction with Phoenicia-East Branch Trail. Left on yellow to Denning Lean-to (2.8m) and parking area at end of Denning Road. Right on yellow 0.7m to parking area on County Rt. 47.

WESTERN CATSKILLS
Ulster and Sullivan Counties

[LB]	**Long Pond-Beaverkill Ridge Trail**	300-04
	Red [G7/F7] Map #43	

0.00	Turn left at junction of Basily and Willowemoc Roads, 0.3m north of Round Pond. Yellow trail to right is Neversink-Hardenburgh Trail. Follow red markers.
2.00	Road junction. Turn sharp left.
2.40	Cars can be driven to this point. Trail leaves road to right.

3.80	Pass spur trail going left to Long Pond Lean-to (0.2m).
4.25	Cross stream on snowmobile bridge; reach junction with Flugertown Road. Left on road goes to Willowemoc. Follow road right 0.1m, then turn left off road and start up Beaver Kill Ridge. Yellow-marked Mongaup-Willowemoc Trail starts here, following same route.
5.00	Mongaup-Willowemoc Trail (yellow), also a snowmobile trail, parts and goes left 3.2m to Mongaup Pond. Follow red markers.
5.60	Gradual climb becomes steeper. Spring.
6.10	Reach ridge line. Sand Pond below on left. Trail follows ridge.
7.35	Junction with blue Mongaup-Hardenburgh Trail: left to Mongaup Pond (2.9m) or right to Beaver Kill Road and Hardenburgh (3.2m).

[MH] Mongaup-Hardenburgh Trail   304-06
Blue [F7/G6] Map #43

0.00	Start of trail at end of campsite road.
0.30	Junction with snowmobile trail near north end of Mongaup Pond. Follow blue markers north up Mongaup Mountain.
1.60	Summit of east peak of Mongaup Mountain (2928'). Trail turns east.
2.70	Summit of peak; follow along ridge.
3.20	Pass red Long Pond-Beaverkill Ridge Trail going right to Long Pond (3.75m).
4.75	Summit of peak (3224'). Trail follows a ridge north, off the Beaver Kill Ridge.
6.40	Swinging bridge and Beaver Kill Road. Left for Hardenburgh (2.8m) or right 0.7m for Quaker Clearing and start of Neversink-Hardenburgh and Dry Brook Ridge Trails.

[MW] Mongaup-Willowemoc Trail   308
Yellow [F7] Map #43

0.00	Start of trail at junction with snowmobile

trail at southeast end of Mongaup Pond near
campsite #38.

1.05   Saddle between two ridges. Begin descent.

2.10   Cross Butternut Brook on bridge. Trail
follows downstream and then swings left.

2.85   Trail crosses woods road that goes right to
Flugertown Road and left to Sand Pond
(private).

3.20   Join Long Pond-Beaverkill Ridge Trail. Continue ahead; now with both yellow and red
markers.

3.65   Trail ends at Flugertown Road. Long Pond-
Beaverkill Ridge Trail (red) turns right on
road for 0.1 mile, and soon turns left and re-
enters woods.

Delaware County

[CM]	**Campbell Mountain Trail**	324-25
	Blue [B6/C6] Map #44	

0.00   Junction of Campbell Mountain Road and
Trout Pond Trail. Parking available. Follow
markers north.

1.10   Campbell Mountain Lean-to.

2.40   Trail crosses Rt. 206. Room for parking.

3.40   Summit of Brock Mountain (2760').

5.50   End of trail. Start of Little Spring Brook and
Pelnor Hollow Trails.

[LT]	**Little Pond Trail**	312-14
	Yellow [E6/D6] Map #44	

0.00   Start of trail at end of road on west side of
Little Pond (State Campground). Branch of
trail also begins on east side of pond.

0.20   North end of pond. Follow trail up, paralleling inlet stream.

1.00   Pass ruins of old farm, pond and fields with
fine view to east.

| 1.60 | Junction with Touch-Me-Not Trail in col west of main peak. Left on red markers to Beech Hill Road, about 3.5m. Right on red markers back to campground, about 2.0m. | |

[LS] **Little Spring Brook Trail**   **324**
Yellow [C6/B6] Map #44

| 0.00 | Junction of Campbell Mountain and Pelnor Hollow Trails (both blue). Follow yellow markers southerly along old Little Spring Brook. |
| 0.60 | State land and trail end. Town road leads 1.1m to Rt. 206. |

[MS] **Mary Smith Trail**   **319**
Red [C6/D6] Map #44

0.00	Junction with Pelnor Hollow Trail 0.8m south from old Little Spring Brook Road.
1.20	Holiday and Berry Brook Road, with parking area on east side. Cross road.
4.50	Mary Smith Hill Road, which leads north to Rt. 30 and south to Lew Beach. From here the red Middle Mountain Trail goes east.

[MM] **Middle Mountain Trail**   **317-18**
Red [D6] Map #44

0.00	Start of trail on Mary Smith Road at junction with red Mary Smith Trail. Proceed east, ascending steeply.
0.90	Summit of Middle Mountain (2975').
1.50	Summit of Beech Hill (2844').
2.00	Beech Hill Road. 0.25m south is start of red Touch-Me-Not Trail going to Little Pond State Campground.

[MP] **Mud Pond Trail**   **326-27**
Blue [A6/A7] Map #44

| 0.00 | Start of trail at lean-to on north shore of Trout Pond at fork with Trout Pond Trail, also blue-marked. This is 1.4m north from |

Russell Brook Road parking area and 1.9m south from Campbell Brook Road. Mud Pond Trail also has yellow snowmobile markers.

0.75 End of moderate climb to 2500'.
1.40 Trail skirts the north and then the west sides of field.
1.75 Junction with tote road, also marked as a snowmobile trail. Mud Pond is 0.25m to the right, with road continuing to a dead end at state land line. Left on road 1.0m for Russell Brook parking area and start of Trout Pond Trail.

[PH] **Pelnor Hollow Trail** **322-25**
    Blue [C6/C7] Map #44

0.00 Start at junction with Campbell Mountain (blue) and Little Spring Brook (yellow) Trails. Proceed in a southeasterly direction.
0.80 Junction with Mary Smith Trail (red).
3.10 Pelnor Hollow Lean-to.
4.00 State land and trail end. Town road leads south 1.5m to Berry Brook Road.

[TO] **Touch-Me-Not Trail** **312-16**
    Red [E6/D6] Map #44

0.00 Start of trail at parking area near beach at Little Pond State Campground.
0.50 Summit of Touchmenot Mt. (2760').
1.25 Junction, in col, with Little Pond Trail. Left on yellow returns to campground (1.6m). Continue ahead on red uphill.
2.50 Summit of Cabot Mt. (2970'). Descend.
4.00 End of trail on Beech Hill Road. Middle Mountain Trail is 0.25m north.

[TP] **Trout Pond Trail** **326-27**
    Blue [A7/B6] Map #44

0.00 Russell Brook Road about 0.5m south of

junction with Morton Hill Road. Follow blue
markers on old tote road alongside Trout
Pond outlet stream.

0.90   Trout Pond. Lean-to at far end of dam.

1.40   Trout Pond inlet and lean-to. Trail turns
right. Blue-marked trail to left, behind lean-
to, is Mud Pond Trail. Spring nearby.

3.30   Trail crosses Campbell Brook Road.

5.40   Campbell Mountain Road, parking area and
beginning of Campbell Mountain Trail.

WEATHER INFORMATION

National Weather Service
  (212) 315-2704 or 2705; 10 A.M. - 4 P.M.
Albany (recorded) (518) 476-1122
Kingston (recorded) (914) 331-5555
Sullivan County (recorded) (914) 791-9555

BUS INFORMATION

Adirondack Trailways
  Route 23 & 23A Windham, Hensonville, Haines Falls
Pine Hill Trailways
  Route 28 Phoenicia, Big Indian, Margaretville
New York City (212) 947-5300
Kingston   (914) 331-0744
Albany   (518) 436-9651

STATE CAMPSITES

North Lake in Greene County on County Route 18,
three miles northeast of Route 23A in Haines Falls.
Can reserve sites through Ticketron. Allows access
to Kaaterskill Falls, Mountain House site and Escarpment Trail (south end). Busy campsite.

Woodland Valley in Ulster County five miles south
of Route 28, on Woodland Valley Road, junction is one
mile west of Phoenicia. In beautiful valley, fine trout
fishing, access to Wittenberg-Cornell-Slide Mountain
Trail and Phoenicia-East Branch Trail to Giant Ledge.

Devils Tombstone in Greene County on Route 214 at south end of Stony Clove, four miles south of the village of Hunter. Small campsite with access to Devil's Path.

Beaverkill in Sullivan County seven miles north of Livingston Manor near the hamlet of Lew Beach. Excellent trout fishing, short drive to Delaware County system of trails in Western Catskills.

Mongaup Pond in Sullivan County on Mongaup Pond Road three miles north of Debruce which is accessed by Route 17 at Livingston Manor. Access to Mongaup-Hardenburgh and Mongaup-Willowemoc Trails.

Little Pond on Delaware-Ulster County border off County Route 54, three and a half miles north of Lew Beach. Nice setting in Western Catskills with access to Touch-Me-Not and Little Pond Trails.

HIKING & OUTDOOR CLUBS

N.Y.-N.J. Trail Conference
G.P.O. Box 2250
New York, N.Y. 10116
(212) 685-9699

Catskill 3500 Club
41 Morley Drive
Wyckoff, NJ 07481
(201) 447-2653

Catskill Center for Conservation & Development, Inc.
Arkville, NY 12406
(914) 586-2611

Appalachian Mountain Club
New York City Office:
202 East 39th Street
New York, NY 10016
(212) 986-1430

Adirondack Mountain Club
174 Glen Street
Glens Falls, NY 12801
(518) 793-7737

DEC OFFICES

Region 3 Headquarters - *Ulster & Sullivan Counties*
21 South Putt Corners Road
New Paltz, NY 12561
(914) 255-5453

Region 4 District Office - *Schoharie & Delaware Counties*
Jefferson Road
Stamford, NY 12167
(607) 652-7364

Region 4 Sub-Office - *Greene County*
439 Main Street
Catskill, NY 12414
(518) 943-4030

USEFUL PUBLICATIONS

CATSKILL RELATED

Adams, Arthur G., Roger Coco, Harriet Greenman and Leon R. Greenman. GUIDE TO THE CAT-SKILLS. Walking News, Inc., New York. 1975. This book contains much information on the Catskill region, similar to a small encyclopedia.

Bennet, John and Seth Masia. WALKS IN THE CAT-SKILLS. The East Woods Press, Fast & McMillan, Inc., Charlotte, NC. 1977. A conversational trail book, which is somewhat outdated.

Burroughs, John. IN THE CATSKILLS. Reprinted by Hope Farm Press, Cornwallville, NY. 1974. Selections from the writings of the great naturalist who introduced the Southern Catskills to the world through his enjoyable essays. A must for Catskill purists.

THE CATSKILL CANISTER. Catskill 3500 Club, Inc., c/o Cyrus B. Whitney, 41 Morley Drive, Wyckoff, NJ 07481. Publication printed quarterly by the Club with information on sponsored hikes and clean-ups, and essays written by members. $3.00 yearly subscription.

THE CATSKILL CENTER NEWS. The Catskill Center for Conservation and Development, Arkville, NY. Updates on political, social and natural in the region.

CATSKILL TRAILS. New York State Department of Environmental Conservation, Albany, NY. Short basic description of major hiking trails.

CATSKILL TRAILS. New York-New Jersey Trail Conference, G.P.O. Box 2250, New York, NY 10116. 1987. Complementary topographical hiking maps to this guidebook. Five-map set printed in four colors showing the entire Catskill region in detail. Waterproof and tearproof.

DeLisser, Richard Lionel. PICTURESQUE CAT-
SKILLS, GREENE COUNTY AND PICTUR-
ESQUE ULSTER. Reprinted by Hope Farm Press,
Cornwallville, NY. 1967 & 1968. A fascinating
look at the Catskills by local historian. A must
read for true Catskill enthusiasts. Many interesting photos.

Haring, H.A. OUR CATSKILL MOUNTAINS. G.P.
Putnam's Sons, New York. 1931. Early history of
the region with emphasis on early mountain industries.

Hoffer, Audrey and Elizabeth Mikols. UNIQUE
NATURAL AREAS IN THE CATSKILL RE-
GION. The Catskill Center for Conservation &
Development, Arkville, NY. 1974. Work by two
graduate students from Yale School of Forestry.

KAATSKILL LIFE. The Delaware County Times, 56
Main Street, Delhi, NY 13753-9991. Well-done
quarterly magazine about the region.

Kudish, Michael. VEGETATIONAL HISTORY OF
THE CATSKILL HIGH PEAKS. Ph.D. Thesis.
Reprinted by University Microfilms, Ann Arbor,
Michigan. 1973. Interesting reading for hikers
interested in geology, floral distribution, old
roads and virgin forest areas. Part of his works
available through the Catskill Center.

Longstreth, T. Morris. THE CATSKILLS. The Century
Company, NY. 1918. Description of explorations
of old roads and trails in early 1900's.

Mack, Arthur C. ENJOYING THE CATSKILLS. Outdoor Publications, Ithaca, NY. 1972. Simple
guide to touring the region, especially by automobile.

McMartin, Barbara and Peter Kick. FIFTY HIKES IN
THE HUDSON VALLEY. Backcountry Publications, Inc. Woodstock, VT. 1985. Includes some
selected hikes in the Catskills.

Mitchell, John G. THE CATSKILLS: LAND IN THE SKY. The Viking Press, NY. 1977. Beautiful color photos of the mountains through the seasons accompanied by the author's essays.

New York-New Jersey Trail Conference. NEW YORK WALK BOOK. Doubleday, NY. 1984. Useful for all of southeastern New York; well-written chapter on the Catskills. Fine maps in back of book.

Rockwell, Charles. THE CATSKILL MOUNTAINS AND THE REGION AROUND; THEIR SCENERY, LEGENDS, AND HISTORY: WITH SKETCHES IN PROSE AND VERSE BY COOPER, IRVING, BRYANT, COLE AND OTHER. Reprinted by Hope Farm Press, Cornwallville, NY. 1973. Description of travels through the region from the 1860's.

Smith, Anita M. WOODSTOCK: HISTORY AND HEARSAY. Catskill Mountain Publishing, Saugerties, NY. 1959. Tough to get, but worth the effort. Interesting fireside readings of local folk tales.

Van Zandt, Roland. THE CATSKILL MOUNTAIN HOUSE. Rutgers University Press, New Brunswick, NJ. 1971. The story of the first and foremost of the great hotels and what it meant to America's romantic period.

BACKPACKING

Barker, Harriet. SUPERMARKET BACKPACKER. Contemporary Books, Inc., Chicago, IL. 1977.

Bunnelle, Hasse and Backpacker Magazine. THE BACKPACKERS FOOD BOOK. Simon and Schuster, NY. 1981.

Danielsen, John A. WINTER HIKING & CAMPING. Adirondack Mountain Club, Glens Falls, NY. 1986.

Drew, Edwin P. THE COMPLETE LIGHT-PACK

CAMPING & TRAIL-FOOD COOKBOOK.
McGraw-Hill, NY. 1977

Fletcher, Colin. THE COMPLETE WALKER III.
Alfred A. Knopf, NY. 1986.

Fleming, June. THE WELL FED BACKPACKER. Vintage Books, NY. 1986.

Greenspan, Rick and Hal Kahn. BACKPACKING: A HEDONIST'S GUIDE. Moon Publications, Chicago, IL. 1985.

Hart, John. WALKING SOFTLY IN THE WILDERNESS. Sierra Club Books, San Francisco, CA. 1984.

ORIENTEERING & NAVIGATION

Fleming, June. STAYING FOUND. Vintage Books, NY. 1982.

Kals, W.S. LAND NAVIGATION HANDBOOK. Sierra Club Books, San Francisco, CA. 1983.

Kjellstrom, Bjorn. BE AN EXPERT WITH MAP & COMPASS. Charles Scribners' Sons, NY. 1976.

SURVIVAL & FIRST AID

Allen, Dan H. DON'T DIE ON THE MOUNTAIN. New Hampshire Chapter, Appalachian Mountain Club, New London, NH. 1982.

Angier, Bradford. HOW TO STAY ALIVE IN THE WOODS. MacMillan Publishing Company, NY. 1962.

Auerbach, Paul S., M.D. MEDICINE FOR THE OUTDOORS. Little, Brown and Company, Boston, MA. 1986.

Brown, Tom, Jr. and Brandt Morgan. TOM BROWN'S FIELD GUIDE TO WILDERNESS SURVIVAL. Berkley Books, NY. 1985.

Forgery, William, M.D. WILDERNESS MEDICINE. ICS Books, Pittsboro, IN. 1979.

McQuilkin, Robert. COMFORT BELOW FREEZING. Anderson World, Inc.

Olsen, Larry Dean. OUTDOOR SURVIVAL SKILLS.
Pocket Books, NY. 1976.
Reifsnyder, William. WEATHERING THE WILDER-
NESS. Sierra Club Books, San Francisco, CA.
1980.
Risk, Paul H. OUTDOOR SAFETY AND SURVIVAL.
John Wiley & Sons, NY. 1983.
Shanks, Bernard. WILDERNESS SURVIVAL.
Universe Books, NY. 1980.
Wilkerson, James A., M.D. MEDICINE FOR MOUN-
TAINEERING. The Mountaineers, Seattle, WA.
1985.

FLORA & FAUNA

Brockman, C. Frank. A GUIDE TO FIELD IDEN-
TIFICATION OF TREES OF NORTH
AMERICA. Golden Press, NY. 1968.
Stokes, Donald. A GUIDE TO FIELD IDENTIFICA-
TION OF TREES OF NORTH AMERICA. Little,
Brown and Company, Boston, MA. 1976.

The Audubon Society Field Guide Series:
Bull, John and John Farrand, Jr. NORTH AMERICAN
BIRDS (EASTERN REGION). Alfred A. Knopf,
NY. 1977.
Little, Elbert L. NORTH AMERICAN TREES
(EASTERN REGION). Alfred A. Knopf, NY.
1980.
Niering, William A. NORTH AMERICAN WILD
FLOWERS (EASTERN REGION). Alfred A.
Knopf, NY. 1980
Whitaker, John O., Jr. NORTH AMERICAN MAM-
MALS. Alfred A. Knopf, NY. 1980.

The Peterson Field Guide Series:
Munrie, Olaus, J. ANIMAL TRACKS. Houghton Miff-
lin Company, Boston, MA. 1976.
Burt, William, H. and Richard P. Grossenheider.
MAMMALS OF NORTH AMERICA NORTH OF

MEXICO. Houghton Mifflin Company, Boston. MA. 1976.

Peterson, Roger Tory. BIRDS EAST OF THE ROCKIES. Houghton Mifflin Company, Boston, MA. 1980.

Peterson, Roger Tory & Margaret McKenney. WILD-FLOWERS OF EASTERN AND CENTRAL NORTH AMERICA. Houghton Mifflin Company, Boston, MA. 1968.

INDEX

NEW YORK-NEW JERSEY TRAIL CONFERENCE BOOK STORE

The **New York - New Jersey Trail Conference** is a non-profit federation of over 5,000 individuals and 70-plus hiking and environmental organizations working to build and maintain trails and to preserve open space.

Formed in 1920, the founders built the first section of the Appalachian Trail in 1923. Today our trail network covers over 800 miles.

The Conference is supported by membership dues, publication sales and donations... along with thousands of hours of volunteer time. Members receive the bimonthly newspaper, *The Trail Walker*, can purchase our maps and guides at a discount, avail themselves of the extensive Conference Library located at the Trail Conference Headquarters...and more.

BOOKS

Appalachian Trail Guide for NY-NJ
with 6 maps
Detailed description of A.T. from Conn. border to Delaware Water Gap. Includes relocations & those proposed. Includes 6 multi-color waterproof maps with 20 ft. contours. 175 pages. ISBN 0-917953-29-0.

Guide to the Long Path
with 8 maps/key
Comprehensive guide to this trail which extends 216 miles from the George Washington Bridge to the northern Catskills, including a new section near Kaaterskill High Peak. Includes facilities, services, access, camping. Divided for day hikes. 60 pages. ISBN 0-9603966-4-0.

Circuit Hikes in Northern New Jersey
A complete guide to 20 hikes in the New Jersey Highlands that can be walked without the need for a car shuttle or retracing steps. Text and maps by Bruce Scofield. Photos. 80 pages. ISBN 0-9603966-3-2.

New York Walk Book
Indispensable regional reference book for the hiker. Trail descriptions with 23 full color maps. Also geology, history, hiking tips and much more. Hikers 'bible' since 1923. Full index and magnificent sketches. Doubleday. 400 pages. ISBN 0-385-15584-0.

Day Walker
Diverse range of day walks and hikes in NY-NJ metropolitan area; many reachable by public transit. For people of all ages and abilities—ideal for families with children. Includes trails, backcountry lanes, old cemeteries, historical towns, city parks and gardens. Maps and sketches. Doubleday. 223 pages. ISBN 0-385-14140-8.

The Pine Barrens of Ronkonkoma
An expanded guide for the hiker to the Long Island Pine Barrens. Trails and woods roads with accompanying maps. Delightful background text by Lawrence G. Paul. 28 pages. ISBN 0-9603966-5-9.

Hiking the Catskills
Written and designed by Lee McAllister and Myron Steven Ochman. They spent years combing the Catskill Forest Preserve to prepare this delightful and personal guide. All state-maintained trails and trailless areas (*"Off The Beaten Path"*) are covered in depth. A complete reference guide. Over 150 photos and illustrations with maps included. ISBN 0-9603966-6-7. *Fits in your pocket!*

MAPS

Our award-winning map sets are printed in four or five colors on a plastic material that is both *waterproof* and *tear resistant*. All have at least 100' contour lines.

Harriman—Bear Mt. Trails
Two Map Set
Indexed. Complete trail system. Also includes lakes, mines, beaches, parking, x-c ski trails, woods roads, shelters, viewpoints and park boundaries. Appalachian Trail and Long Path. Historical Notes.

North Jersey Trails
Two Map Set
Includes trail systems in Ringwood, West Milford, Ramapo Mts. Also, Wawayanda St. Park, Norvin Green and Hewitt St. Forests. Features Greenwood Lake (NY/NJ), Bearfort Mt. and the Wyanokies. Viewpoints, lakes, parking and multi-shaded park lands. Appalachian Trail and Historical Notes.

West Hudson Trails
Two Map Set
Includes Orange County's (NY) Storm King Mt., Black Rock Forest and Schunemunk Mt. Marked trails, viewpoints, lakes, parking, woods roads for x-c ski. Historical Notes.

East Hudson Trails
Three Map Set
Includes Putnam County's (NY) Hudson Highlands and Fahnestock State Parks. Features Sugarloaf Mt., Breakneck Ridge, Canopus Lake, Anthony's Nose, Appalachian Trail, Beacon Mt., more. Boundaries, viewpoints, parking and Historical Notes.

Catskill Trails
Five Map Set
The four-county Catskill Park with complete trail index and guide on map backs. Magnetic north-south navigation lines, easy-to-read green overprint of state-owned land. All marked and many unmarked trails, woods roads, viewpoints, parking, campgrounds, leantos and springs.
Special: *Order both the Catskill Trails Five Map Set and our HIKING THE CATSKILLS book and save!*

Shawangunk Trails
Three Map Set
Mohonk, Minnewaska and the Ellenville Watershed with a large scale map (20' contours) of the detailed Lake Mohonk area. Magnetic north-south navigation lines, a multi-shaded green overprint for public access land, points of interest, swimming areas, many types of trails. First easy-

to-read maps of this truly magnificent area. Published in association with the Mohonk Preserve.

South Taconic Trails
One Map
(Three detailed extension maps on the reverse)
Views abound in this area where NY, Conn. and Mass. come together. Riga Lake, Bear and Alander Mts., Bashbish Falls, Mts. Everett and Race. Appalachian Trail, shelters, woods roads, viewpoints and parking. Your *ticket* to this less-traveled area.

South Kittatinny Trails
Two Map Set
Delaware Water Gap National Recreation Area at Worthington State Forest, including sections in Penna. New Jersey's most popular hiking area: Appalachian Trail, Sunfish Pond, Mts. Tamma and Minsi. All marked trails and many unmarked ones. Viewpoints, camping, parking and multi-shaded park lands.

North Kittatinny Trails
Two Map Set
High Point State Park and Stokes State Forest with northern sections of Delaware Water Gap National Recreation Area. Appalachian Trail, Stony Lake, Sunrise Mt., Buttermilk Falls, Tillman Ravine. All marked trails and many unmarked ones. Viewpoints, camping, parking and multi-shaded park lands.
Special: *Order both Kittatinny Sets at the same time and save!*

Please write for membership information, a local hiking club list, and/or a complete publications catalogue. **GPO Box 2250, NYC 10116**

NOTES